THIRD EDITION

GETTING FUNDED

A COMPLETE GUIDE TO PROPOSAL WRITING

MARY S. HALL

Copyright 1988 by Mary Hall
Getting Funded: A Complete Guide to Proposal Writing
Third Edition

Formerly published as
Developing Skills in Proposal Writing

First edition published September 1971
Second edition published September 1977

ISBN 0-87678-070-2
LC 88-070400

Published and distributed by:
Continuing Education Publications
Portland State Unviersity
P.O. Box 1491
Portland, Oregon 97207

(503) 725-4891

ABOUT THE AUTHOR

Dr. Mary Stewart Hall is currently Vice President of Corporate Contributions of the Weyerhaeuser Company (A Fortune 500 firm) and Executive Director and a Trustee of the Weyerhaeuser Company Foundation. During 1986-87, she served as President of the Pacific Northwest Grantmakers Forum (a five-state association of foundations, trusts and corporate giving programs). She is a member of the Contributions Council of the Conference Board and a Director of Independent Sector (a national organization of the largest private donors and nonprofit institutions). She has served in a variety of advisory capacities to the Council on Foundations.

She has worked with grants and contracts for over twenty years. Dr. Hall began her career as a staff member with the U.S. Congress and was involved in the development of much of the early educational and social grant-in-aid legislation. In 1965, she organized and directed one of the first full-time staffs devoted to securing external funds for a major state university. While Director of Federal Relations at the University of Oregon, she also began editing *Federal Notes*. This biweekly newsletter quickly became a best known source of information on funding for educators and social scientists throughout the nation. In 1968, her office was expanded to provide assistance and information on external funding for the entire Oregon State System of Higher Education.

She became Associate Superintendent of Public Instruction in Oregon during 1972. While serving in this capacity, she supervised staffs who annually distributed more than $50 million in grant-in-aid funds to educational agencies in the state.

Interspersed throughout this period, Dr. Hall served as a professor of educational administration and political science. She has received a number of awards for her own research and training interests, including Project New Resources. This program, financed by the Office of Economic Opportunity, was one of the first federal awards to train grants specialists.

She is the author of nine books and a variety of articles, monographs and refereed papers. Many of these have dealt with intergovernmental relations, grants and contract administration, private fundraising, or program planning and evaluation. Dr. Hall has been a consultant to many international, national, state and local agencies as well as private foundations and corporate giving programs. She is a frequent conference speaker and continues her involvement with higher education through serving as a Visiting Lecturer or Executive-In-Residence.

She received her B.S., M.S. and Ph.D. from the University of Oregon. In 1984, she was graduated from the Executive Management Program of the Graduate School of Business at Stanford University.

ACKNOWLEDGEMENTS

Special thanks to Dona Beattie, Assistant Dean, Division of Continuing Education, Portland State University, who assisted with the research for this edition.

TABLE OF CONTENTS

ILLUSTRATIONS

INTRODUCTION

The circumstances facing those seeking grant-in-aid funds have altered significantly since the second edition of this book was issued in 1977. These differences can be separated into two categories: *who gives* and *who gets*.

CHANGES IN WHO GIVES

● Although the annual rate of growth has slowed (and since 1976, declined), federal grants-in-aid have increased from around $65 billion to over $100 billion (Office of Management and Budget).

● However, when adjusted for inflation, these types of federal outlays actually decreased some 14 percent between FY 1980 and FY 1986 (Abramson and Salamon).

● U.S. spending for research and development has achieved new historic heights (even in constant dollars). But since 1980, more than half of all national R & D has been funded by the private sector (National Science Board).

● State and local governments have become less significant sources of grants and contracts, mainly because of the substantial decrease in their share of federal funds. In FY 1977, these sources received 11.4 percent of federal outlays (excluding payments to individuals). By FY 1987, this had declined to an estimated 5.3 percent of federal funds (Office of Management and Budget).

● Corporations have become the fastest growing source of charitable giving, even during a period of economic instability. While corporate income before taxes in 1985 was one-third larger than in 1976, corporate contributions were three times larger (The Conference Board).

● Although the rapid annual increase in cash gifts by corporations is predicted to slow in the years ahead, growth in gifts of equipment, products and other in-kind resources is expected to continue (The Conference Board).

● Assets and giving by community foundations are another expanding area. Assets of the twenty-five largest community foundations increased 22.2 percent from 1985 to 1986, while their grants jumped by almost 9.5 percent (AAFRC Trust for Philanthropy).

● The number of foundations increases each year, although the rate of growth has slowed somewhat since the big spurt in 1950-59. Currently, more than 25,000 private foundations are tracked by the Foundation Center.

● Those states with the largest number of foundations (accounting for over 60 percent of the total) are California, Illinois, Michigan, New York, Pennsylvania and Texas.

● Funding by the private sector may be even more important in years ahead because of a significant push by several national bodies to increase giving by individuals, foundations and corporations.

CHANGES IN WHO GETS

● In terms of federal grants-in-aid, the big winner has been health-related institutions, with organizations and institutions providing other social services the largest losers. Between FY 1982 and FY 1986, federal outlays for health care and research (excluding payments to individuals) increased some 20 percent in constant dollars. By comparison, similar type outlays for the social welfare fields (especially employment and training projects) declined by 42 percent (Abramson and Salamon).

● Substantial reductions in federal grants (in constant dollars) have also affected elementary and secondary education, programmatic support of higher education, environment/conservation and, to a lesser extent, arts and culture (Abramson and Salamon).

● Education was the biggest recipient of charitable gifts by corporations, accounting for 38 percent of business dollars in 1985. The next largest beneficiaries of corporate support that year were (in rank order) health and human services, civic and community activities, culture and the arts and "other" (The Conference Board).

● Health and welfare fields also did well in competing for private foundation grants, receiving over half of all foundation dollars in 1985 (welfare with 26.2 percent and health with 23.5 percent). The next largest recipients of foundation grants were (in rank order): education, cultural activities, science and technology, social science and religious causes (The Foundation Center).

● An analysis of shifts in the types of organizations and institutions now receiving both private foundation and corporate dollars suggests that public agencies are becoming increasingly successful in competing in arenas previously the exclusive domain of private nonprofit applicants.

● Population size does not appear to be the major factor in terms of which states receive the most money from private foundations. In 1985, the top five recipient areas (by geography) were New York, California, the District of Columbia, Pennsylvania and Utah (The Foundation Center).

While these statistics demonstrate some of the dramatic differences in the world of grantsmanship since 1977, one thing has not changed: *There is still fierce competition among an increasing number of applicants for both public and private grants.* It is even more important that one know how to prepare an effective proposal.

This book is based on two fundamental assumptions: *First, there is social value in writing proposals to seek funding from private and governmental sources.* The application process is one of the most democratic means we know of matching those who

have ideas for the improvement of society with those who have the resources to support such progress. Individuals and organizations that have the creativity, drive, perseverance and capacity to submit successful requests not only deserve the additional resources and prestige that grants can bring, but they are a primary means of creating desirable social change.

Second, there is no special mystique about proposal writing. Anyone with a good, well-planned idea, appropriate research on sources of support and the ability to communicate effectively in writing can do a successful job of preparing a funding request. There are, however, some ways of approaching this task and some specific procedures that can be profitably adopted by the novice, or by those seeking new sources of support. This book is intended as a basic primer to share some of those techniques and experience.

The book is also aimed specifically at those situations where external funds must be sought through an application of more complexity than a simple letter. The letter or direct mail solicitation, whether aimed at individuals, a firm or foundations, is more typically described in books labeled *fundraising.* Such books may also suggest other methods of securing support through testimonial dinners, memberships, fees-for-services, auctions and other types of special events.

The preparation of a proposal normally follows a well-established pattern which, in many respects, is analogous to the traditional planning process found in the literature on management. By viewing proposal development as a process, one can begin to recognize repetitive steps which must be completed for any application and can build a reservoir of experiences to be applied to the development of any funded project. To aid this recognition, the book itself is organized along a logical pattern of planning, beginning first with a discussion of ideas for projects and ending with considerations about submission, negotiation and project renewal.

As with the earlier editions, the book is divided into two major parts. Part I deals with the planning and information collection which should be accomplished prior to the actual writing of a proposal. Entitled "The Preproposal Phase," these chapters place increased emphasis on such significant skills as assessing the capability to compete and selecting the appropriate funding source. In line with recent trends, substantial details are provided on foundations and corporations.

These chapters also focus on the unique considerations which must be given to planning applications submitted in response to *Requests for Proposals* (RFPs). These formal solicitations for specified services desired by a funding source still represent one of the major vehicles through which sponsored project funds are received. They are discussed from several perspectives throughout the first five chapters.

Part II of the book deals with the actual writing of a proposal and each chapter focuses on a specific component usually found in such documents. The chapters are designed so that the reader may gain a step-by-step understanding of the ingredients necessary for a successful application.

As in the first section of the book, the actual discussion of proposal preparation in this edition places great emphasis on effectively competing for grants from corporations and foundations.

These chapters are also intended to apply to all competitive applications. The only type of proposal content not addressed specifically is an application for governmental *formula programs*. Under these programs, specified agencies are eligible for definite amounts of money (usually computed on the basis of a formula outlined in the enabling legislation) and such funds are awarded as a matter of course if the applicant correctly fills out the necessary forms and meets the appropriate deadline.

Three additional terms are used frequently throughout the book and should be understood at this point. *Sponsored project* refers to an activity or program financed by funds which have been obtained from application to a source other than the agency administering the project. The term *externally-funded* is also used to categorize this type of project.

The words *grant* and *contract* will also appear several times. These words are often used in conjunction with each other, yet they represent two distinct types of awards from funding sources and may require different types of information in the proposal document.

In general, a *contract* is given for a project where the funding source has already identified the need, identified the expected outcomes for the project,

selected an acceptable cost range and estimated the time required to complete the project. The funding source is thus faced with simply choosing the best among possible candidates to carry out the project. Its choice will be based on such issues as previous experience, geographical location, quality of personnel or favorable budget. It also expects to exert strict management control over whomever receives the contract. There are several kinds of contracts commonly in use, including *fixed-price, straight-cost-reimbursement, cost-plus-fixed fee* and *cost sharing*. These classifications are generally distinguished by the manner in which the budget for the contract is negotiated. In general, contracts are usually awarded for projects solicited through a Request for Proposal (RFP).

A *grant*, on the other hand, is typically awarded for projects where most or all of the factors outlined above have not yet been determined. Some observers feel that proposals for grants thus require more ingenuity and creativity than those submitted for contracts. Grants are frequently awarded for experimental projects or for projects for which the idea and purpose of the award have been suggested by the recipient. In general, grants are frequently characterized by greater latitude in shifting funds among budget categories, more flexibility in the timetable necessary for completing various elements of the project, and more freedom in the methods used to accomplish the intended outcomes.

The debate over whether grants or contracts are more advantageous to the recipient has continued for many years and opinions still differ. In most cases, however, it is the funding source rather than the applicant who determines which type of award will be made. But knowing the type of award most likely to be selected and the relationship between the characteristics of grants and contracts and their respective proposal content is the job of the applicant.

Other terms unique to the field of proposal development will be defined as they appear throughout the book.

CHAPTER REFERENCES

AAFRC Trust for Philanthropy, *Giving USA: 32nd Annual Issue* (New York: AAFRC Trust for Philanthropy, 1987).

Abramson, A. J., and L.M. Salamon, *The Nonprofit Sector and the New Federal Budget* (Washington, D.C.: Urban Institute Press, 1986).

National Science Board, *Science Indicators: The 1985 Report* (Washington, D.C.: National Science Board, 1985).

Office of Management and Budget, *Historical Tables, Budget of the United States Government, FY 1988* (Washington, D.C.: Government Printing Office, 1987).

The Conference Board, *Annual Survey of Corporate Contributions,* 1987 ed. (New York: The Conference Board, 1987).

The Foundation Center, *Grants Index,* 15th ed. (New York: The Foundation Center, 1986).

PART ONE
THE PREPROPOSAL PHASE

PROPOSAL IDEAS

This chapter outlines some of the key characteristics of project ideas and shows the impact that the source of an idea may have on the timing and content of a proposal document.

CHARACTERISTICS OF PROJECT IDEAS

It is important, at the outset, to determine some of the key characteristics of a project for which you might write a proposal. Most sources of funding, whether public or private, restrict their awards by at least one of the four considerations mentioned below:

● **What is the function of the project you are proposing?** Examples might include research, development, demonstration, training, service, technical assistance, general organizational support, facilities, equipment purchases and so forth.

● **In what field is your project?** Some of the standard categories include education, health, social welfare, civic or community improvement, arts, cultural, science and technology, religion or environmental/conservation.

● **Who will benefit from your project?** Types of clientele or project participants might include the low-income, infants, youth, families, the elderly, the unemployed, the homeless, refugees, persons of certain race, ethnicity or sex and so forth.

● **What are the geographic parameters of your project?** Is it oriented towards urban or rural areas? Is it local, statewide, nationwide or international?

Identifying clearly as many of the appropriate descriptive characteristics of your project idea as you can will assist you in delimiting the search for the most likely sources of support. They provide the keys for unlocking the information contained in the indexes of the *Catalog of Federal Domestic Assistance*, *The Foundation Directory* and other such funding publications described in Chapter 4. They are also essential to your ability to identify data to support the need for your project or to see whether someone else has already carried out your project ideas. More information on both of these issues is provided in Chapter 3.

ORIGINS OF PROJECT IDEAS

It is also crucial to know whether your proposal is for an idea that originated primarily with the submitting agency, or is for a purpose suggested (at least in part) by the funding source. The former are usually called *unsolicited* and the latter, *solicited*. This distinction will have clear implications for communications with potential funding sources and for the content and timing of the proposal itself.

An *unsolicited* idea is one which is created by the person or organization seeking funds who, at this point, has no idea whether it will be of interest to any potential donors. From the viewpoint of the applicant, these are frequently the most interesting and important projects. As will be discussed later, however, they are often the most difficult to fund.

A *solicited* idea, on the other hand, is one which has been suggested in at least general terms by the funding source itself. There has been a definite trend in recent years towards such solicited projects by federal and state agencies, as well as certain foundations and corporations. Many observers feel that this movement is being fueled by the increasing demand on sponsored project funds which has forced funders to be more specific about what they want to have accomplished.

There are at least two ways in which *solicited projects* are initiated.

The first is a Request for Proposal (RFP) which describes the type of program to be mounted, the outcomes intended and the criteria to be used in selecting recipients of the funds. The funder may also specify the time to be permitted for the project, a range of acceptable costs, the geographical area or clientele to be served, and, in some cases, the actual procedures or methods to be used. The document may also list the type of qualifications needed by those eligible to respond and detail the type of information to be submitted.

Learning about RFPs from private foundations and corporations can be tricky. They seldom maintain standard mailing lists for automatic distribution, but typically send the RFP to organizations with whom they are already familiar. Watching newsletters and other sources of information on current activities of foundations and corporations is the most likely way to learn of these opportunities.

Monitoring the availability of RFPs from federal or state agencies is much simpler. Most are required to publicize the availability of such funds prior to selecting award recipients. Their communication method is usually publications designed to solicit governmental contracts (see Chapter 4) or, in some cases, public announcements in major daily newspapers.

Some governmental sources are, at the same time, adopting measures to restrict the number of copies of the complete RFP document or contract specifications they must issue. It is now a fairly common practice for such agencies to require that interested groups furnish a statement of capability or complete a form requesting placement on a bidder's list. Having this prepared in advance can help one respond to RFPs that have short timelines.

A second approach used by funding sources for solicited projects is the so-called "program announcement." This approach is most commonly used by those governmental or private donors that want to support projects of a particular type or in a specific field, but that wish to leave considerable flexibility to applicants in proposing how to design and carry out the program.

Program announcements come in many formats. Some federal agencies, for example, include all of their program announcements in an annual catalog. Others (including most private sources) issue separate booklets or pamphlets when they want to announce a particular program competition.

Whether for public or private sources, program announcements usually include:

● A description of the nature of the problem the donor is trying to solve.

● Topical areas or categories of projects for which proposals may be submitted.

● Eligibility requirements for applicants.

● Deadlines.

● What information must be submitted (and sometimes in what form).

● The selection criteria and process.

● Sometimes, announcements include the amount of money available.

Those who wish to respond to a program announcement are usually expected to propose the specific objectives, outcomes or deliverables to be achieved; the best methodology or approach to follow; and the appropriate timeline, staff, budget or other resources required. Since program announcements from private foundations are not as common as those from governmental agencies, an example of the former is included in Attachment 1.

Program announcements from either public or private sources are difficult to monitor. There is no single foolproof method to use in learning of these opportunities in time to develop a successful response.

The most dependable way that such groups can hope to receive program announcements is to: a) identify all governmental or private sources which might provide monies of interest to the group; b) send letters to these sources and ask to be placed on their routine mailing lists for all future program announcements and application forms; and c) routinely monitor those governmental and private news sources which identify upcoming funding opportunities. Chapter 4 discusses some of these sources of information.

As noted before, the classification of a project idea as either being *solicited* or *unsolicited* will affect the preliminary communications with the funding source, the anticipated timetable for securing funds, and the proposal content itself.

IMPACT ON COMMUNICATION WITH THE FUNDING SOURCE

Most proposals take a great deal of time and effort to prepare. The submitting agency should, therefore, determine in advance whether the idea for the proposal is consistent with the interests of potential grantors and whether the application will receive serious consideration once it is written. In the case of *solicited* project ideas, this preliminary correspondence will focus on discussions such as the attractiveness of the proposed program approach and the proposed project outcomes. The chances that the proposal will be funded, once submitted, are enhanced by getting these kinds of reactions well in advance. In the case of *unsolicited* ideas, however, these initial discussions must first determine whether the development of a completed proposal is even warranted. It is unwise to risk any great quantity of time and effort on a proposal for an unsolicited idea whose major purpose, direction and cost has not been checked in advance with potential funding sources. Guidance on how to carry out this communication is provided in Chapter 4.

IMPACT ON PROPOSAL TIMELINE

With applications for *solicited* ideas, a definite submission deadline and a date on which to expect notification of the proposal's acceptance or rejection is usually well established. The sample timetable provided in Chapter 5 will provide some guidance for the amount of time commonly associated with preparation and approval of these kinds of applications.

In the case of *unsolicited* ideas, however, the applicant must first determine whether a proposal is warranted. This requires additional delay, ranging from only a few days if an inquiry into possible funding sources can be made by telephone and assurance of the idea's relevancy is received verbally, to several months if the funding agency asks for a preliminary draft or abstract of the proposal.

In addition, the *unsolicited* idea may not be appropriate to a well-defined program category and even if

it is of interest to a funding source, no formal application deadline may exist. This is particularly true if the application is to be considered for financing with a funding source's discretionary monies. On occasion, a potential funding source will accept an unsolicited proposal with the understanding that if monies are still available at year end, it will be considered after the agency or foundation completes its regular application review and selects projects within its most immediate priorities. It is not uncommon for applicants attempting to fund an *unsolicited* idea to spend several years locating support. This is especially true if the decision is made first to try to influence the content of authorizing legislation and thus move the idea into the solicited category.

IMPACT ON PROPOSAL CONTENT

The *unsolicited* proposal also faces an additional hurdle in that it must include the same type of information required in *solicited* applications, but also do a better-than-average job of convincing the funding source of the merit of the idea, the need for the program, and the capability of the submitting agency to administer a successful project. As a result, the components of the proposal document covering these topics take on additional significance.

In most cases, the group developing an *unsolicited* proposal will want to follow the same proposal format and complete the same application forms as those used by the funding source for *solicited* requests. However, this too should be checked in advance with potential funding sources. Some agencies do have separate guidelines or content requirements for *unsolicited* projects.

As noted earlier, *unsolicited* ideas are normally the most difficult to finance as the number of donors limiting awards to predefined priorities (and in some cases, predefined projects) increases. One observer of the national scene now estimates that funds distributed through contract solicitation and Requests for Proposals account for over 50 percent of monies distributed through direct applications to the federal government. Increasing use of these solicited project mechanisms by state agencies (either concerned with distributing their own or federal funds) is also apparent. Private foundations and corporations are also expanding their use of the *solicited* project approach, particularly when they have decided to mount a major initiative to resolve a particular problem area or to provide national leadership in a particular field of service.

This trend indicates that a greater burden is now placed on you to keep in touch with potential funding sources and to respond to funding solicitations with more efficiency and effectiveness. Too, you must have a greater capacity to assess your own ability to compete successfully for these prespecified opportunities. All proposals require an investment for their development and it is only reasonable to do this when the chances for success are relatively high.

CHAPTER REFERENCES

Catalog of Federal Domestic Assistance (Washington, D.C.: Government Printing Office, 1986).

The Foundation Directory, 10th ed. (New York: The Foundation Center, 1985).

EXAMPLE OF A PROGRAM ANNOUNCEMENT FROM A PRIVATE FOUNDATION

Fred Meyer
Charitable Trust

PROGRAM GUIDELINES   AGING *and*
INDEPENDENCE

BACKGROUND

PROGRAM OBJECTIVES

With dramatic increases in the number of older citizens, it becomes imperative that this country develop more ways to maintain and prolong their independence and enhance their quality of life. Our ethics, our politics, and our economy will be enormously affected by the arrangements we develop for the well-being of this group of citizens. Because of the significance of these concerns, the Board of the Fred Meyer Charitable Trust has selected "Aging and Independence" as one of its areas of grantmaking focus.

Prior to making this decision, the Trust held discussions with people in the Northwest and elsewhere who were knowledgeable about the problems and opportunities experienced by our aging citizens. These discussions clearly indicated that the problems are numerous and complex and that the opportunities seem to be more restricted than necessary. The Trust identified several themes that are of widespread concern. Among these are:

1. The primary provider of care for the elderly remains the family, and this informal care system needs to be supported. There is also a need to investigate new methods of improving the effectiveness and capacity of other systems, both informal and formal, which provide support and services to older persons. For those who are cared for in an institutional setting the enhancement of the quality of their life there is of deep concern.

2. Formal services for the elderly are concentrated heavily on the acute, intensive end of the needed continuum of care. The mid-range of services that most directly encourages and enables independence has not been fully developed and needs more support.

3. Even when services exist, there is frequently a problem of impeded access to them. The path to services is often too difficult or circuitous for senior citizens and their caregivers, and improved access to badly needed services is a critical need.

While recognizing there are many other problems facing the elderly that need attention, including poor health and insufficient income, the Trust has decided to concentrate its primary efforts in the areas enumerated above. These areas have received relatively little support from other funding sources. Improvement in them can yield important benefits to older citizens and the society at large. And they offer opportunities in which the limited resources of a private foundation can make a significant difference.

In pursuing its goal of assisting the prolongation of independence of aging citizens, the Trust will concentrate primarily on the following program areas:

1. ACCESS

The Trust will be interested in proposals that promote easier and fuller access for senior citizens to existing services in the community. Particular emphasis will be given to better informational systems and simplified entry into the service system. Examples of such projects might include: linkage of one service system to another, single entry into the service network, development of community focal points, and case management.

2. DELIVERY

The Trust will be interested in proposals that develop and test new methods of service delivery. Particular emphasis will be given to projects that promote effective and efficient ways of providing services in the least intensive and intrusive manner and setting. Of special interest will be those projects that utilize natural networks, families, and communities in addressing the needs of the elderly.

3. SPECIAL POPULATIONS

Within the general framework of the concerns described alone, the Trust will be particularly interested in proposals that address the special needs of three underserved and/or little understood populations:

a. Isolated elderly—This isolation may be due to the rural nature of the community of residence or the inability to reach community services due to poverty or frailty.

b. Minority elders—Cultural and/or language barriers may prevent minority seniors from services offered by the community.

c. The very old—Because so few seniors lived to ages of 85 and older until recently, little is known about their special physical and emotional needs, and there is a need to increase our knowledge about this group.

ELIGIBILITY & REVIEW CRITERIA

*T*he focus of the Trust's effort will be on projects that explore and demonstrate productive and cost-effective ways to prolong the period of independence and enhance the quality of life. The Trust cannot fund the replication of such projects everywhere they are needed. Instead the Trust will emphasize support to model projects, the results of which can be disseminated to other communities. By encouraging innovation and the testing of alternative approaches, the Trust hopes that it can promote long-range benefits to our society and its older citizens. An important consideration in selecting grantees will be the plans and potential of the project to instruct others in how to provide more efficient and helpful services.

*W*hen it is appropriate and useful, projects that exhibit cooperation between different agencies and systems will be of special interest to the Trust. The Trust will also encourage projects that include productive roles for senior citizens.

*T*he Trust will normally make grants only to organizations that are tax-exempt under Section 501(c)(3) of the Internal Revenue Code and are not "private foundations" as defined under Section 509(a) of the Code. Under certain circumstances grants can be made to public educational institutions and governmental units.

*O*rganizations in Alaska, Idaho, Montana, Oregon, and Washington are eligible to apply. Grant requests from outside this region are not invited.

*T*he Trust generally will *not* provide the basic funding of food, shelter, or health care, although projects that improve the delivery of services in these areas may be considered. Also the Trust generally will *not* fund projects that focus on income maintenance, construction of buildings, or basic biomedical research.

*P*roposals should demonstrate that the project:

✦ supports the program objectives described in this announcement

✦ has outcomes that are clear and amenable to evaluation

✦ if successful, could be sustained after the grant period

✦ has been discussed with others in the community or field and is not unnecessarily duplicative

✦ includes a clear plan for dissemination of results

APPLICATION PROCEDURES & TIMETABLE

CONTACT PERSON

*W*hen a proposal is submitted, it must conform to the Trust's application procedure. A copy of our application guidelines may be obtained by writing or calling the Trust office.

*T*he current deadline for submitting proposals addressing "Aging and Independence" is July 1, 1986. Action by the Trustees of the Fred Meyer Charitable Trust ordinarily will not come in less than four months from the time a complete proposal is received. In many instances the time for consideration may be longer because of the time needed for investigation.

*A*ll inquiries regarding this program should be directed to:

Marty Lemke,
Program Officer
Fred Meyer Charitable Trust
1515 S.W. Fifth, Suite 500
Portland, Oregon 97201
(503) 228-5512

ASSESSING YOUR CAPABILITY

This chapter provides a checklist for use in determining an organization's general capability to engage in successful grantsmanship. It also discusses methods of judging the capability to respond to a specific Request for Proposal (RFP).

As noted in the introduction, competition for sponsored project funds is increasing each year. In earlier days, an individual or organization with a good idea could almost be assured of getting it supported. Success is no longer so easily guaranteed. Not only must organizations wishing to secure external funds be willing to provide the requisite support services, but they must also become more effective in judging whether the efforts required for a proposal's development are justifiable.

This discussion is divided into two parts. The first covers a series of questions designed to establish the overall capability of an organization to successfully participate in securing external funds. While the discussion cannot be exhaustive, it does identify a series of questions which should be considered prior to significant investments in proposal development. The second discussion deals with considerations for evaluating the likelihood of success in responding to a Request for Proposal. It suggests information which should be secured by a potential applicant before the requested proposal is written. RFPs have become such an important source for funding that they deserve special attention in assessing individual or institutional capabilities.

Because of its emphasis on general capability, this chapter is designed primarily for the use of individuals who oversee efforts to secure sponsored project funds. However, the checklist can also be used by individuals wishing to assess their individual capability or to determine whether their current employer is the best sponsor for a particular idea. It may be that the individual can seek a more effective sponsor by joining in a consortium or by selecting a co-applicant at another institution or organization.

CHECKLIST FOR ASSESSING YOUR INSTITUTION OR AGENCY

❏ **DOES YOUR ORGANIZATION HAVE A STRATEGIC PLAN?** Put succinctly, has your organization gone through the thoughtful discipline of recently reviewing its mission, the needs or assumptions upon which that mission is based, determining its goals, setting its priorities, defining the program, services and activities required to achieve those priorities, analyzing the resources required (including people, money, facilities and so forth), identifying the gaps in existing resources and deciding on strategies for filling these gaps?

It is chic now to downplay the importance of strategic planning. But the days of simply submitting a proposal to "get money" are long gone, if they ever existed.

All applications cost the submitting institution or agency. Sometimes this is obvious, such as dollars required for matching funds and the release of staff for time to develop proposals. Sometimes the costs are less apparent, such as the impact of assigning a key staff member to a sponsored project, or focusing on areas where external funds are available to the neglect of other functions more essential to the organization's basic mission.

Organizations can no longer afford to support the submission of every project of interest to one of their employees. Some universities have now learned this lesson; most have not. Even nonprofits are beginning to be aware of the importance of a strategic plan to their ability to attract the right kind of funding (Barry, 1986).

The prime consideration in deciding whether to authorize proposal development (or submission) should be whether the proposed project will contribute to achieving the goals or solving the needs of the organization and those it serves. If such goals and needs have not been formally identified, administrators have little basis on which to judge the potential impact of a proposed project.

Perhaps of equal importance, this lack of direction and overall organizational planning is usually apparent to potential funding sources. This further inhibits success.

❑ **HAVE YOU ASSESSED THE COMPETENCE OF YOUR INSTITUTION?** Because this is such an important topic, there are a variety of more specific questions which should be considered. These include:

● Do you understand the "competitive advantages" of your organization? Have you identified those factors in your structure, clientele, location, history or staff which might make you particularly visible or attractive to potential sources of support?

● Do you know the reputation of your organization? Have you examined records of previous funds received by your group and do you know whether the sources for these awards were satisfied with your performance? Have you assessed other aspects of your organizational reputation which might enhance or impede your chances for grants or contracts?

● Are you aware of the capability of your staff? Have you surveyed the professional standing and reputation of your employees and do you know where your particular strengths lie? Are there individuals with specific talents for project development or administration available to you?

● Do you have appropriate external sources of professional or political support? Do your staff, governing boards and previous or current clientele have effective relationships with individuals who serve in decision-making capacities over grant or contract awards? What kind of political support can you count on from necessary local, state or federal officials? While these relationships will seldom outweigh a poorly-written proposal, a bad project

idea or the lack of other essential capabilities, they may be important in securing needed information or in demonstrating support essential to successful implementation of a proposed project.

● Do you have the necessary legal basis? Many funding sources require that an organization be declared tax-exempt by appropriate state or federal government agencies. Others have legal requirements governing corporations and for-profit organizations. These should be carefully checked and compared against the status of your organization to determine eligibility for external funds. You should also determine compliance with other legal requirements, such as assurances of non-discrimination or of protection of human subjects (see chapter 6 for a more detailed listing of these requirements).

● Have you considered appropriate fiscal impacts? Do you have the necessary ability to provide required matching dollars or services? Do you have the capability to release staff from their other duties to quickly respond to funding opportunities? Can your organization continue the program when the external funds end, and, if not, what will be the impact?

● Do you have the financial resources to hire (if necessary) the expertise to direct a major or complex fundraising effort? More importantly, do you have the experience within your organization to effectively select and manage such expertise?

● Has your organization thought through which aspects of its current operation are most likely to be appealing to external donors (assuming funds are being sought for support of ongoing activities)? As an example, one civic group tried unsuccessfully for several years to enlist several corporate donors to underwrite the costs of issuing the agency's newsletter. The group would have been far better advised to seek support for some of their community services and to pay for the costs of the newsletter out of their annual membership fees.

● Do you have the necessary flexibility for securing external funds? Frequently, staff assignments or responsibilities are fixed well in advance. Organizations unable to reassign individuals or temporarily relieve key staff of on-going responsibilities could not effectively manage or implement an externally-funded project even if they could secure the funds.

● What are your options for collaboration with others? Can you work with other institutions, organizations or individuals in consortia, sub-contract or consultant roles? This frequently will determine the range of funding possibilities open to you and your likelihood of marshaling the necessary resources to compete with others.

● Does your organization provide appropriate rewards? Is there any incentive for your staff to invest the time and energy necessary to secure external funds? Have you considered the impact of such rewards on other staff who do not receive such awards?

❏ **DOES YOUR ORGANIZATION HAVE THE ESSENTIAL SUPPORT SYSTEMS?** Most individuals experienced in securing external funds feel there are at least five basic kinds of services which should be provided, in varying degrees, within any organization that expects to successfully secure grants or contracts. These include:

● Information systems to monitor sources of funds, relevant legislative action, application deadlines and changes in application forms. Such systems may also provide a variety of other services including preliminary discussions with a funding source, assistance with proposal development and so forth.

● Statistical services that can quickly identify sources for or secure needed data on the community, state, organization, clientele, facilities, budget or other information necessary to document either the need for a project or to establish organizational eligibility.

● Policymaking systems that can expeditiously reach decisions about whether a proposal should be developed, and allocate the resources needed to prepare the application. Other important kinds of decision-making include fixing the responsibility for: reviewing and approving the proposal prior to submission; negotiating with the funding sources; project administration, fiscal management and reporting; evaluation and program reporting; and refunding.

● Reference systems that provide either computerized or manual searches for determining whether the project idea has already been funded elsewhere, or to assist with compilations of related research.

● Business systems to assist with defining all types of resources needed for the project and for providing appropriate fiscal management and reporting if a project is funded.

There are other types of assistance which may also be essential to the proposal developer and which should either be provided for by the submitting organization or secured from others. These include appropriate secretarial services, media services (if the proposal will require art work or technical comments on the use of media for product development), copying or printing services, computer services, editing or reviewing services, and sources of technical advice on aspects of the project which may be outside of the expertise of the proposal writer.

The level of such services will obviously vary from organization to organization. But individuals who do not have access to these basic systems, at least in some minimal form, will find it more difficult to compete for external funds.

If you do not have such support systems, don't give up. On the contrary, a realistic assessment of your organization's capabilities may either prompt development of the necessary services (this may, in fact, be the purpose for one of the first grants you write) or it may encourage you to plan submission of a project through another agency that has the requisite competence. Most of these systems are also essential to the successful management of a project. It is better to take corrective action prior to proposal development rather than wait until the project is funded and it begins to fail.

ASSESSMENT OF CAPABILITY FOR RESPONDING TO REQUESTS FOR PROPOSALS

Documents entitled Requests for Proposals (RFPs) are increasingly being used by state and federal agencies and some private foundations to select recipients of sponsored project funds. The rise in the use of RFPs may be traced to the impact of decreasing government funds and an increase in competition among potential applicants. Funding sources must now attempt to identify their highest priorities with more precision. They must also maximize the probable success of achieving desired outcomes by carrying out more planning on possible projects prior to the awarding of funds. The RFP document grows out of this increased attention to pre-planning. Agencies also feel that the use of the RFP lessens the possibility of charges of unfair competition for scarce dollars.

There is no uniform format for RFPs. However, most carry at least the following information: purpose of the award and desired outcomes; instructions to applicants about how and when to respond to the RFP; details on the technical content of the desired program, including specification of expected tasks or products (usually called the "scope of work"); details on legal issues or requirements affecting the award; and a set of forms.

In judging whether to submit a response to the RFP, the content of the document itself must be evaluated as well as the capabilities of the potential applicant. In making this evaluation, you should apply criteria of: *eligibility, interest, feasibility, flexibility, capability* and *competitiveness*. The following checklist speaks to these criteria.

❑ **Are you eligible to respond to the RFP?** Some Requests for Proposals will carry explicit eligibility requirements detailing the types of agencies or institutions which may submit a proposal. More often, these criteria are implicit. For example, the document may require applicants to have specific kinds of prior experience or be able to mount a project within a specific geographic setting. Organizations that cannot meet either the implicit or explicit eligibility criteria will probably not be considered seriously for the award.

❑ **Is the RFP compatible with your interests?** Organizations should focus their proposal-writing efforts on projects that will help achieve their goals or meet the needs of the institution and its clientele. For a variety of reasons, if the proposed purposes of the RFP do not meet these criteria, the opportunity for funds should probably be ignored.

❑ **Is the RFP feasible?** Sometimes proposals are requested for projects that are simply impossible to implement successfully. The factors which the potential applicant should consider in assessing feasibility include: the number of products or "deliverables" expected; the amount of time available; the amount of money to be awarded (this frequently is expressed in the RFP as the amount of staff time, i.e. staff-days, that the funding source is willing to support); the availability of the necessary technology or knowledge; the environment in which the project must be implemented (funding sources sometimes overlook the impact of an unfavorable political climate or local opposition to a proposed project); the degree to which cooperation or participation by other agencies or individuals are required; the decision-making process for the project; and the kinds and amount of monitoring, reporting and evaluation data that must be furnished. If the RFP as originally written is not feasible, you should determine if the funding source is willing to entertain suggested modifications that will increase chances of success. If not, don't apply for this one.

❑ **Is the RFP flexible?** At least two kinds of flexibility should be considered in assessing an RFP. The first deals with the degree of flexibility available to you in responding to the RFP. Can alternative methodology or approaches be suggested for completing the "scope of work?" Will the funding source entertain revisions in the suggested products and/or services as long as you can demonstrate that the original purposes of the RFP will be achieved? This type of flexibility is critical in determining whether your interest and capabilities can be matched to the funding opportunity offered by the RFP. Secondly, how much flexibility appears to be available in managing the project? It is almost impossible to anticipate every event or factor that will impact on a project. Does the funding source appear to be aware of this? Has it specified or will it approve processes necessary for negotiating needed changes once the project is under way? If not, you should carefully consider the consequences of responding to the RFP unless you are extremely experienced in managing projects of the type requested.

❑ **Are you capable of implementing the RFP?** The evaluative criteria included in the RFP are an important consideration in assessing the adequacy of your staff and organizational capability. These criteria indicate the degree to which factors such as previous experience, available support services, staff qualifications, and content of the proposal itself will be considered in selecting recipients for the award. You can use the criteria for doing a self-evaluation prior to writing the proposal. You should consider whether it will be possible to free up necessary staff during the period required for the proposed project. Also to be considered is whether you can afford to submit a competitive budget. Some organizations have various support services which they can contribute to a project without charge. Others must consider all externally-funded projects to be essentially self-supporting. While the amount of a proposal's budget is seldom the sole reason for a particular award, it does play a role in tightly-contested decisions.

❏ **How competitive will you be?** A criterion closely associated with the issue of capability is your overall competitiveness. This means not only trying to determine who else will be competing for the award, but it also includes understanding the political context of the RFP. The names of potential opponents can usually be determined by asking the funding source for a list of other organizations to whom the RFP has been sent. Many funding sources also schedule a so-called "bidders conference" prior to the date when a completed proposal is expected. In addition to providing additional details on the RFP and answering questions for applicants, the conference is a good means of determining which other groups are interested in the funds.

A second issue to be considered is whether another organization already has the inside track. In theory, if the funding source intends to give an award to an already-selected recipient, it is supposed to declare the project a "sole-source offering" and publicly announce its intentions. For various reasons, this may not be done. Identifying RFPs that are already "locked up" is sometimes difficult, even for organizations that have a good informational pipeline. But experienced proposal writers claim the content of the RFP itself may give the necessary clues. They look for (a) the amount of detail provided in the RFP, and (b) the degree to which the RFP mentions related projects already under way or work that has been completed by another organization prior to issuing the RFP. They claim that an overly-detailed "scope of work" statement frequently means the project has been tailored to plans and ideas of a specific organization. And they note that organizations whose prior or related work is frequently mentioned in the RFP may already have the competitive edge on this award. Recognizing these clues in an RFP provides the basis for gathering further information prior to investing the time needed for a completed proposal.

Finally, you should assess the potential impact of political issues surrounding the award. It may be that the RFP has been developed in response to criticism from a particular source, or in response to legislative action sponsored by a particular group or individual. Relationships between these "influentials" and other potential applicants should be considered.

Other information which it may be wise to collect prior to writing a response to an RFP is mentioned in Chapter 3.

A WORD TO BEGINNERS

At about this stage in the development of a project idea, the question arises as to whether a beginner really has a chance to attract external funds. An analysis of institutional and individual capability may have produced a discouraging picture. What do you do if the requisite support services or prior experience do not exist? Is it really worth the effort to pursue the idea any further?

The answer is, "yes." There are two reasons why the novice should not become unduly discouraged at this point. *First, the preparation and submission of the proposal is of benefit even if the first attempts to get it funded fail.*

● Experience only comes with trying. Many proposals (including those of the more experienced) are submitted and revised several times before they are finally successful. During each failure, you gain valuable information and insight into how to improve future applications. Eventually this pays off and future chances of attracting funds are substantially increased.

● The time and effort invested in preparing a proposal that is really of interest is never lost. The submitting organization may find that a well-planned proposal can be implemented, albeit more slowly, with the use of local dollars. Also, the effort invested in exploring a topic and identifying prior research and related efforts can oftentimes be translated into a successful professional publication. This produces professional rewards for you even if external funds are never secured.

Second, the potential applicant can take some immediate steps to improve apparent areas of weakness. A more extensive discussion of possible approaches is provided in Chapter 12, but some of the most common follow:

● The decision can be made to ask a more experienced colleague to serve as principal investigator or project director in the application. This is a time-honored approach in helping to secure funds for ideas of interest to less experienced persons.

● Efforts can be initiated to join in a collaborative venture with another group (internal or external to the organization) that has the requisite support services or more experience and reputation in the project's area. By joining enthusiasm with experience, this team approach is often successful.

● You can become more realistic in choosing likely sources of support. A decision can be made at this point to focus on those sources where the competition may be less keen, such as money available from a discretionary fund within the organization itself, awards from state agencies, smaller or regional private foundations, local businesses, or small grant programs within federal agencies.

The proposal writer should never forget that many billions of dollars are issued each year for grants and contracts. And each year a substantial amount is awarded to individuals who are submitting their first proposals.

CHAPTER REFERENCE

Barry, B. W., *Strategic Planning Workbook for Nonprofit Organizations* (St. Paul, MN: Amherst H. Wilder Foundation, 1986).

DEVELOPING THE IDEA

This chapter indicates the steps which may be followed in refining the idea for a proposal and discusses the importance of gathering data and building support and involvement of others during the planning phase.

A MODEL FOR PROPOSAL DEVELOPMENT

The planning and writing of a proposal is, in many ways, akin to implementing a special type of planning process. Figure 1 details the general model of proposal development followed in organizing this book. Many of the steps will be familiar to those knowledgeable of the literature on planning and management.

The portions of Figure 1 to be touched on in this chapter are shown with a shaded background. Prior steps have been covered in earlier chapters and the remainder of the model will be covered elsewhere in the book. Refer to Figure 1.

ASSESSING THE NEED FOR AN IDEA

A reference was made earlier to an assumption of the author that no special mystique surrounds the ability to write proposals. It is now time to share another assumption: before setting pen to paper, the organization or individual developing a request for sponsored project funds has an obligation to do a thorough job of assessing the need for a proposal's idea, considering both local conditions and societal problems as a whole.

If necessary, this argument could be presented totally in terms of morality. As there are not sufficient financial resources available to meet all of society's needs, those dollars which *are* requested and approved should be used to the best possible purpose.

However, there are sound, pragmatic reasons why a thorough analysis of the proposed idea and its

impacts, both good and bad, should be undertaken before the proposal document is completed. Not the least of these reasons is that the project might actually be funded and the applicant held responsible for delivering what may unwittingly have been promised. Important considerations behind the assessment of need are:

● It will avoid your expending considerable effort on inadvertently duplicating other projects. Meador (1985) found that over one-third of all proposals submitted to an agency seeking innovative ideas were for projects that had already been tried elsewhere. The effort put into these proposals was largely wasted because their authors had not done basic homework.

● Every agency or institution has a variety of problems that require attention. In meeting one need through the receipt of external funds, the organization may ignore or postpone solution of another. Such a decision and its implications should be carefully considered.

● In competing for sponsored project funds, an organization also commits some of its own resources. While this may involve only personnel and expenses for proposal development (in itself sometimes quite costly), it may also require matching dollars or services. Sometimes the agency is also expected to continue the project with its own revenue once the external funding ends.

● The receipt of a grant or contract always has some side effect, often unexpected, on the agency administering the program. To the extent that these influences can be identified in advance, the agency can make decisions about how to ameliorate harmful effects or capitalize on beneficial results. For

FIGURE 1　　　　　　　　　　　　　　　　　　　**DEVELOPING THE IDEA**

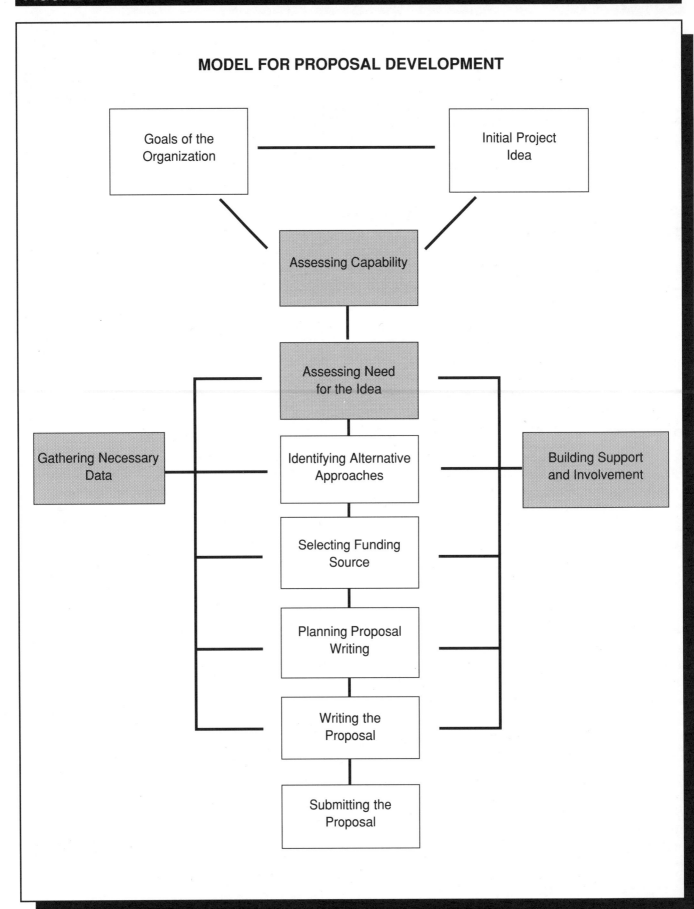

MODEL FOR PROPOSAL DEVELOPMENT

This handout taken from *Getting Funded: A Complete Guide To Proposal Writing* by Mary Hall, 1988.
Available from Continuing Education Publications, P.O. Box 1491, Portland, OR 97207.

example, a new grant or contract may result in major changes in the structure of the agency. New types of expertise and professional interests may be brought into the agency and this will leave different values, interests and expectations, even if the specific personnel involved are later terminated. It may mean that program priorities will be shifted, often for extended periods, as the community or population served comes to expect and demand continuation of a program started with outside funds. Facilities and equipment supported by the grant or contract will need to be maintained. The funding source may require that the population to be served be involved in the project's planning and operation. This may dramatically affect future relationships between the organization and its community or clientele.

● All donors ask: "Is this project concerned with the needs of the clients or the needs of the applicant?" If the needs of those to be served have not been assessed, it will be impossible to document a compelling rationale for the right answer to this question in your proposal.

Factors to be considered in analyzing the need for a particular project's idea will vary. However, the following checklist may be useful in prompting other questions which should be asked during this process.

❏ *What specific needs are addressed and for whom?*

❏ *Why should these particular needs and this specific population receive attention at this time?* Viewed another way, what is likely to happen if this particular project is not implemented now?

❏ *Who else is working on these needs, either locally, regionally or nationally?* What have they learned that is applicable to your project? What evidence do you have that your efforts do not unnecessarily duplicate those of others?

❏ *Is the need really solvable?* What evidence do you have that your program can really make a difference?

❏ *Is the need one of the top priorities in your institution's strategic plan?* Equally important, do you have the capability to initiate this effort at the present time?

❏ *Is the need seen as especially important by those groups or organizations whose support and involvement is critical to the success of the project?*

❏ *What constraints or difficulties should be anticipated in meeting the need?*

Space does not permit a discussion of the alternative techniques available for conducting a needs assessment. Those unfamiliar with this process can secure appropriate literature on the subject by consulting their local library. Bauer (1984) has a chapter particularly useful to nonprofit organizations.

However accomplished, the end products of this process should include:

● A clear-cut statement of the problem(s) that the project will try to address.

● A good description of the population(s) to be served by the project.

● A list of factors which indicate why the idea should receive priority for funding.

● An understanding of the previous literature, research, or work that has addressed this same problem and knowledge of whether the specific project idea has already been tried in another context.

● An identification of additional data on the need that should be proposed for collection during the operation of the project.

While a needs assessment is most commonly associated with shaping demonstration, training or service projects, it is also a critical step in the development of a research proposal. In addition to answering relevant questions in the checklist posed earlier, the information collected during the analysis of needs is important later in shaping both the "problem statement" and the "related research" components of the research proposal (see Chapter 8). The following checklist suggests some additional questions which might be considered in analyzing a research idea.

❏ *Why is the proposed research needed?* What gap in a body of knowledge or methodology does it propose to complete?

❏ *How significant is the proposed idea?* Are there additional research breakthroughs that can be anticipated later because of this project's contributions?

❑ *What prior research has been done on either the proposed content or methodology and what have been its flaws?*

❑ *What is the theoretical base for the study?* What evidence exists that this base is sound or at least is worth further exploration?

In order to complete the analysis of need, you may wish to consult one or more of the information sources listed at the end of this chapter. These sources are particularly useful in identifying previous research or securing regional or national data to be compared to local information about the problem.

DEFINING THE APPROACH

For any given problem there may be a variety of approaches to both the solution and its implementation. Once a need is clearly defined, the next step in refining the project idea is to consider as many alternative methods for solution as possible and to analyze the respective merits or disadvantages of each. A community faced with serious unemployment, for example, may either institute a large training effort aimed at existing occupations or may emphasize the identification and development of new kinds of jobs. The former approach may more quickly decrease the level of unemployment, but it may also result in placing individuals in lower-paying positions, occupations that are seasonal or temporary, or jobs where there may shortly be an oversupply.

Having made a choice on the particular approach to take, the applicant must also decide on the best method of implementation. Should the training be preceded by some type of educational activity? Should it be conducted in a institution or on the job? Should the employer be subsidized for hiring an individual trained in the project and, if so, for how long? Each choice again has to be analyzed for its potential benefits or problems.

In selecting possible options and weighing their merits the following questions are illustrative of those that should be considered.

● *What has been the experience of other organizations or individuals in launching similar projects?*

● *What does the research or existing literature show about the success or failure of similar approaches in the past?* And does this same literature suggest new and innovative techniques that might be attempted?

● *What are the priorities of the potential funding sources?* Is one approach clearly of more interest to them than another?

● *What will be the anticipated short-term and long-term impact of each approach in solving the particular problem?* And if a particular group of subjects or population is involved in the project, how will it be affected?

● *What is the anticipated cost-benefit for each approach?* In order to answer this question, you may need to detail the expected payoffs for each option and compare these against the resources needed to carry each one out.

● *Which approach is most suitable to the capabilities and interests of those who are proposing the idea?*

● *Which approach will appear most dramatic or unusual?* While this should not be the sole criterion used in making the final decision, it may definitely have a bearing on how likely the proposal is to be funded.

● *Which approach is most feasible for being replicated by other organizations with a similar need?* Many funding sources only support projects that will produce products or processes that can later be used by others.

It should be assumed that personnel doing a thorough job of refining the project idea will probably change positions several times about which is the best solution to the need. New information causes the continuous reassessment of options. This will be true once the project is under way, as well as before the proposal is actually written. In fact, one experienced proposal writer pointed out, only partly in jest, that she always counted on her current project to prompt ideas for at least two future proposals. She said she was always thinking of better ideas or better approaches when it was too late to apply them to the current situation.

GATHERING STATISTICAL DATA

Many novices and even some experienced proposal writers overlook the importance of statistical data to the development and refinement of the project idea or the role that it should play in the application itself. Statistical data is needed, for example, to:

● Help prove the need for the project, particularly in your locale.

● Help refine an approach to the need (for example, by suggesting that one type of effort has been shown to be more effective than others in the past).

● To document the degree to which your organization has previously been successful (either with this or other clientele).

While it may be commonly understood that statistical data will be required in applications to governmental sources, applicants often forget to pay attention to providing such information in requests to private foundations and corporations. While these sources will not want to be bombarded with pages of charts and graphs, they will want sufficient data included to answer the types of questions which any sensible reviewer would ask. Chapter 14 provides many examples of selection criteria used by private sources. Review those when deciding what type of data to collect during the preproposal phase.

Applications to national sources (whether governmental or private) should almost always contain some type of comparative data to place your needs in the appropriate context. For example, data showing that the juvenile delinquency rate in your town is twice as high as neighboring areas and perhaps five times as high as regional or national levels will help justify the need for a project more than any emotional appeals or political maneuverings.

Comparative data is also useful in supporting a request to private sources for even a small portion of your agency's annual operating budget. All donors will want to know what impact your services are having and how this equates to others performing similar work.

Unfortunately, the difficulties facing those trying to gather regional and national data have

increased in recent years. Much information is still collected by the federal government, but is no longer compiled, analyzed or periodically issued in an easily accessible manner. One has to be more creative these days in searching out some of this material. The attachment to this Chapter will suggest the variety of sources that may be used.

The beginning point, however, is still your local or state reference library. Developing a good working relationship with key individuals in these institutions will pay many dividends.

BUILDING SUPPORT AND INVOLVEMENT

It is assumed that key personnel in the applicant organization will have been consulted at some point during the processes outlined thus far and will have been given the opportunity to participate in preliminary discussions and decisions. But before carrying the idea for the sponsored project any further, you should give some thought to the matter of involving and informing other affected individuals or groups.

● Top-level administrators or governing boards of the organization. Since they will have to sanction the completed proposal eventually, it is wiser to identify and deal with any concerns while the project is still in the design phase.

● Affected agencies or groups within the community. Private donors are particularly interested in the degree of local support for most projects and they also want assurances that the project is not inappropriately duplicative of others' services.

● The population to be served or studied. Their willing participation cannot be taken for granted and may, in fact, need to be documented in the application.

● Relevant state agencies or organizations. In many fields, a state agency or organization has been designated to oversee program development, resource allocation or the provision of technical services to local groups planning new projects. They may be a good source of information on the results of similar projects in the past, serve as potential sources of funds themselves, or be willing to help with endorsements to regional or national sources.

● The state agency administering A-95 (a circular issued by the Federal Office of Management and Budget). This requirement insures that state and local government bodies have an opportunity to review and comment on all relevant projects prior to their submission for federal funds. The A-95 staff is a good source for finding out if similar projects have been submitted to the federal government from groups within the state in the past. They can also advise how much lead time to provide for this review once your proposal is completed.

● Local representatives of foundations or corporations whom you are likely to be approaching. They can often spot issues that will strengthen your applications and they may be able to suggest other possible sources of support.

● Program officers in the federal agency to whom you may be sending the proposal. Sladeck and Stein (1983) have some helpful tips on how to use these individuals' expertise in designing a project and even writing the proposal.

CHAPTER REFERENCES

Bauer, D.G., *The "How-To" Grants Manual* (New York: Macmillan, 1984).

Meador, R., *Guidelines for Preparing Proposals* (Chelsea, Lewis Publishers, 1985).

Sladek, F.E., and E.L. Stein, "Funding Agency Contacts: Letting Them Help," *Grants Magazine,* vol. 6, no. 1 (March 1983), 19-31.

EXAMPLES OF SOURCES OF INFORMATION FOR IDEA REFINEMENT

SELECTED COMPUTERIZED INFORMATION SEARCH SERVICES

There are now several hundred computerized information systems available from public or commercial sources that can be helpful in determining the originality of an idea, prior research related to an idea or statistical data useful in explaining the need for a project. A first step is to consult one of the following documents that provide brief descriptions of these data services:

Complete Guide to Dial-Up Data Bases, Datapro Research Corporation, 1805 Underwood Boulevard, Delran, NJ 18075.

A periodic inventory of computerized information systems, with the most recent edition issued in 1985. Arranged alphabetically and easy to use.

Directory of On-Line Databases, Cuadra/ Elsevier, 52 Vanderbilt Avenue, New York, NY 10017.

An annual listing of computerized information sources, with periodic supplements during the year.

A REPRESENTATIVE SAMPLE OF SOME OF THESE COMPUTERIZED SERVICES FOLLOWS:

AMA/NET, Socio-Economic Bibliographic Information Base, American Medical Association, 535 N. Dearborn, Chicago, IL 60610.

This service provides bibliographic citations to non-clinical aspects of health care and monitors more than 700 journals. Coverage includes economics, education, ethics, international relations, legislation, medical practice, political science, psychology, public health, statistics and sociology. It is updated monthly.

American Statistics Index, Congressional Information Service, Inc., 4520 East-West Highway, Suite 800, Bethesda, MD 20814.

A guide to statistical and other information published by the United States government. Monthly update.

Associated Press, VU/Text Information Services, Inc., 1211 Chestnut Street, Philadelphia PA 19107.

A service to access the full text of all stories distributed through AP since January 1, 1985. Stories can be searched for by word, as well as by date or headline. Daily update.

Comsearch.

A computerized database on grants made by private foundations. Can be accessed by a customized inquiry or, in some fields, hardcopies of prior listings can be purchased. Prices vary. Write: The Foundation Center, 79 Fifth Avenue, New York, N.Y. 10003.

Congressional Information Service. CIE, Inc., 4520 East-West Highway, Washington, D.C. 20014.

This covers most activities and publications of the U.S. Congress, including hearings, committee reports and special documents. These are excellent and often overlooked sources of expert testimony and statistical data as well as descriptions of social needs. *The CIE Index* may be ordered to determine what material is available on particular subjects.

DIALOG, Dialog Information Services, Inc., 3460 Hillview Avenue, Palo Alto, CA 94304.

Contact this commercial firm's marketing department for a description of one of the largest computerized information services in the world. It currently contains over 280 databases in a broad scope of disciplines. There are many different ways to subscribe to the service and you may find DIALOG available through your local university library. A catalog for the service was issued most recently in early 1987.

CONTINUED

Educational Resource Information Clearing-houses. ERIC, National Institute of Education, Washington, D.C. 20014.

The federal government supports several centers throughout the country that collect and disseminate information on selected educational topics such as higher education, handicapped education or early childhood education. In addition to reviewing and abstracting journal and periodical articles in their respective fields, the centers monitor books, project reports, speeches, unpublished manuscripts, dissertations, state and federal documents, and other sources of information on research, current practice or discussion. Most university libraries and state departments of education have access to the ERIC system.

National Technical Information Service. NTIS, 5285 Port Royal Road, Springfield, VA 22161.

This is the central source for the public sale of all federally-sponsored research, development and engineering reports or other analyses prepared by federal agencies, their grantees or contractors. NTIS is also a central source of federally generated machine-processable data files. These documents can be identified through customized searches or through a variety of catalogs or hardcopies of previously prepared bibliographic listings.

State Housing, Construction and Finance, Chase Econometrics, 150 Monument Road, Bala Cynwyd, PA 19004.

This system maintains national, regional and state data on demographics, population, housing, households, finances, housing stock, economics, consumer price indices, mortgage rates, and employment and mortgage organizations. Its ability to generate comparative information makes it valuable in many fields.

SCISEARCH, Institute for Scientific Information, 3501 Market Street, University City Science Center, Philadelphia, PA 19104.

A multidisciplinary index to over 4,000 journals in engineering, physical, biological and natural sciences. Updated biweekly. This organization also operates Social SCISEARCH (covering 1,400 social science publications 3,300 journals in disciplines such as biomedicine).

EXAMPLES OF SOURCES OF STATISTICAL DATA

Digest of Educational Statistics, Center for Statistics, U.S. Department of Education, Washington, D.C. 20202.

This standard source of nationwide data covers major characteristics of all aspects of elementary, secondary and higher education (including institutional, faculty and student information) and includes both historical data and projected trends.

Federal Information Sources and Systems 1984, Information Handling and Support Facility, General Accounting Office, Box 6015, Gaithersburg, MD 20877.

Describes about 1,700 federal information systems, including document centers, clearinghouses, research centers and libraries. Also lists a variety of federal publications.

Project Summaries, Division of Science Resources Studies, Directorate for Scientific, Technological and International Affairs, National Science Foundation, Washington, D.C. 20550.

This document describes, for each fiscal year, the studies which this agency has carried out or contracted for to track basic science and technology information (such as level of resources, output and impact). It also tells in what form this data is available and when the next update is expected. Examples of the types of studies conducted include an analysis of the supply, demand and labor markets for scientists and engineers; the level of resources available to historically black colleges and universities and their sources; and trends in basic research.

Research in Progress: 1984-85, Independent Sector, 1828 L Street NW, Washington, D.C. 20036.

This directory, which will be updated periodically, provides a brief description of research projects on philanthropy, voluntary action, and not-for-profit activity. A number of these studies include statistical data on trends in various fields of service as well as sources of authoritative citations on different types of projects and their effectiveness. The book is organized by major

disciplines and issue areas and contains several different types of indexes.

Requirements for Recurring Reports to the Congress, U.S. General Accounting Office, Information Handling and Support Facility, P.O. Box 6015, Gaithersburg, MD 20877.

This free directory (last issued in 1984) describes approximately 2,900 recurring reporting requirements of the U.S. Congress. It is an invaluable tool for quickly determining the type of information routinely collected throughout the federal system. It has two sections. The Citation Section is organized by agency and contains, for each reporting requirement, a synopsis of the requirement, a descriptive abstract, budget data, authorizing legislation, relevant congressional committees, geographic coverage and public availability. The Index Section provides access to the Citation Section by subject, agency, congressional committee, law and budget function. Once you know what information is collected, you can then contact the appropriate agency to get the necessary data.

State Administrative Officials Classified By Function: 1985-86, Council on State Governments, Iron Works Pike, Box 11910, Lexington, KY 40578.

This document provides the name and contact information for those who fill key administrative roles in all state agencies throughout the U.S. It has both a state agency and subject category index and may be helpful in identifying those to communicate with in gathering comparative data from other states.

Washington Information Directory, 1985-86, Congressional Quarterly, Inc., 1414 22nd Street NW, Washington, D.C. 20037.

A list of 5,000 government agencies, committees and nongovernmental associations considered authoritative sources on specialized information. Several indexes, including by subject area.

SELECTING THE FUNDING SOURCE

This section describes the methods to use in identifying the appropriate funding sources, lists the types of information to secure from the funding source prior to the preparation of the proposal, and suggests techniques for communicating with the funding source before the proposal is submitted.

IDENTIFYING THE FUNDING SOURCE

Let us briefly review the steps which thus far have been completed in the proposal development process:

● An idea has been identified, its key characteristics analyzed, and a decision made on whether it is a solicited or unsolicited project.

● A review of the applicant organization's capability has been completed, basic systems needed to support the proposal's development have been secured and a decision has been made that the idea is compatible with the agency's mission and priorities.

● The validity of the need for the project has been substantiated, a clear statement of the problem to be solved has been developed and appropriate statistical data and related research have been obtained.

● Several options for meeting the need and implementing the project have been brainstormed. These have been tested against related research, local interest and capabilities, prior experience with similar ideas, possible impact, feasibility and degree of innovativeness.

● A tentative decision has been made about the best approach to the project. This will soon be tested against the interests of potential funding sources and may later be refined or revised if necessary.

● The potential project has been explained to other interested individuals and groups. Support for the goals and methods of the project has been generated, potential roles in the project have been identified and matters of coordination and cooperation have been discussed.

It is now time to answer the critical question: *Where are the most likely sources of money to carry out this idea?*

Many proposal writers are too narrowly focused when they enter this search. They think: "Well, if it is a science project, obviously we should approach the National Science Foundation." But perhaps the project's approach involves new methodology for training technicians (an idea that might appeal to some corporations), or it is intended to benefit students from disadvantaged backgrounds (a mission of many foundations, corporations and other private sector donors), or the project's success may benefit the economy in a particular locale (thus qualifying for sources with a special interest in that geography or the state's economic development agency).

At this point it may be useful to revisit the discussion on project characteristics in Chapter 1 and brainstorm as many alternative ways of viewing the idea as possible. This will help to insure that all potential types of support are at least identified and considered.

DIFFERENCES BETWEEN PUBLIC AND PRIVATE FUNDING

Some projects can qualify equally well for public or private support, but most will probably appeal more readily to one or the other. While difficult to generalize (and subject to a variety of opinions), there are some key differences between the two that may assist in narrowing at least the initial focus to one or the other. Apart from the obvious difference that private sources prefer not to fund causes or functions for which significant amounts of public funding are available, there are some other distinctions, as outlined in Table 1.

The remainder of this chapter is divided into two sections: Part I, discussing public sources of funding, and Part II, describing the private sector.

PART I:

PUBLIC SOURCES OF FUNDING
◼ **FEDERAL AGENCIES**
◼ **STATE AND LOCAL AGENCIES**

FEDERAL GOVERNMENT AGENCIES

There are literally hundreds of separate grant-in-aid programs supported through the federal government, managed by a large bureaucracy of departments, bureaus and offices. Although the availability of such funds is declining (in constant dollars), the federal government still represents the largest source of support for those seeking external funding.

The government conveniently provides many of the tools necessary to identify which federal programs are most likely to match your interests. The seven major ones are briefly outlined below:

● *Catalog of Federal Domestic Assistance*, Superintendent of Documents, U.S. Government Printing Office, Washington, D.C. 20402. Cost—$38.00. This is the official guide to all federal programs authorized by public law. It will answer most of your basic questions about any programs, although financial data and deadlines given should always be double checked with the administering agency.

● *Federal Assistance Programs Retrieval System (FAPRS)* is a computerized question-answer system designed to give more rapid access to most of the same information provided in the *Catalog*. Customized searches can be done by subject area, applicant eligibility criteria or type of assistance desired. Every state has designated access points where FAPRS searches may be requested. You can get further

information by contacting your local Member of Congress (who may do the search for you at no cost) or by writing to: Federal Domestic Assistance Catalog Staff (WKU), General Services Administration, Ground Floor, Reporters Building, 300 7th Street SW, Washington, D.C. 20407.

● *Federal Register*, Superintendent of Documents, U.S. Government Printing Office, Washington, D.C. 20402. Cost--$345/year. This is the official news publication of the government, including announcements of public meetings, availability of new programs, changes in regulations and deadlines.

● *U.S. Government Manual*, Superintendent of Documents, U.S. Government Printing Office, Washington, D.C. 20402. Cost—$24. This handbook describes all federal agencies and their responsibilities, and gives the names of key officials.

● *Commerce Business Daily*, Superintendent of Documents, U.S. Government Printing Office, Washington, D.C. 20402. Cost—$248/year. This is the required mechanism for announcing upcoming contracts and Requests for Proposals, as well as those selected for such awards.

● *Federal Executive Telephone Directory*, Carroll Publishing, 1058 Thomas Jefferson Street NW, Washington, D.C. 20007. Cost--$140. Names, addresses and telephone numbers of key governmental personnel. Issued six times a year.

● *Agency Catalogs, Newsletters, Program Announcements and RFPs*. Once you know which agencies typically administer funds of interest to you, write to their public information office and ask to be put on the mailing list for further publications.

You will usually find that the above resources are already available somewhere in your organization. If not, they can be used at your nearest Government Repository Library (the location of which can be requested from Chief of the Library, Department of Public Documents, U.S. Government Printing Office, Washington, D.C. 20402).

Other sources of information on federal funding are described in Attachment 1.

TABLE 1   **SELECTING THE FUNDING SOURCE**

DIFFERENCES BETWEEN PUBLIC AND PRIVATE SOURCES OF FUNDING

ADVANTAGES

Public	Private
1. Purpose set by legislation.	1. More likely to focus on emerging issues, new needs, populations not yet organized to be large "special interests."
2. Focus on functions usually impacting significant groups in society.	2. Will often allow their funds to be pooled with other sources.
3. Have the most money.	3. Some can make very large grants.
4. More likely to make big grants/contracts.	4. Better source of start-up or experimental funds.
5. More likely to pay all project costs.	5. Proposals need not be complex or lengthy.
6. More likely to cover indirect costs.	6. Can be much more flexible in responding to unique needs and circumstances.
7. Easier to identify and to keep current.	7. Seldom have bureaucratic requirements to follow in administering grants.
8. Have known application processes and firm deadlines.	8. Carry more stature and prestige.
9. Use prescribed formats for proposals.	9. Can often provide forms of help other than just cash.
10. Known possibilities of renewal.	10. Usually have fewer applicants.
11. Lots of staff, with resources for technical assistance.	11. Can generally be much more informal.
12. Funds available to wider array of organizations (such as forprofit, as well as nonprofit or other public units).	12. Often better sources for more local needs and smaller agencies.
13. Are accountable to elected officials if funders obviously don't follow the rules.	

DISADVANTAGES

Public	Private
1. Are much more bureaucratic.	1. Average grant size usually smaller.
2. Proposals must be much more lengthy and require a variety of compliances.	2. Priorities can change very rapidly, thus making continuation support more difficult to predict.
3. Often require institutional cost-sharing and matching.	3. Applicants have limited influence on the decisionmaking process.
4. Many more requirements to follow once funds are received.	4. Information on their policies and procedures more difficult to track. This requires more lead-time for research.
5. Reviewers tend to favor established applicants.	5. Some unwilling to pay all project costs and most do not cover indirect costs.
6. Sometimes difficult to sell really new ideas or high-risk approaches.	6. Limited number of staff lessens opportunities for preliminary discussion/site visits.
7. Cost to applicant of securing such funds and carrying out projects usually much higher.	7. May not be very forthcoming about why you were rejected, thus making it difficult to compete more effectively the next time.
8. Changing political trends affect security of some programs and continued availability of funds.	

This handout taken from *Getting Funded: A Complete Guide to Proposal Writing* by Mary Hall, 1988.
Available from Continuing Education Publications, P.O. Box 1491, Portland, OR 97207.

INFORMATION TO GATHER ON EACH FEDERAL PROGRAM

You will need to determine most, if not all, of the information listed in Table 2 on those federal programs to which you might apply. The majority can be obtained from the publications cited previously or in this chapter's attachment, through computerized searches, or follow-up calls and letters.

Some find it helpful to record the responses to these informational categories on worksheets. This allows the information to be quickly confirmed and more easily updated. Bauer (1984) and Seltzer (1986) provide several sample worksheets.

Once you have secured all of the printed matter available on the program, you face the issue of how to gather the more "informal" information. Personal visits to federal agency officers are seldom practical for the less experienced writer or individuals in smaller agencies.

You might, therefore, find it profitable to prepare a written letter briefly describing your project and to send it to the agency administrator, indicating that you will be calling to discuss this by telephone (you may need to call more than once, but persevere). You can also use this letter to contact others in your locale who have successfully competed under this program (you will find that out through lists of past grants) and those who have previously served as proposal reviewers for the agency (this will also be available from most agencies).

Some of the issues you might want to probe further with these folks include:

● Do they agree that your project addresses an important need?

● Does it seem that you have thought of a good way to solve this problem?

● What could be changed to strengthen your chances?

● How closely does the project match the program priorities and selection criteria of this particular funding source?

● What number of awards under this program during the past two years went to those applying for the first time?

● What components of the proposal appeared to be most important to the reviewers last year?

● What were the most common mistakes made by those applying to this program?

● What kind of information do applicants seldom provide that the agency would like to see in the proposal?

● Are there any discretionary funds, unsolicited proposal funds or as yet unannounced programs in this agency for which your project might qualify?

● Can the individual suggest other federal programs under which your project might have a higher priority?

To the newcomer, this seems like a lot of information to gather (often in a short period of time), but Figure 1 may help you to visualize an overview of the investigation process. Some of these steps can be assigned to others and not all will need to be completed for every project.

The time and effort that you put in at this stage will have considerable payoff later when you have been able to narrow your proposal writing down to those federal programs where you are most likely to be successful.

STATE AND LOCAL GOVERNMENT AGENCIES

State and local government agencies have at least four reasons for serving as sources of grant or contract funds:

● They are designated as recipients for federal monies (usually block grants) which must then be redistributed to local applicants.

● They receive a grant or contract themselves and want to identify others to perform part of the project's requirements.

● They are designated as the administrator of a grant-in-aid program established by the state legislature, county, borough or city council and must then choose recipients for these funds.

TABLE 2   **SELECTING THE FUNDING SOURCE**

KINDS OF INFORMATION NEEDED ON POTENTIAL
FEDERAL FUNDING SOURCES

❏ Correct name for the grant-in-aid program or program category.

❏ Correct name and address of administering agency.

❏ Name, title and telephone number of key administrator.

❏ Major purpose of legislation that authorized program.

❏ Latest regulations governing program and any indication they may change in the near future.

❏ Current priorities of the program and if these may change.

❏ Eligibility requirements for applicants.

❏ Appropriations in current FY and amount projected for next year.

❏ What portion of these sums will likely be retained for continuation awards and how much will be available for new grants.

❏ The required proposal format plus any accompanying forms.

❏ The compliance requirements, individual agency policies or Office of Management and Budget policies pertaining to the program.

❏ Whether a preliminary letter or abstract is required or a capability statement necessary to receive a full RFP.

❏ Application deadlines (there may be more than one per year).

❏ Dates of expected proposal review and notification.

❏ The application and review process, including the latest selection criteria.

❏ The rating form used last year in the selection criteria.

❏ The names and affiliations of those who served as proposal reviewers. You may not be able to get this for the upcoming round of competition, but you will for agencies that have standing panels as well as those who served last year. It might be worth a check in your professional directories to see the type of organization they represent, their personal backgrounds and professional interests.

❏ A list of the grants or contracts awarded under the program during the past two years, including amounts.

❏ The tendency of the agency to cut budget requests. You can determine this by asking for copies of funded proposals (which are a matter of public record, although you may need to pay a copying charge) and comparing this to the amount actually reported for the grant on the above list.

❏ Details on any restrictions placed on the use of the program's funds.

❏ Requirements for matching funds or cost sharing.

❏ Policies towards renewals and samples of renewal application forms.

❏ Requirements for reports once the grant or contract is received and other information on project administration (these are usually contained in a separate document available from each agency).

❏ Whether a state or local government plays any role in the program administration or selection process and, if so, the names and telephone numbers of those in your area.

This handout taken from *Getting Funded: A Complete Guide to Proposal Writing* by Mary Hall, 1988.
Available from Continuing Education Publications, P.O. Box 1491, Portland, OR 97207.

HOW TO ORGANIZE YOUR SEARCH FOR POTENTIAL FEDERAL FUNDING SOURCES

Step 1:
Consult major directories and draw up list of possibilities. Identify needed information.

Step 2A:
Contact Member of Congress. Request FAPRS printout on identified sources and also search for other possible sources. Ask for Public Laws and House/Senate hearings on latest amendments to all pertaining programs.

Step 2B:
Write agency head to get latest copy of program announcement, application forms, deadlines, other general information. Ask about FY budget and estimates on sums for new grantees. Get list of past grants.

Step 3:
Consult local library to secure latest *Federal Register* regulations, names and telephone numbers of new sources turned up by FAPRS. Check FY budget data in latest Office of Management and Budget report.

Step 4:
Write agency head of any new sources and get same information as Step 2B.

Step 5:
Review basic information you have received and select the most promising sources.

Step 6:
For refined list, send the agency head a project draft and follow it up with a telephone call. Ask for copies of any funded proposals in which you are interested, plus any other information you haven't been able to find.

Step 7:
For refined list, identify local grantees and pick their brains on how to improve the odds for your success.

Step 9:
Consolidate all you have learned and select the most likely funding source. Develop timeline to prepare proposal for next suitable deadline.

Step 8:
For refined list, identify local reviewers and seek their guidance on program chances.

● They wish to purchase a particular product or service to help implement some aspect of their responsibilities.

Abramson and Salamon (1986) have noted that these bodies are becoming less important sources of funds, particularly to nonprofits, as federal outlays to other governmental sources are beginning to decline. In all but a few states, local appropriations do not appear to be increasing sufficiently to offset the impact of these federal reductions.

However, state and local governments have two distinct advantages over federal agencies: One, their personnel are usually more accessible; and two, the competition for funds is unlikely to be as intense. They thus represent good sources for the beginning proposal writer or those who are considering a project which should clearly be supported by public, as opposed to private, funds.

State and local agencies that distribute federal monies can be identified through the information sources discussed previously or outlined in Attachment 1. The process of identifying other funding from such bodies is more difficult.

In the case of state agencies, two beginning points are a) the annual *State Administrative Officials Classified by Function* issued by the Council on State Governments, and b) your state's agency directory or handbook (normally available from your local library or the office of your Secretary of State). From these, you can compile a list of those individuals heading functions most directly related to the needs and interests of your organization.

A follow-up call or letter to these individuals, briefly describing your project and asking if they have relevant grants or contract programs is the next appropriate step. After asking that they send you any printed material on their programs, you should then seek a personal appointment if at all possible.

In all preliminary contacts of this type, the potential applicant should try to achieve four goals:

● *to determine whether the state group is a potential source of funds for this particular project;*

● *if so, to get all of the necessary information to prepare a successful application* (generally, this will be similar to that outlined previously on federal programs);

● *to ascertain the overall interests and priorities of the agency so that you will know if it is worthwhile to maintain continuing contact; and, if appropriate,*

● *to establish some communication system that will lead to notification of future grant and contract opportunities.*

To aid this last goal, it is wise to send or take along a general statement of capabilities for the administrator's files. This should include, at a minimum, a description of your agency or organization, including its mission, date established, legal basis, general areas of expertise or ongoing services, type of staff, a brief summary of the range of their experience, and any special or unique factors (such as data-processing capability, desk-top publishing experience and so forth).

For sources of support (other than federal monies) from county, city or borough governments, the best beginning place is the local telephone book. In some locales, a regional council of government (COG) still exists. Staff in these agencies can also be helpful in pointing you in the right direction.

As a final note, many individuals make the mistake of assuming that state or local agencies are automatically not interested in supporting research. In fact, they annually fund significant numbers of studies on issues appropriate to their jurisdictions. Such bodies are particularly fertile hunting ground for those seeking both a topic and support for a doctoral dissertation. Most frequently, these arrangements are established through a consulting contract, personal services agreement or internships rather than a grant-in-aid.

PART II:

PRIVATE SOURCES OF FUNDING

- ■ **FOUNDATIONS**
- ■ **CORPORATIONS**
- ■ **PROFESSIONAL ASSOCIATIONS AND TRADE ASSOCIATIONS**
- ■ **OTHER**

PRIVATE FOUNDATIONS

The world of private foundations can often be a bewildering and sometimes frightening prospect to the novice proposal writer. Cartoons have depicted these institutions as being comprised of pompous officials (usually male) in pinstripe suits, sitting in elegant surroundings in some highrise in Manhattan, tossing millions of dollars to kneeling supplicants, most of whom haven't a clue as to why they are being favored or rejected.

As with all cartoons, there may have been elements of truth in these characterizations. But donors and those who work for them have made great strides in the past decade in reducing the barriers between grantmakers and grantseekers.

● An increasing number of foundations now hire staff members from the same types of organizations they are funding. The person you meet across the desk may well have held a job similar to yours not too long ago.

● Corporate foundations, in large numbers, now use a process of calling on local employees of their parent firms to serve as volunteer "points of contact" in those communities in which they have major operations.

● A growing number of foundations issue printed guidelines and annual reports.

● The rise of community foundations has increased the likelihood of private monies being available to resolve needs that are of only local concern.

● Regional Area Groups (RAGs) of donors now exist in all parts of the country. Most have some type of annual program to help grantseekers learn more about the interests of their members and compete more effectively for private resources. The Council on Foundations maintains communication with over twenty such RAGs. The most prominent of these, along with a name and information on how to make contact, are described in Attachment 6.

● The Foundation Center and the Council on Foundations (among others) offer an array of informational services making it easier to identify foundations, track their interests and be aware of their grantmaking policies and procedures.

● Finally, it should not be forgotten that most of these organizations were created for the purpose of "doing good." They are genuinely interested in the ideas of those (in their particular field of emphasis) who are "out on the firing line" providing services and trying to improve society.

The foundations themselves face some special problems. Understanding these will assist in your communications and relationships with such organizations.

● The current tax laws are not especially encouraging to new foundation formation and fewer than 300 foundations with assets over $1 million have been created since the 1970s.

● The total number of grants that foundations can provide is minuscule when compared to the potential impact of the cutback in federal funds in fields traditionally of interest to nonprofits.

● Only a little more than 1,000 of the 25,000 private foundations have professional staff. Most of these staffs are small.

● The vast majority of the foundations in the U.S. are themselves very small, with assets under $1 million.

TYPES OF PRIVATE FOUNDATIONS

There are four generally accepted classifications of private foundations. Their major characteristics are shown in Figure 2.

FIGURE 2   SELECTING THE FUNDING SOURCE

GENERAL CHARACTERISTICS OF FOUR TYPES OF FOUNDATIONS

Foundation Type:	Independent Foundation	Company-sponsored Foundation	Operating Foundation	Community Foundation
Description	An independent grant-making organization established to aid social, educational, religious or other charitable activities.	Legally an independent grantmaking organization with close ties to the corporation providing funds.	An organization which uses its resources to conduct research or provide a direct service.	A publicly-supported organization which makes grants for social, educational, religious or other charitable purposes in a specific community or region.
Source of Funds	Endowment generally derived from a single source such as an individual, a family, or a group of individuals. Contributions to endowment are limited as to tax deductibility.	Endowment and annual contributions from a profit-making corporation. May maintain small endowment and pay out most of contributions received annually in grants, or may maintain endowment to cover contributions in years when corporate profits are down.	Endowment usually provided from a single source, but eligible for maximum tax deductible contributions from public.	Contributions received from many donors. Usually eligible for maximum tax deductible contributions from public.
Decision-making Body	Decisions may be made by donor or members of donor's family, by an independent board of directors or trustees, or by a bank or trust officer acting on donor's behalf.	Decisions made by board of directors often composed of corporate officials, but which may include individuals with no corporate affiliation. Decisions may also be made by local company officials.	Decisions generally made by independent board of directors.	Decisions made by board of directors representing the diversity of the community.
Grantmaking Activity	Broad discretionary giving allowed but may have specific guidelines and give only in a few specific fields. About 70% limit their giving to local area.	Giving tends to be in fields related to corporate activities or in communities where corporation operates. Usually give more grants but in smaller dollar amounts than independent foundations.	Makes few, if any, grants. Grants generally related directly to the foundation's program.	Grants generally limited to charitable organizations in local community.
Reporting Requirements	Annual information returns 990-PF filed with IRS must be made available to the public. A small percentage issue separately printed annual reports.	Same as preceding.	Same as preceding.	IRS 990 return available to public. Many publish full guidelines or annual reports.

Source: *The Foundation Directory*, 10th ed., New York: The Foundation Center, 1985.

TYPES OF FOUNDATION AWARDS

In 1985, foundations granted about $4.3 billion in sums ranging from as small as $100 to awards in excess of several millions of dollars. Although it is hard to generalize, these grants typically went for the following purposes:

● **General support.** These awards are intended to assist with the normal ongoing work of the applicant as outlined in the proposal that has been submitted. There is a trend towards smaller and fewer grants of this nature, since most foundations like to tie their funds to some definite purpose.

● **Endowment.** This is one of the most desirable awards from the perspective of the applicant but, again, an increasingly difficult grant type to secure. In an endowment, the donor may specify a purpose for the grant, but provide sufficient money for the purpose to be carried out by using only the earnings on the award (the bulk of which is invested by the applicant). This permits perpetual support for the grant's purpose.

● **Program or project grants.** These are the most common form of foundation grant and they are designated for a specific type of activity, research, service or event. Applications for such awards need to be able to specify how the success of the effort can be measured or judged.

● **Fellowships/scholarships.** These awards, to support the work of specific individuals, may be a part of a program or project grant. But sometimes they are solely for the purpose of student assistance. In most cases, the foundations give such awards to institutions or organizations which, in turn, select the particular student to receive the funds. However, some foundations make such awards directly to individuals.

● **Capital grants.** Typically, these refer to awards for buildings and/or equipment. Some foundations specialize in making grants only for these purposes.

● **Loan guarantees.** Although used infrequently, some foundations will agree to serve as a guarantor on a loan an applicant is seeking from commercial sources.

● **Program-related investment.** As an adjunct to normal grantmaking, a relatively small number of foundations will also consider making a direct investment of some of their assets in the applicant organization, with the understanding that the funds (and perhaps a modest rate of return) will eventually be returned to the donor. Examples of fields where this is most common include community development, rural cooperatives, low-income housing and minority enterprises.

Within most of these major types of grant categories, there may also be additional variations. Some foundations want their awards to be used as *seed money*, to help plan a new enterprise or assist with its initiation. Others want their grants to be used as *pilot awards*, to demonstrate the effectiveness of some new model or approach, usually with the understanding that if the effort is successful, continuation funds will be sought elsewhere. And finally, a large number of foundations make *matching* or *challenge* grants, indicating that they will provide a certain sum of funds for some purpose if additional monies are raised elsewhere. Sometimes the precise amount which must be secured to qualify for the initial award is specified and sometimes not.

Finally, it should be noted that private foundations are incorporated in all states. According to the AAFRC Trust for Philanthropy, the six states with the highest concentration of foundations (accounting for nearly 60 percent of the total) are, in rank order, California, Illinois, Michigan, New York, Pennsylvania and Texas.

FOUNDATION RECIPIENTS

Most foundations must limit their awards to private, nonprofit, tax-exempt organizations that have been certified by the Internal Revenue Service as qualifying under Section 501(c)(3) of the Code. For those who are not familiar with the steps necessary to qualify for this status, a particularly useful discussion is found in Seltzer (1987). Additionally, some foundations will make awards to public entities (as defined under Section 170(c) of the Code). A small number of foundations will also make grants directly to individuals.

Most foundations have the options of also making an award to an organization that is not tax-exempt, but would be considered eligible by the Internal Revenue Service if it applied. This case frequently comes up when a foundation is hoping to make an

TABLE 3   SELECTING THE FUNDING SOURCE

DISTRIBUTION OF GRANT BY SUBJECT AREA, 1985, OF SOME 1,200 FOUNDATIONS

SUBJECT	$ AMOUNT	NO. GRANTS	% OF TOTAL
Cultural Activities			
General	$69,374	1,400	3.9
Art & Architecture	63,995	882	2.4
History	28,191	543	1.5
Language & Literature	30,064	539	1.5
Media & Communications	25,339	586	1.6
Music	42,241	1,164	3.2
Theater & Dance	35,031	1,132	3.1
TOTAL CULTURAL ACTIVITIES	294,236	6,246	17.2
Education			
General	22,787	478	1.3
Adult & Continuing	22,267	203	0.6
Elementary & Secondary	57,808	1,472	4.1
Higher (General)	227,955	3,656	10.1
Vocational	7,109	250	0.7
TOTAL EDUCATION	337,925	6,059	16.8
Health			
General	26,878	449	1.2
Medical & Health Education	73,949	711	2.0
Medical Care & Treatment	155,690	1,908	5.3
Medical Research	120,618	800	2.2
Mental Health	29,086	618	1.7
Public Health	67,570	1,523	4.2
TOTAL HEALTH	473,790	6,009	16.6
Religion			
General	24,420	527	1.5
Religious Education	13,841	175	0.5
TOTAL RELIGION	38,261	702	2.0
Science			
General	31,763	320	0.9
Life Sciences	31,499	344	0.9
Physical Sciences	28,096	605	1.7
Technology	86,096	997	2.7
TOTAL SCIENCE	177,454	2,266	6.2
Social Science			
General	18,958	291	0.8
Anthropology	6,146	75	0.2
Economics	18,224	390	1.1
Law & Legal Education	10,201	269	0.7
Political Science	115,633	1,827	5.0
TOTAL SOCIAL SCIENCE	169,162	2,852	7.8
Welfare			
General	126,072	4,002	11.0
Business & Employment	59,700	1,634	4.5
Community Affairs	94,284	1,811	5.0
Consumer Interests	1,067	41	0.1
Crime & Law Enforcement	11,146	334	0.9
Environment & Energy	59,637	1,180	3.2
Equal Rights & Legal Services	43,669	764	2.1
Recreation	58,175	1,168	3.2
Rural Development	20,594	294	0.8
Urban Development	48,230	958	2.6
TOTAL WELFARE	522,574	12,186	33.4
TOTAL GRANTS	2,013,401	36,320	100.0

Source: *The Foundation Grants Index, 15th edition*, New York: The Foundation Center, 1985.

award to an overseas organization. However, the foundation must usually retain "expenditure oversight" of the grant and, in addition, file special reports with the IRS. This tends to limit this particular option.

INFORMATION TO SECURE ON PRIVATE FOUNDATIONS

As with federal agencies, there is a list of questions you will want to answer before deciding whether or not to approach a particular foundation. Some of these are outlined in Table 4.

RESEARCHING FOUNDATIONS

STEP 1. Determine which of the informational resources listed in Attachment 2 are available to you locally. Check in your own organization, with your local library, at the nearest university, or call The Foundation Center (800-424-9836) to identify the location of their nearest regional or cooperating library. The last has free access to most of the Center's publications and many of its services. While you are making that call, determine whether the Center has an existing COMSEARCH document in your subject area and, if the price seems reasonable, order it.

If you are pressed for time and have the necessary resources, you may also want to consider asking the Center to do a customized search of their database for you.

STEP 2. Consult the various directories and other publications and prepare a list of potential sponsors. Think about the purpose of your organization or project as broadly as possible (it may be helpful to again review the discussion on project characteristics in Chapter 1). But note any of the foundation's geographic or eligibility restrictions; these are seldom flexible.

STEP 3. After developing a general list of potential donors, begin to narrow this down to the most likely. You can do this by checking the more detailed entries in the Foundation Center's *Source Book Profiles* (there are versions for both private and corporate foundations). The *Grants Index* and *Grants Index BiMonthly* will give you a more realistic picture of the

actual type of awards made by your sources and the kinds of organizations that most frequently receive their awards, as well as the amounts.

At about this same time, write or call the foundations on your list and ask for copies of their annual reports, guidelines or other printed material. It is not necessary to furnish them with a description of your project or organization simply to get their printed material. Almost 2,000 foundations have something to send and most will forward it promptly.

STEP 4. For those still left on your list, you may want to consult their latest 990 PF (a form they must submit annually to the Internal Revenue Service that includes a list of all their grantees, details on finances, giving interests and restrictions, and application procedures and deadlines). A sample of one is provided in Attachment 3. This is often the only source of information on smaller foundations. You can secure copies on specific foundations by contacting the Internal Revenue Service (call your local office to determine the procedure) or by looking at these in The Foundation Center's libraries. Often the Center's copies are two to three years out of date, but it may be the only information you have.

STEP 5. Start talking to other people. Begin with those in your own organization who may know something about the foundation. Call friends in other agencies that have received money from these sources. There may be a particular foundation that has already funded your organization several times in the past; call its staff to see if they have any suggestions or observations to make that will help you assess your possibilities.

STEP 6. Assess your organization's relationship to the funder. Be certain to check your organization's historical files to find out if you have ever received a grant from them before, and, if so, if the project was completed satisfactorily. Do any members of your staff or board know a member of the foundation staff or its board? In the case of unstaffed foundations, lawyers or trust officers may handle the initial correspondence, so see if you have any linkages to them.

STEP 7. Finally, narrow down your prospects to the most likely. The author suggests that you always, whenever possible, send an initial letter of inquiry before submitting a formal proposal. It is also recommended that you submit such a letter before

TABLE 4   **SELECTING THE FUNDING SOURCE**

KINDS OF INFORMATION NEEDED ON PRIVATE FOUNDATIONS

❑ What is the correct name of the foundation, its address and telephone number?

❑ Name, title, telephone number and address of primary contact person. Is this also the person to whom all grant requests should be submitted?

❑ Names (and, if possible, backgrounds) of donors, trustees and officers.

❑ Names and titles of staff (if any) and their backgrounds.

❑ Do they have a local or regional representative with whom you may talk? What role does this person play in the selection process?

❑ Any geographic restrictions on their grants?

❑ What kinds of organizations are eligible to apply? Individuals?

❑ Primary stated purposes of the foundation.

❑ Subject areas in which they make awards.

❑ Program categories and current priorities.

❑ Recent grants, including amounts.

❑ What type of awards do they seem to prefer (i.e. challenge, seed money)?

❑ What types of grants or purposes will they not support?

❑ What is the amount of their assets? In the most recent year that you can verify, how much did they pay out for grants? How much of this was for new, rather than continuation, awards?

❑ Is there a maximum or minimum amount on their grants?

❑ What is the average-sized grant and typical range of awards?

❑ Will they consider all of the costs of a project or only a specified percentage?

❑ Do they cover indirect costs? If not, will they pay for direct costs of some overhead functions in a project application?

❑ Do they have selection criteria and, if so, what are they?

❑ What is their application process? Deadlines? If none, do they operate on a calendar year?

❑ Do they have an application form? Instructions to applicants on what to submit? What attachments do they want?

❑ Do they want a letter of inquiry prior to receiving a proposal?

❑ What is their selection process? How far in advance should you submit a proposal before you can expect a decision?

❑ Do they use non-staff reviewers? If so, is it possible for you to get their names and affiliations?

❑ What is their policy on renewal? Do they indicate any definite limit on how many years they will support an organization or project?

❑ Will they assist in funding a project that is also receiving federal or other public monies?

This handout taken from *Getting Funded: A Complete Guide to Proposal Writing* by Mary Hall, 1988. Available from Continuing Education Publications, P.O. Box 1491, Portland, OR 97207.

trying to seek a personal appointment to discuss your project.

Many foundations (both corporate and private) ask for an initial letter of inquiry. The wording of this document is important. Some foundations may actually consider a grant on the basis of this letter alone. Others will not accept a later proposal if they have given a "discouraging" reply to the initial communication.

Figure 3 provides an example of an actual letter of inquiry submitted to a private foundation. Its writer did such an effective job that the foundation made a commitment to the project simply based on this initial document and the information gained during the subsequent visit.

The letter is a good model because it:

● Opens with a brief statement about the organization.

● Immediately gives the purpose of the letter.

● Provides a short description of the proposed project.

● Indicates that the project relates to the foundation's mission.

● Documents the need for the project.

● Indicates that there is support for the effort among the necessary participating organizations by the fact of their cost-sharing.

● Lets the foundation know how much money is likely to be requested and for how long support is needed.

● Shows that thought has been given as to how to continue the service later.

● Establishes credibility with the foundation by bringing along a person well known to (and liked by) the foundation head. As it happens, this person is also an expert in the subject.

● Alerts the foundation to an upcoming telephone call and indicates the information the potential applicant would like to have in advance.

The letter was also placed on appropriate letterhead, spelled the names of the foundation and the contact person correctly, used that person's correct

title, and had no grammatical or typographical errors. These are all important considerations in the initial inquiry.

CORPORATIONS

Charitable giving by corporations can be viewed as somewhat of an anomaly: *Why should organizations created solely for the purpose of making money give it away?*

The full history, rationale and outlook for corporate philanthropy is yet to be documented. But in 1982, the Council on Foundations commissioned the firm of Yankelovich, Skelly and White, Inc. to survey the officers of major companies to determine their attitudes on this matter.

Fully 59 percent said that "business has an ethical responsibility to make contributions to nonprofit organizations." Reasons cited referred to the "enlightened self-interest" of having good health, social welfare, arts, cultural and educational institutions in the communities where their plants and officers were located. Others spoke about the perceived importance to their "public image" of giftmaking. Still others, speaking about the potential impact of lowered tax rates, cited responsibilities to cover some of the social obligations previously funded by the federal government.

Whatever the reason, a growing and significant percentage of the many thousands of large and small firms in the country serve as potential sources of charitable support. In 1985, these dollars were estimated by The Conference Board to have increased 10 percent. The 439 firms tracked that year gave sums in excess of $4.4 billion.

In addition to corporate foundations (described in the previous section), corporations provide support through:

● Direct cash giving programs.

● Donations of equipment, facilities, land, products, employee services and other "in-kind" assistance.

● "Cause-related marketing" (a phrase referring to when a firm promotes its products in a way that produces cash income for a nonprofit or other charitable recipient).

SAMPLE LETTER OF INQUIRY TO A FOUNDATION

The Foundation Name
Address
City, State Zip

Dear Dr._____:

    The XYZ organization is a private nonprofit agency that has taken the lead in providing temporary shelter for young "street people" in ABC city. I am writing to see if you would consider a proposal to expand the employment and counseling services available to these youth.

    Our organization currently operates four shelters serving 75 young people each night. This is an increase of 30 percent from last year. Our major goal is to convince these young people to seek some form of additional education, to become employed, and, where appropriate, to return home.

    We believe our chances of accomplishing this would be improved by a person working among the shelters who could direct our residents to the alternative education, employment, health and mental health counseling services available throughout the city. Your foundation has expressed a special interest in the coordination of services to young people. We hope that you will give our project further consideration.

    The other community services involved have pledged their cooperation. They agree that a major problem in reaching these young people is the "in-take" process and that this can best be initiated at our shelters. We estimate the cost of this project the first year at $____, of which $_____ will be provided by the cooperating agencies. We would like you to consider a proposal for the remainder. If we can prove that our service is effective, we would qualify next year for some of the demonstration funds available through _____ agency.

    I will be calling shortly to seek an appointment to discuss this project. Ms. _____ of DEF agency, one of your past grantees, will be accompanying me. She is helping in the design of this project.

    In the meantime, would you please mail me your application guidelines and any instructions for preparing a completed request. A copy of our 501(c)(3) letter is attached.

                             Sincerely,

                             Name of sender

TABLE 5   **SELECTING THE FUNDING SOURCE**

BENEFICIARIES OF CORPORATE SUPPORT 1984-1985

	1985 436 Companies		1984 415 Companies	
	Thousands Dollars	% of Total	Thousands Dollars	% of Total
Health and Human Services				
Federated drives:				
United Ways			191,353	13.2
Other federated campaigns			2,538	0.2
National health organizations			16,427	1.1
National human service organizations			14,576	1.0
National youth organizations			4,666	0.3
Hospitals:				
Capital grants			24,666	1.7
Operating grants			7,092	0:5
Employee matching gifts for hospitals			1,920	0.1
Local youth organizations			21,751	1.5
Agencies for senior citizens and elderly				
Other local health and human service agencies			71,206	4.9
Capital grants excluding hospitals				
Employee matching gifts for health and human services			1,645	0.1
Subcategories unspecified			42,107	2.9
TOTAL HEALTH AND HUMAN SERVICES	494,109	29.2	399,948	27.7
Education:				
Higher education institutions:				
Unrestricted institutional operating grants			38,719	2.7
Student financial aid (funded through college or university)			26,080	1.8
Departmental grants			63,110	4.4
Special project or research grants			112,143	7.8
Capital grants			30,309	2.1
Employee matching gifts for higher education			72,238	5.0
Grants to state and national fund-raising groups			13,014	0.9
Precollege educational institutions:				
Employee matching gifts for precollege education			3,756	0.3
Public school support			13,737	1.0
All other support			8,629	0.6
Scholarships and fellowships (other than those reported above)			22,991	1.6
Education-related organizations:				
Economic education			11,684	0.8
All other support			17,090	1.2
Other			70,221	4.9
Subcategories unspecified			57,949	4.0
TOTAL EDUCATION	650,005	38.3	561,670	38.9

	1985 436 Companies		1984 415 Companies	
	Thousands Dollars	% of Total	Thousands Dollars	% of Total
Culture and Art:				
Music			19,673	1.4
Museums			30,450	2.1
Public TV and radio			18,677	1.3
Arts funds or councils			8,429	0.6
Theaters			9,358	0.6
Cultural centers			14,637	1.0
Dance			3,495	0.2
Libraries			2,538	0.2
Employee matching gifts for culture and art			8,928	0.6
Other			16,076	1.1
Subcategories unspecified			22,549	1.6
TOTAL CULTURE AND ART	187,536	11.1	154,711	10.7
Civic and Community Activities:				
Public policy organizations			15,334	1.1
National community improvement organizations			30,483	2.1
National environment and ecology organizations			77,964	5.4
National justice and law organizations:				
System research, reform, alternatives			2,666	0.2
Litigation, defense, advocacy			1,653	0.1
Other national organizations			7,602	0.5
Municipal or statewide improvements			7,781	0.5
Community improvement:				
Neighborhood or community-based groups			13,860	1.0
Housing			14,378	1.0
Economic development/employment			9,910	0.7
Legal systems/services			1,790	0.1
Local environment and ecology			19,149	1.3
Other local organizations			36,426	2.5
Subcategories unspecified			32,606	2.3
TOTAL CIVIC AND COMMUNITY ACTIVITIES	279,508	16.5	271,602	18.8
Other				
Religious activities			513	
Women's causes				
Groups in U.S. whose principal objective is aid in other countries			19,513	1.4
Activities other than above			27,819	1.9
Subcategories unspecified			8,538	0.6
TOTAL OTHER	83,549	4.9	56,383	3.9
GRAND TOTAL	1,694,707	100.0	1,444,313	100.0

Source: The Conference Board, Washington D.C. 1987.

It is impossible to generalize about the information needed on businesses and how to approach them when you consider that they range from the small grocery store on the corner (who might donate a product to an auction or take an ad in a local non-profit publication) to some of the largest firms in the world. This discussion will, therefore, be limited to those that are sufficiently large to (a) have an identifiable source of contact for their philanthropy, and (b) normally require applications. This reduces the number of potential corporate donors to approximately 2,500.

According to the annual surveys of The Contributions Council, this last category of firms is most likely to be found in the following industries (in rank order of size): electrical machinery and equipment, petroleum and gas, transportation equipment, chemicals, food/beverage and tobacco, and insurance. In 1985, gifts by firms in these categories exceeded at least $100 million per industry. Those industries with grants in the $50 to $99 million range were (by rank order of size): telecommunications, banking, pharmaceuticals, utilities, and retail and wholesale trade.

There is one important point to be gained from the above (in addition to stimulating thought about those firms most likely to make grants): The biggest givers tend primarily to be in the "manufacturing" industries, yet the growth in both profit and employment is increasingly in the "non-manufacturing" fields. This trend may have unfortunate consequences in years ahead.

In 1985, 436 of these corporations were analyzed to determine the fields to which they made gifts. The results are shown in Table 5.

INFORMATION TO SECURE ON CORPORATIONS

Much of the information you will need to know about corporations is similar to that listed previously about foundations. The obvious items are listed in Table 6.

Attachment 4 provides citations to a variety of publications that describe corporations with charitable activities or that monitor changes in their priorities and personnel. Again, you will find many of these in your local public or university library.

Using these materials to provide a potential prospect list involves considering the following issues:

❏ Does the firm have any significant business, facility or number of employees in your community?

❏ Is the nature of the firm's business related in any way to the type of project which you are attempting to support?

❏ Does your organization produce basic research which has any unique or direct tie to the firm's business?

❏ Does your organization deal with issues that are of unique importance to the firm or its industry?

❏ Does your institution educate or train people who are employed in significant numbers by the firm?

❏ Is there any unique benefit to be gained by the firm from being associated with your project? Publicity? Visibility with key customers?

❏ Is your nonprofit the most important in your field in the community? Phrased another way, are you the firm's best "investment" if they want to do something in your field?

❏ Does the firm sell substantial products or services to your primary constituency?

The more "yes" answers, the better your chances.

Once you have developed your "most likely" prospect list, it is again important to develop an initial letter of inquiry. Most firms require that charitable requests (whether for cash or "in kind") be first submitted in writing.

The letter in Figure 3 can be modified for this purpose by explaining why you think your project should be of interest to the firm (as opposed to a foundation). The questions listed earlier may help you think through this rationale. Chapter 7 also provides several models for how to start your letter with statements of project purpose that also tie to the interests of the potential donor.

INFORMATION TO SECURE ON CORPORATIONS

❏ What is the correct name of the firm, its address and telephone number?

❏ Who is in charge of its giving? That person's name, title and address? Also get the same for its marketing function.

❏ What are the firm's philanthropic interests? Priorities?

❏ Do they seem to prefer grants of a particular type?

❏ What are their selection criteria and process?

❏ What is their budget, average-sized gift, range of gift?

❏ Do they have printed material on their charitable activities? This is likely to be the case with all large donors.

❏ Do they have a required form? Application deadlines?

❏ Do they use a committee to make decisions and, if so, who is on this?

❏ What role does their local management play in the process?

❏ Should applications start with this local manager or be sent directly to headquarters?

❏ What other kinds of resources, in addition to cash, have they been known to give others in the past?

❏ Will they give awards to organizations that also receive funds from federated campaigns to which they contribute?

❏ What kinds of restrictions, if any, do they have on eligible applicants or fields of service?

Finally, give some thought to whether you have any special access to the firm that will insure that your request is given thorough consideration. This may be someone on your staff or board who knows a senior manager in the firm who can be asked to forward the inquiry to the contributions officer. This is perfectly acceptable as long as no "pressure" is implied in the transmittal. You may also have good relationships with another firm whose senior executive would be willing to send a note along with your letter. None of these techniques guarantees you a positive response, but they may help with timely consideration.

ASSOCIATIONS

There are three categories of "associations" that may be potential sources for projects of sufficient size to warrant a proposal: professional associations, trade associations and labor unions. Attachment 5 provides citations to sources of information on all three.

Professional associations number in the thousands and range from well-known civic organizations, such as Rotary, to lesser-known groups connected with specific academic disciplines. Many of these have "small grants" programs, offer scholarships and fellowships, or have significant annual award competitions.

Trade associations are made up of businesses in the same industry or product lines. In recent years, a number of these have formed their own "foundations." They collect annual sums from their members and then redistribute some or all of the money to other applicants. They are seldom public about their interests and once you have identified a group who might be interested in your project, it is best to pick up the telephone and talk to their key executives.

Labor unions are also an often forgotten, but growing source of project support, particularly for services or issues of direct relevance to their membership. Examples might be those who want to support independent policy studies on the impact of imports on their employment or those who are interested in medical research on some health-related issue of particular concern to their workers.

CHAPTER REFERENCES

Abramson, A.J., and L.M. Salamon, *The Nonprofit Sector and the New Federal Budget* (Washington, D.C.: Urban Institute Press, 1986).

Bauer, D.G., *The "How-To" Grants Manual* (New York: Macmillan, 1984).

Platzer, L.C., *Annual Survey of Corporate Contributions*, 1987 ed. (New York: The Conference Board, 1987).

Seltzer, M., *Securing Your Organization's Future* (New York: The Foundation Center, 1987).

State Administrative Officials Classified by Function (Lexington, KY: Council on State Governments, 1986). See Chapter 3 for address.

White, A., and J. Barolomeo, *Corporate Giving: The Views of Chief Executive Officers of Major American Corporations* (Washington, D.C.: Council on Foundations, 1982).

SOURCES OF INFORMATION ON PUBLIC FUNDING

Academic Research Information Systems. Usually weekly; prices vary by field. ARIS, The Redstone Building, 2940 16th Street, Suite 314, San Francisco, CA 94103.

Issues newsletters on the medical sciences, social and national sciences, and creative arts and the humanities. Gives leads to upcoming RFPs, grant announcements, deadline changes and new program policies. Write for latest costs.

CBD Online. United Communications Group, 9701 Georgia Avenue, Suite 800, Silver Springs, MD 20910.

This computerized information system, updated daily, describes all U.S. government procurement and contract award information similar to that printed in the *Commerce Business Daily.* For those who can afford it, CBD provides additional lead time in responding to requests with a very short deadline.

City Hall: An Important Resource for Your Organization, by C. Derfner. $3.00 plus $2.00 handling. The Grantsmanship Center, P.O. Box 6210, 650 S. Spring Street, Suite 507, Los Angeles, CA 90014.

Reprint from *Grantsmanship Center NEWS.* One of the few detailed studies of how an organization secured a grant from a city government.

Contracting with the Federal Government, by F.M. Alston et al. 1984. $55. John Wiley and Sons, Inc., 605 Third Avenue, New York, NY 10158.

A helpful book for those interested primarily in contracts. Includes forms, regulations, methods for getting on bidders' lists and other basic details.

Federal Agency Guides, Office of Federal Programs, American Association of State Colleges and Universities, One Dupont Circle, Suite 700, Washington, D.C. 20036.

Summaries of major programs in federal agencies, with the names of key contacts. Issued only to member institutions, but you may be able to borrow copies from a member in your town. Particularly valuable on lesser known programs and new programs not yet covered in FAPRS. Another useful publication from this source is their *Federal Program Special Report.*

Federal Grants and Contracts Weekly. $191/year. Capitol Publications, Inc., 1300 N 17th Street, Arlington, VA 22209.

Gives a weekly update on contracting opportunities, upcoming grants, an alert on RFPs and profiles of various government agencies.

Getting Grants, by Craig Smith and Eric Skjei. 1981. $16.00. Harper and Row, 10 E. 53rd Street, New York City, N.Y. 10022.

Useful discussions on research government grants, including histories of successful proposals.

Grant Proposals that Succeeded, by Virginia White. 1984. $22.50. Plenum Press, 233 Spring Street, New York, NY 10013.

Step-by-step description of preparing successful proposals, including the negotiations process.

GRANTS Database. Oryx Press, 2214 North Central at Encanto, Phoenix, AZ 85004-1483. Several books in the system at varying prices.

This publisher issues a variety of documents listing government (and sometimes, private) sources for grants and contracts. It sells a *Directory of Research Grants* ($110); *Directory of Biomedical and Health Care Grants* 1987 ($74.50); *Directory of Grants in the Physical Sciences* 1987 ($74.50); and *Directory of Grants in the Humanities,* 1987 (74.50).

Grants Magazine. 4 issues per year, $65. Plenum Press, 233 Spring Street, New York, NY 10013.

An excellent periodical covering issues on both public and private funding.

Health Grants and Contracts Weekly. $152/year. Capitol Publications, Inc., 1300 N 17th Street, Arlington, VA 20009.

Alerts to upcoming grants and RFPs in health and medical fields.

The "How-To" Grants Manual, by D.G. Bauer. 1984. $19.95. Macmillan Publishing Company, 866 Third Avenue, New York, NY 10022.

Developed in cooperation with the Council on Education, this is one of the best of recent books on getting grants from the federal government.

SOURCES OF INFORMATION ON PRIVATE FOUNDATIONS

America's Newest Foundations. 1987. $74.95. The Taft Group, 5130 MacArthur Blvd., NW, Washington, D.C. 20016.

> Profiles of foundations formed in the last five years. Indexed by location, areas of interest and names.

Chronicle of Non Profit Enterprise. $23 for 6 issues. Chronicle of Non Profit Enterprise, 138 Wyatt Way NE, Bainbridge Island, WA 98110.

> A lively newsletter covering national news on corporations and foundations as well as interesting projects by nonprofits. Always includes at least one lengthy interview with a significant professional in the field of philanthropy.

COMSEARCH, The Foundation Center, 79 Fifth Avenue, New York, NY 10003.

> This is a customized search of information on over 24,000 private foundations maintained in the Center's computerized databases. Prices vary according to length of search. Also write the Center to determine the price and availability of already-completed COMSEARCH documents available in paper or microfiche. Examples of the latter include a list of the 1,000 largest foundations by total giving, regional listings, and over 114 lists by subject area. New ones are being produced all the time, so periodically ask for the Center's catalog.

Council on Foundations Newsletter. Biweekly. Free to members: $60/year for non-members. Council on Foundations, 1828 L Street, NW, Washington, D.C. 20036.

> Current information on issues affecting foundations and the people involved with them. Especially helpful on legislation.

Donor Briefing. $150 for 26 issues. Donor Briefing, Box 183, 1340 W. Irving Park Road, Chicago, IL 60613.

> Draws on a broad array of printed sources covering philanthropy, and abstracts those of particular interest to donors and donees. Subscription price includes first class mail delivery.

The Foundation Directory, edition 10, 1985. $65. The Foundation Center, 79 Fifth Avenue, New York, NY 10003.

> Contains profiles on over 4,400 of the largest U.S. foundations. Organized by the state in which the foundation is incorporated, with other helpful indexes, including by subject area.

The Foundation Directory Supplement. 1985. $35. The Foundation Center, 79 Fifth Avenue, New York, NY 10003.

> More recent information on over 1,000 of the foundations described in *Edition 10*. As with the basic directory, includes index by subject, donors, officers and trustees, foundation name.

Foundation Fundamentals: A Guide for Grantseekers, by Patricia Read. Third edition, 1986. $9.95. The Foundation Center, 79 Fifth Avenue, New York, NY 10003.

> A basic guide to foundations, tips on approaches and presentations.

The Foundation Grants Index, **edition 15**, 1986. $44. The Foundation Center, 79 Fifth Avenue, New York, NY 10003.

> Lists 36,000 grants made in the past year. Includes subject, geographic and recipient indexes. Also has several useful statistical tables on trends in foundation giving.

The Foundation Grants Index Bimonthly. $28 for 6 issues. The Foundation Center, 79 Fifth Avenue, New York, NY 10003.

> Lists over 2,000 recent grants each issue. Useful way to monitor changing trends in larger foundations.

Foundation Grants to Individuals, **fifth edition**, 1986. $18. The Foundation Center, 79 Fifth Avenue, New York, NY 10003.

> The only publication available devoted entirely to foundations that give to the individual.

Foundation News. Bimonthly. $24/year. Council on Foundations, Inc., 1828 L Street, NW, Washington, D.C. 20036.

> Articles and news reports on issues affecting foundations. Useful for tracking key personnel and board changes as well as publications.

How to Write Successful Foundation Proposals, by Joseph Dermer. 1980. $11.50. Public Service Materials Center, 111 N Central Avenue, Hartsdale, NY 10530.

> Provides examples of presentations that have been successful.

Index of Progressive Funders, 1985-86 edition. $40. Public Media Center, 466 Green Street, San Francisco, CA 94133.

> Directory of funding sources for public interest and progressive nonprofit organizations.

National Data Book, eleventh edition, 1987. $60. The Foundation Center, 79 Fifth Avenue, New York, NY 10003.

>A two-volume listing of 24,859 active foundations in the U.S. For each entry, gives foundation name and address, name of principal officer, fiscal data, citations to those publishing annual reports and the IRS number to help you locate tax returns.

Researching Foundations, Parts I and II. $3.00 each. The Grantsmanship Center, 650 S. Spring Street, Suite 507, Los Angeles, CA 90014.

>Reprints from earlier articles in the *Grantsmanship Center NEWS* on researching foundations, including the use of regional directories.

Securing Your Organization's Future, by Michael Seltzer. 1987. $19.95. The Foundation Center, 79 Fifth Avenue, New York, NY 10003.

>Comprehensive guide on private source fundraising, including many helpful tips on approaching private foundations.

Source Book Profiles. 1987. $285. The Foundation Center, 79 Fifth Avenue, New York, NY 10003.

>The profiles run on a two-year publishing cycle which updates comprehensive details on 500 of the largest foundations. For each profile, gives foundation name, address, telephone number, contact person, officers, trustees, principal staff, full fiscal data, background history, list of publications, funding cycles, policies, application guidelines, and analysis of grant interests and policies. You can order prior year volumes at a price discount.

Taft Foundation Reporter, 17th edition. 1986. $297. The Taft Group, 5130 MacArthur Blvd., NW, Washington, D.C. 20016.

>Profiles of over 500 of the largest national and regional private foundations. May also be ordered as part of the total Taft Foundation Information System, which includes *Foundation Giving Watch* and *Foundation Updates* (annual subscription of $377 plus $15 for postage and handling).

The Art of Winning Foundation Grants, by Howard Hillman and Karin Abarbanel. 1975. $14. Public Service Materials Center, 111 N. Central Avenue, Hartsdale, NY 10530.

>Describes how to research foundations as well as approach them.

The Associates Program. $325. The Foundation Center, 79 Fifth Avenue, New York, NY 10003.

>This annual membership fee gives you ten free calls, or 2-1/2 hours of answers per month of customized searches of the Center's computerized databases.

The Bread Game: The Realities of Foundation Fundraising, Herb Allen (ed). Revised edition 1981. $9.95. Regional Young Adult Project, 944 Market Street, #705, San Francisco, CA 94102.

>Useful tips on dealing with foundations, especially pitched at grassroots nonprofit organizations.

THE FOUNDATION CENTER

The Foundation Center is an independent national service organization established by foundations to provide an authoritative source of information on private philanthropic giving. In fulfilling its mission, The Center disseminates information on private giving through public service programs, publications, and a national network of library reference collections for free public use. The New York, Washington, D.C., Cleveland, and San Francisco reference collections operated by The Foundation Center offer a wide variety of services and comprehensive collections of information on foundations and grants. The Co-operating Collections are libraries, community foundations, and other nonprofit agencies that provide a core collection of Foundation Center publications and a variety of supplementary materials and services in subject areas useful to grantseekers.

Over 100 of the network members have sets of private foundation information returns (IRS Form 990-PF) for their states or regions which are available for public use. These collections are indicated by a + next to their names. A complete set of U.S. foundation returns can be found at the New York and Washington, D.C. collections. The Cleveland and San Francisco offices contain IRS returns for those foundations in the midwestern and western states respectively.

Because the collections vary in their hours, materials and services, it is recommended that you call each collection in advance. To check on new locations or current information, call toll free 1-800-424-9836.

WHERE TO GO FOR INFORMATION ON FOUNDATION FUNDING

REFERENCE COLLECTIONS OPERATED BY THE FOUNDATION CENTER

+The Foundation Center
79 Fifth Avenue
New York, NY 10003
212-620-4230

+The Foundation Center
1001 Connecticut Avenue, NW
Washington, D.C. 20036
201-331-1400

+The Foundation Center
Kent H. Smith Library
1442 Hanna Building
1422 Euclid Avenue
Cleveland, OH 44115
216-861-1933

+The Foundation Center
312 Sutter Street
San Francisco, CA 94108
415-397-0902

COOPERATING COLLECTIONS

ALABAMA

+Birmingham Public Library
2020 Park Place
Birmingham 35203
205-226-3600

Huntsville-Madison County
Public Library
108 Fountain Circle
P.O. Box 443
Huntsville 35804
205-536-0021

+Auburn University at
Montgomery Library
Montgomery 36193-0401
205-271-9649

ALASKA

+University of Alaska,
Anchorage Library
3211 Providence Drive
Anchorage 99504
907-786-1848

ARIZONA

+Phoenix Public Library
Business and Sciences Department
12 East McDowell Road
Phoenix 85004
602-262-4782

+Tucson Public Library
Main Library
200 South Sixth Avenue
Tucson 85701
602-791-4393

ARKANSAS

+Westark Community
College Library
Grand Avenue at Waldron Road
Fort Smith 72913
501-785-4241

+Little Rock Public Libary
Reference Department
700 Louisiana Street
Little Rock 7220l
501-370-5950

CALIFORNIA

Inyo County Library-Bishop
Branch
210 Academy Street
Bishop 93514
619-872-8091

Peninsula Community
Foundation
1204 Burlingame Avenue
Burlingame, 94011-0627
415-342-2505

+California Community
Foundation
Funding Information Center
3580 Wilshire Blvd., Suite 1660
Los Angeles 90010
213-413-4719

+Community Foundation for
Monterey County
420 Pacific Street
Monterey 93942
408-375-9712

California Community
Foundation
4050 Metropolitan Drive
Orange 92668
714-937-9077

Riverside Public Library
3581 7th Street
Riverside 92501
714-787-7201

California State Library
Reference Services, Rm. 309
914 Capital Mall
Sacramento 95814
916-322-0369

+San Diego Community
Foundation
625 Broadway, Suite 1015
San Diego 92101
619-239-8815

+The Foundation Center
312 Sutter Street
San Francisco 94108
415-397-0902

Orange County Community
Development Council
1440 East First Street, 4th Floor
Santa Ana 92701
714-547-6801

+Santa Barbara Public
Library
Reference Section
40 East Anapamu
P.O. Box 1019
Santa Barbara 93102
805-962-7653

Santa Monica Public Library
1343 Sixth Street
Santa Monica 90401-1603
213-458-8603

Central Sierra Arts Council
229 South Shepherd Street
Sonora 95370
209-532-2787

North Coast Opportunities, Inc.
101 West Church Street
Ukiah 95482
707-462-1954

COLORADO

Pikes Peak Library District
20 North Cascade Avenue
Colorado Springs 80901
303-473-2080

+Denver Public Library
Sociology Division
1357 Broadway
Denver 80203
303-571-2190

CONNECTICUT

D.A.T.A.
880 Asylum Avenue
Hartford 06105
203-278-2477

+Hartford Public Library
Reference Department
500 Main Street
Hartford 06103
203-525-9121

D.A.T.A.
81 Saltonstall Avenue
New Haven 06513
203-776-0797

DELAWARE

+Hugh Morris Library
University of Delaware
Newark 19717-5267
302-451-2965

FLORIDA

+Volusia County Public
Library
City Island
Daytona Beach 32014
904-252-8374

+Jacksonville Public Library
Business, Science, and
Industry Department
122 North Ocean Street
Jacksonville 32202
904-633-3926

+Miami-Dade Public Library
Florida Collection
One Biscayne Boulevard
Miami 33132
305-579-5001

+Orlando Public Library
10 North Rosalind
Orlando 32801
305-425-4694

+University of West Florida
John C. Pace Library
Pensacola 32514
904-474-2412

Selby Public Library
1001 Boulevard of the Arts
Sarasota 33577
813-366-7303

+Leon County Public
Library
Community Funding
Resources Center
1940 North Monroe Street
Tallahassee 32303
904-478-2665

Palm Beach County
Community Foundation
324 Datura Street, Suite
311
West Palm Beach 33401
305-659-6800

GEORGIA

+Atlanta-Fulton Public
Library
Ivan Allen Department
1 Margaret Mitchell Square
Atlanta 30303
404-688-4636

HAWAII

Community Resource
Center
The Hawaiian Foundation
Financial Plaza of the
Pacific
111 South King Street
Honolulu 96813
808-525-8548

+Thomas Hale Hamilton
Library
General Reference
University of Hawaii
2550 The Mall
Honolulu 96822
808-948-7214

IDAHO

+Caldwell Public Library
1010 Dearborn Street
Caldwell 83605
208-459-3242

ILLINOIS

+Belleville Public Library
121 East Washington Street
Belleville 62220
618-234-0441

DuPage Township
300 Briarcliff Road
Bolingbrook 60439
312-759-1317

+Donors Forum of Chicago
208 South LaSalle Street
Chicago 60604
312-726-4882

+Evanston Public Library
1703 Orrington Avenue
Evanston 60201
312-866-0305

+Sangamon State Univer-
sity Library
Shepherd Road
Springfield 62708
217-786-6633

INDIANA

Allen County Public Library
900 Webster Street
Fort Wayne 46802
219-424-7241

Indiana University North-
west Library
3400 Broadway
Gary 46408
219-980-6580

+Indianapolis-Marion
County Public Library
40 East St. Clair Street
Indianapolis 46204
317-269-1733

IOWA

+Public Library of Des
Moines
100 Locust Street
Des Moines 50308
515-283-4259

KANSAS

+Topeka Public Library
Adult Services Department
1515 West Tenth Street
Topeka 66604
913-233-2040

+Wichita Public Library
223 South Main
Wichita 67202
316-262-0611

KENTUCKY

Western Kentucky Univer-
sity
Division of Library Services
Helm-Cravens Library
Bowling Green 42101
502-745-3951

+Louisville Free Public
Library
Fourth and York Streets
Louisville 40203
502-584-4154

LOUISIANA

+East Baton Rouge Parish
Library
Centroplex Library
120 St. Louis Street
Baton Rouge 70821
504-389-4960

+New Orleans Public
Library
Business and Science
Division
219 Loyola Avenue
New Orleans 70140
504-596-2583

+Shreve Memorial Library
424 Texas Street
Shreveport 71104
318-226-5894

MAINE

+University of Southern
Maine
Center for Research and
Advanced Study
246 Deering Avenue
Portland 04102
207-780-4411

MARYLAND

+Enoch Pratt Free Library
Social Science and History
Department
400 Cathedral Street
Baltimore 21201
301-396-5320

MASSACHUSETTS

+Associated Grantmakers
of Massachusetts
294 Washington Street
Suite 501
Boston 02108
617-426-2608

Boston Public Library
Copley Square
Boston 02117
617-536-5400

Western Massachusetts
Funding Resource Center
Campaign for Human De-
velopment
Chancery Annex
73 Chestnut Street
Springfield 01103
413-732-3175 ext. 67

Walpole Public Library
Common Street
Walpole 02081
617-668-5497 ext. 340

+Grants Resource Center
Worcester Public Library
Salem Square
Worcester 01608
617-799-1655

MICHIGAN

+Alpena County Library
211 North First Avenue
Alpena 49707
517-356-6188

University of Michigan—
Ann Arbor
Reference Department
209 Hatcher Graduate
Library
Ann Arbor 48109-1205
313-764-1149

+Henry Ford Centennial
Library
16301 Michigan Avenue
Dearborn 48126
313-943-2337

+Purdy Library
Wayne State University
Detroit 48202
313-577-4040

+Michigan State University
Libraries
Reference Library
East Lansing 48824
517-353-9184

+Farmington Community
Library
32737 West 12 Mile Road
Farmington Hills 48018
313-553-0300

+University of Michigan—
Flint Library
Reference Department
Flint 48503
313-762-3408

+Grand Rapids Public
Library
Sociology and Education
Department
Library Plaza
Grand Rapids 49502
616-456-4411

+Michigan Technological
University Library
Highway U.S. 41
Houghton 49931
906-487-2507

MINNESOTA

+Duluth Public Library
520 Superior Street
Duluth 55802
218-723-3802

+Southwest State Univer-
sity Library
Marshall 56258
507-537-7278

+Minneapolis Public Library
Sociology Department
300 Nicollet Mall
Minneapolis 55401
612-372-6555

Rochester Public Library
Broadway at First Street,
SE
Rochester 55901
507-285-8002

Saint Paul Public Library
90 West Fourth Street
Saint Paul 55102
612-292-6311

MISSISSIPPI

Jackson Metropolitan
Library
301 North State Street
Jackson 39201
601-944-1120

MISSOURI

+Clearinghouse for
Midcontinent Foundations
Univ. of Missouri, Kansas
City
Law School, Suite 1-300
52nd Street and Oak
Kansas City 64113
816-276-1176

+Kansas City Public
Library
311 East 12th Street
Kansas City 64106
816-221-2685

+Metropolitan Association
for Philanthropy, Inc.
5585 Pershing Avenue
Suite 150
St. Louis 63112
314-361-3900

+Springfield-Greene
County Library
397 East Central Street
Springfield 65801
417-866-4636

MONTANA

+Eastern Montana College
Library
Reference Department
1500 N. 30th Street
Billings 59101-0298
406-657-2262

+Montana State Library
Reference Department
1515 E. 6th Avenue
Helena 59620
406-444-3004

NEBRASKA

University of Nebraska,
Lincoln
106 Love Library
Lincoln 68588-0410
402-472-2526

+W. Dale Clark Library
Social Sciences Depart-
ment
215 South 15th Street
Omaha 68102
402-444-4826

NEVADA

+Las Vegas—Clark County
Library District
1401 East Flamingo Road
Las Vegas 89109
702-733-7810

+Washoe County Library
301 South Center Street
Reno 89505
702-785-4190

NEW HAMPSHIRE

+The New Hampshire
Charitable Fund
One South Street
Concord 03301
603-225-6641

Littleton Public Library
109 Main Street
Littleton 03561
603-444-5741

NEW JERSEY

Cumberland County Library
800 E. Commerce Street
Bridgeton 08302
609-455-0080

The Support Center
17 Academy Street, Suite
1101
Newark 07102
201-643-5774

County College of Morris
Masten Learning Resource
Center
Route 10 and Center Grove
Road
Randolph 07869
201-361-5000 ext. 470

+New Jersey State Library
Governmental Reference
185 West State Street
Trenton 08625
609-292-6220

NEW MEXICO

Albuquerque Community
Foundation
6400 Uptown Boulevard
N.E.
Suite 500-W
Albuquerque 87110
505-883-6240

+New Mexico State Library
325 Don Gaspar Street
Santa Fe 87503
505-827-3824

NEW YORK

+New York State Library
Cultural Education Center
Humanities Section
Empire State Plaza
Albany 12230
518-474-7645

Bronx Reference Center
New York Public Library
2556 Bainbridge Avenue
Bronx 10458
212-220-6575

Brooklyn in Touch
101 Willoughby Street
Room 1508
Brooklyn 11201
718-237-9300

+Buffalo and Erie County
Public Library
Lafayette Square
Buffalo 14203
716-856-7525

Huntington Public Library
338 Main Street
Huntington 11743
516-427-5165

Queens Borough Public
Library
89-11 Merrick Boulevard
Jamaica 11432
718-990-0700

+Levittown Public Library
Reference Department
One Bluegrass Lane
Levittown 11756
516-731-5728

SUNY/College at Old
Westbury Library
223 Store Hill Road
Old Westbury 11568
516-876-3201

+Plattsburgh Public Library
Reference Department
15 Oak Street
Plattsburgh 12901
518-563-0921

Adriance Memorial Library
93 Market Street
Poughkeepsie 12601
914-485-4790

+Rochester Public Library
Business and Social
Sciences Division
115 South Avenue
Rochester 14604
716-428-7328

+Onondaga County Public
Library
335 Montgomery Street
Syracuse 13202
315-473-4491

+White Plains Public Library
100 Martine Avenue
White Plains 10601
914-682-4488

NORTH CAROLINA

+The Duke Endowment
200 S. Tryon Street, Suite
1100
Charlotte 28202
704-376-0291

Durham County Library
300 N. Roxboro Street
Durham 27701
919-683-2626

+North Carolina State
Library
109-East Jones Street
Raleigh 27611
919-733-3270

+The Winston-Salem
Foundation
229 First Union National
Bank Building
Winston-Salem 27101
919-725-2382

NORTH DAKOTA

Western Dakota Grants
Resource Center
Bismarck Junior College
Library
Bismarck 58501
701-224-5450

+The Library
North Dakota State University
Fargo 58105
701-237-8876

OHIO

+Public Library of Cincinnati
and Hamilton County
Education Department
800 Vine Street
Cincinnati 45202
513-369-6940

+The Foundation Center
1442 Hanna Building
1422 Euclid Avenue
Cleveland 44115
216-861-1933

CALLVAC Services, Inc.
370 South Fifth Street
Suite 1
Columbus 43215
614-221-6766

Lima-Allen County
Regional Planning Commis-
sion
212 N. Elizabeth Street
Lima 45801
419-228-1836

+Toledo-Lucas County
Public Library
Social Science Department
325 Michigan Street
Toledo 43624
419-255-7055 ext. 221

Ohio University-Zanesville
Community Education and
Development
1425 Newark Road
Zanesville 43701
614-453-0762

OKLAHOMA

+Oklahoma City University
Library
NW 23rd at North Black-
welder
Oklahoma City 73106
405-521-5072

+The Support Center
525 NW Thirteenth Street
Oklahoma City 73103
405-236-8133

+Tulsa City-County Library
System
400 Civic Center
Tulsa 74103
918-592-7944

OREGON

+Library Association of
Portland
Government Documents
Room
801 SW Tenth Avenue
Portland 97205
503-223-7201

PENNSYLVANIA

Northampton County Area
Community College
Learning Resources Center
3835 Green Pond Road
Bethlehem 18017
215-865-5358

+Erie County Public Library
3 South Perry Square
Erie 16501
814-452-2333 ext. 54

+Dauphin County Library
System
Central Library
101 Walnut Street
Harrisburg 17101
717-234-4961

Lancaster County Public
Library
125 North Duke Street
Lancaster 17602
717-394-2651

+The Free Library of
Philadelphia
Logan Square
Philadelphia 19103
215-686-5423

+Hillman Library
University of Pittsburgh
Pittsburgh 15260
412-624-4423

+Economic Development
Council of Northeastern
Pennsylvania
1151 Oak Street
Pittston 18640
717-655-5581

James V. Brown Library
12 E. 4th Street
Williamsport 17701
717-326-0536

RHODE ISLAND

+Providence Public Library
Reference Department
150 Empire Street
Providence 02903
401-521-7722

SOUTH CAROLINA

+Charleston County Public
Library
404 King Street
Charleston 29403
803-723-1645

+South Carolina State
Library
Reader Services Depart-
ment
1500 Senate Street
Columbia 29201
803-758-3138

SOUTH DAKOTA

+South Dakota State
Library
State Library Building
800 North Illinois Street
Pierre 57501
605-773-3131

Sioux Falls Area Foundation
404 Boyce Greeley Building
321 South Phillips Avenue
Sioux Falls 57102-0781
605-336-7055

TENNESSEE

+Knoxville—Knox County
Public Library
500 West Church Avenue
Knoxville 37902
615-523-0781

+Memphis Shelby County
Public Library
1850 Peabody Avenue
Memphis 38104
901-725-8876

+Public Library of Nashville
and Davidson County
8th Avenue, North and
Union Street
Nashville 37203
615-244-4700

TEXAS

Amarillo Area Foundation
1000 Polk
P.O. Box 25569
Amarillo 79105-269
806-376-4521

+The Hogg Foundation for
Mental Health
The University of Texas
Austin 78712
512-471-5041

+Corpus Christi State
University Library
6300 Ocean Drive
Corpus Christi 78412
512-991-6810

+Dallas Public Library
Grants Information Service
1515 Young Street
Dallas 75201
214-749-4100

+Pan American University
Learning Resource Center
1201 W. University Drive
Edinburg 78539
512-381-3304

+El Paso Community
Foundation
El Paso National Bank
Building
Suite 1616
El Paso 79901
915-533-4020

+Funding Information
Center
Texas Christian University
Library
Ft. Worth 76129
817-921-7000 ext. 6130

+Houston Public Library
Bibliographic & Information
Center
500 McKinney Avenue
Houston 77002
713-224-5441 ext. 265

+Funding Information
Library
507 Brooklyn
San Antonio 78215
512-227-4333

UTAH

+Salt Lake City Public
Library
Business and Science
Department
209 East Fifth South
Salt Lake City 84111
801-363-5733

VERMONT

+State of Vermont Depart-
ment of Libraries
Reference Services Unit
111 State Street
Montpelier 05602
802-828-3261

VIRGINIA

+Grants Resources Library
Hampton City Hall
22 Lincoln Street, Ninth
Floor
Hampton 23669
804-727-6496

+Richmond Public Library
Business, Science, & Technology Department
101 East Franklin Street
Richmond 23219
804-780-8223

WASHINGTON

+Seattle Public Library
1000 Fourth Avenue
Seattle 98104
206-625-4881

+Spokane Public Library
Funding Information Center
West 906 Main Avenue
Spokane 99201
509-838-3361

WEST VIRGINIA

+Kanawha County Public
Library
123 Capital Street
Charleston 25301
304-343-4646

WISCONSIN

Society for Nonprofit
Organizations
6314 Odana Road
Suite One
Madison 53719
608-274-9777

+University of Wisconsin—
Madison
Memorial Library
728 State Street
Madison 53706
608-262-3647

+Marquette University
Memorial Library
1415 West Wisconsin
Avenue
Milwaukee 53233
414-224-1515

WYOMING

+Laramie County Commu-
nity College Library
1400 East College Drive
Cheyenne 82007
307-634-5853

CANADA

Canadian Center for
Philanthropy
185 Bay Street, Suite 504
Toronto, Ontario M5J1K6
416-364-4875

ENGLAND

Charities Aid Foundation
12 Crane Court
Fleet Street
London EC4A 2JJ
1-583-7772

MARIANA ISLANDS

Northern Marianas College
P.O. Box 1250 CK
Saipan, GM 96950

MEXICO

Biblioteca Benjamin
Franklin
Londres 16
Mexico City 6, D.F.
525-591-0244

PUERTO RICO

Universidad Del Sagrado
Corazon
M.M.T. Guevarra Library
Correo Calle Loiza
Santurce 00914
809-728-1515 ext. 274

VIRGIN ISLANDS

College of the Virgin Islands
Library
Saint Thomas
U.S. Virgin Islands 00801
809-774-9200 ext. 487

EXAMPLE OF A PF 990 - THE ANNUAL FORM THE PRIVATE AND CORPORATE FOUNDATIONS MUST FILE WITH THE INTERNAL REVENUE SERVICE

Form **990-PF**	**Return of Private Foundation**	OMB No. 1545-0052
Department of the Treasury Internal Revenue Service	or Section 4947(a)(1) Trust Treated as a Private Foundation	**1986**
	Note: *You may be able to use a copy of this return to satisfy State reporting requirements.*	

For the calendar year 1986, or tax year beginning _____ , 1986, and ending _____ , 19 ___

Please type, print, or attach label. See Specific Instructions.	Name of organization	Employer identification number
	Address (number and street)	State registration number (see instructions)
	City or town, state, and ZIP code	Fair market value of assets at end of year

If application pending, check here ▶ ☐   Foreign organizations, check here ▶ . . . . . ☐   Please attach check or money order here.

Check type of organization

☐ Exempt private foundation   ☐ 4947(a)(1) trust   ☐ Other taxable private foundation

Section 4947(a)(1) trusts filing this form in lieu of Form 1041, check here and see General Instructions. ▶

If the foundation is in a 60-month termination under section 507(b)(1)(B), check here . . . ▶ ☐

The books are in care of ▶ _____

Located at ▶ _____ Telephone no. ▶ _____

Check this box if your private foundation status terminated under section 507(b)(1)(A) . . . ▶ ☐

Part I	**Analysis of Support, Revenue, and Expenses** (See instructions for Part I)	**(a)** Revenue and expenses per books	**(b)** Net investment income	**(c)** Adjusted net income	**(d)** Disbursements for charitable purpose
Support and Revenue	1 Contributions, gifts, grants, etc. received (attach schedule)				
	2 Contributions from split-interest trusts				
	3 Interest on savings and temporary cash investments				
	4 Dividends and interest from securities				
	5 a Gross rents				
	b (Net rental income (loss) _____)				
	6 Net gain or (loss) from sale of assets not on line 10				
	7 Capital gain net income				
	8 Net short-term capital gain				
	9 Income modifications				
	10 a Gross sales minus returns and allowances .				
	b Minus: Cost of goods sold (attach schedule)				
	c Gross profit (loss)				
	11 Other income (attach schedule)				
	12 Total (add lines 1 through 11)				
Operating and Administrative Expenses	13 Compensation of officers, directors, trustees, etc. . .				
	14 Other employee salaries and wages				
	15 Pension plans, employee benefits				
	16 a Legal fees				
	b Accounting fees				
	c Other professional fees				
	17 Interest				
	18 Taxes (attach schedule)				
	19 Depreciation and depletion				
	20 Occupancy				
	21 Travel, conferences, and meetings				
	22 Printing and publications				
	23 Other expenses (attach schedule)				
	24 Total operating and administrative expenses (add lines 13 through 23)				
	25 Contributions, gifts, grants paid				
	26 Total expenses and disbursements (add lines 24 and 25).				
	27 a Excess of revenue over expenses and disbursements (line 12 minus line 26)				
	b Net investment income (if negative enter -0-) . .				
	c Adjusted net income (if negative enter -0-) . . .				

For Paperwork Reduction Act Notice, see page 1 of the instructions.   Form **990-PF** (1986)

Part II Balance Sheets

Attached schedules should be for end of year amounts only. (See instructions for col. (c).)

		Beginning of year	End of year	
		(a) Book Value	(b) Book Value	(c) Fair Market Value
Assets	1 Cash—non-interest bearing			
	2 Savings and temporary cash investments			
	3 Accounts receivable ▶ _____			
	minus allowance for doubtful accounts ▶ _____			
	4 Pledges receivable ▶ _____			
	minus allowance for doubtful accounts ▶ _____			
	5 Grants receivable			
	6 Receivables due from officers, directors, trustees, and other disqualified persons (see instructions)			
	7 Other notes and loans receivable ▶ _____			
	minus allowance for doubtful accounts ▶ _____			
	8 Inventories for sale or use			
	9 Prepaid expenses and deferred charges			
	10 Investments—securities (attach schedule)			
	11 Investments—land, buildings, and equipment: basis ▶ _____			
	minus accumulated depreciation (attach schedule) ▶ _____			
	12 Investments—mortgage loans			
	13 Investments—other (attach schedule)			
	14 Land, buildings, and equipment: basis ▶ _____			
	minus accumulated depreciation (attach schedule) ▶ _____			
	15 Other assets (describe ▶ _____)			
	16 Total assets (see instructions)			
Liabilities	17 Accounts payable and accrued expenses			
	18 Grants payable			
	19 Support and revenue designated for future periods (attach schedule)			
	20 Loans from officers, directors, trustees, and other disqualified persons			
	21 Mortgages and other notes payable (attach schedule)			
	22 Other liabilities (describe ▶ _____)			
	23 Total liabilities (add lines 17 through 22)			
Fund Balances or Net Worth	**Organizations that use fund accounting, check here ▶ ☐ and complete lines 24 through 27 and lines 31 and 32.**			
	24a Current unrestricted fund			
	b Current restricted fund			
	25 Land, buildings, and equipment fund			
	26 Endowment fund			
	27 Other funds (Describe ▶ _____)			
	Organizations not using fund accounting, check here ▶ ☐ and complete lines 28-32.			
	28 Capital stock or trust principal			
	29 Paid-in or capital surplus			
	30 Retained earnings or accumulated income			
	31 Total fund balances or net worth (see instructions)			
	32 Total liabilities and fund balances/net worth (see instructions)			

Part III Analysis of Changes in Net Worth or Fund Balances

1 Total net worth or fund balances at beginning of year—Part II, column (a), line 31

2 Enter amount from Part I, line 27a

3 Other increases not included in line 2 (itemize) ▶ _____

4 Add lines 1, 2, and 3

5 Decreases not included in line 2 (itemize) ▶ _____

6 Total net worth or fund balances at end of year (line 4 minus line 5)—Part II, column (b), line 31

Part IV   Capital Gains and Losses for Tax on Investment Income

(a) List and describe the kind(s) of property sold, e.g., real estate, 2-story brick warehouse; or common stock, 200 shs. MLC Co.	(b) How acquired P—Purchase D—Donation	(c) Date acquired (mo., day, yr.)	(d) Date sold (mo., day, yr.)
1			

(e) Gross sales price minus expense of sale	(f) Depreciation allowed (or allowable)	(g) Cost or other basis	(h) Gain or (loss) (e) plus (f) minus (g)

Complete only for assets showing gain in column (h) and owned by the foundation on 12/31/69			(l) Losses (from col. (h)) Gains (excess of col. (h) gain over col. (k), but not less than zero)
(i) F.M.V. as of 12/31/69	(j) Adjusted basis as of 12/31/69	(k) Excess of col. (i) over col. (j), if any	

2 Capital gain net income or (net capital loss) · · { If gain, also enter in Part I, line 7 } { If (loss), enter -0- in Part I, line 7 } · · ·

3 Net short-term capital gain (loss) as defined in sections 1222(5) and (6) If gain, also enter in Part I, line 8 (see instructions for line 8) } If loss, enter -0- in Part I, line 8 · · · · · · · · · · }

Part V   Qualification Under Section 4940(e) for Reduced Tax on Net Investment Income

(For optional use by domestic private foundations subject to section 4940(a) tax on net investment income.)

If section 4940(d)(2) applies, leave Part V blank.

Were you liable for section 4942 tax on the distributable amount of any year in the base period? · · · · · · ☐ Yes ☐ No
If "Yes," you do not qualify under section 4940(e). Do not complete this part.

1 Enter the appropriate amount in each column for each year; see instructions before making any entries.

(a) Base period years Calendar year (or fiscal year beginning in)	(b) Qualifying distributions	(c) Net value of noncharitable-use assets	(d) Payout ratio (column (b) divided by column (c))
1985			
1984			
1983			
1982			
1981			

2 Total of line 1, column (d) . . . .

3 Average payout ratio for the 5-year base period—divide the total on line 2 by 5, or by the number of years the foundation has been in existence if less than 5 years. . . . .

4 Enter the net value of noncharitable-use assets for 1986 from Part IX, line 5 . . . .

5 Multiply line 4 by line 3 . . . .

6 Enter 1% of Part I, line 27b . . . .

7 Add lines 5 and 6 . . . .

8 Enter the amount from Part XIII, line 6 . . . .
If line 8 is equal to or greater than line 7, check the box in Part VI, line 1b, and complete that part using a 1% tax rate. See the Part VI instructions.

Part VI Excise Tax on Investment Income (Section 4940(a), 4940(b), 4940(e), or 4948—see instructions)

1 a Exempt operating foundations described in section 4940(d)(2), check here ☐ (attach copy of ruling letter) and enter "N/A" . . . .

b Domestic organizations that meet the section 4940(e) requirements in Part V, check here ☐ and enter 1% of Part I, line 27b . . . .

c All other domestic organizations enter 2% of line 27b. Exempt foreign organizations enter 4% of line 27b . . .

2 Tax under section 511 (domestic section 4947(a)(1) trusts and taxable foundations only. Others enter -0-) . . .

3 Add lines 1 and 2 . . . .

4 Tax under subtitle A (domestic section 4947(a)(1) trusts and taxable foundations only. Others enter -0-) . . . .

5 Tax on investment income (line 3 minus line 4 (but not less than -0-)) . . . .

6 Credits: **a** Exempt foreign organizations—tax withheld at source . . . .

b Tax paid with application for extension of time to file (Form 2758) . . . .

7 Tax due (line 5 minus line 6) . . { Pay in full with return. Make check or money order payable to Internal Revenue Service. ▶

8 Overpayment (line 6 minus line 5) { (Write employer identification number on check or money order.)

(See instructions for information on 1987 estimated taxes.) }

Part VII Statements Regarding Activities

	Yes	No
File Form 4720 if you answer "No" to question 10b, 11b, or 14b or "Yes" to question 10c, 12b, 13a, or 13b unless an exception applies.		
1 a During the tax year, did you attempt to influence any national, state, or local legislation or did you participate or intervene in any political campaign?		
b Did you spend more than $100 during the year (either directly or indirectly) for political purposes (see instructions for definition)? . . . If you answered "Yes" to 1a or 1b, attach a detailed description of the activities and copies of any materials published or distributed by the organization in connection with the activities.		
c Did you file Form 1120-POL?		
2 Have you engaged in any activities that have not previously been reported to the Internal Revenue Service? . . . *If "Yes," attach a detailed description of the activities.*		
3 Have you made any changes, not previously reported to the IRS, in your governing instrument, articles of incorporation, or bylaws, or other similar instruments? . . . . *If "Yes," attach a conformed copy of the changes.*		
4 a Did you have unrelated business gross income of $1,000 or more during the year?		
b If "Yes," have you filed a tax return on Form 990-T for this year?		
5 Was there a liquidation, termination, dissolution, or substantial contraction during the year? . . . . . *If "Yes," attach the schedule required by General Instruction I.*		
6 Are the section 508(e) requirements satisfied either: • by language written into the governing instrument, or • by state legislation that effectively amends the governing instrument so that no mandatory directions that conflict with the state law remain in the governing instrument?		
7 Did you have at least $5,000 in assets at any time during the year? . . . . *If "Yes," complete Part II, column (c), and Part XVI.*		
8 a Enter states to which the foundation reports or with which it is registered (see instructions) ▶ -------------------		
b If you answered 7 "Yes," have you furnished a copy of Form 990-PF to the Attorney General (or his or her designate) of each state as required by the General Instructions? . . . . *If "No," attach explanation.*		
9 Are you claiming status as a private operating foundation within the meaning of section 4942(j)(3) or 4942(j)(5) for calendar year 1986 or fiscal year beginning in 1986 (see instructions for Part XV)? . . . . *If "Yes," complete Part XV.*		
10 Self-dealing (section 4941): **a** During the year did you (either directly or indirectly):		
(1) Engage in the sale or exchange, or leasing of property with a disqualified person?		
(2) Borrow money from, lend money to, or otherwise extend credit to (or accept it from) a disqualified person? . .		
(3) Furnish goods, services, or facilities to (or accept them from) a disqualified person?		
(4) Pay compensation to or pay or reimburse the expenses of a disqualified person?		
(5) Transfer any of your income or assets to a disqualified person (or make any of either available for the benefit or use of a disqualified person)?		
(6) Agree to pay money or property to a government official? (Exception: check "No" if you agreed to make a grant to or to employ the official for a period after he or she terminates government service if he or she is terminating within 90 days.)		

Part VII   Statements Regarding Activities (continued)

		Yes	No
10 b If you answered "Yes" to any of the questions 10a(1) through (6), were the acts you engaged in excepted acts as described in regulations section 53.4941(d)-3 and 4?			
c Did you engage in a prior year in any of the acts described in 10a, other than excepted acts, that were acts of self-dealing that were not corrected by the first day of your tax year beginning in 1986?			
11 Taxes on failure to distribute income (section 4942) (does not apply for years you were a private operating foundation as defined in section 4942(j)(3) or 4942(j)(5)):			
a Did you at the end of tax year 1986 have any undistributed income (lines 6d and e, Part XIV) for tax year(s) beginning before 1986?			
If "Yes," list the years ▶ _____, _____, _____, _____			
b If "Yes" to 11a, are you applying the provisions of section 4942(a)(2) (relating to incorrect valuation of assets) to the undistributed income for ALL such years?			
c If the provisions of section 4942(a)(2) are being applied to ANY of the years listed in 11a, list the years here and see the instructions ▶ _____, _____, _____, _____			
12 Taxes on excess business holdings (section 4943):			
a Did you hold more than a 2% direct or indirect interest in any business enterprise at any time during the year?			
b If "Yes," did you have excess business holdings in 1986 as a result of any purchase by you or disqualified persons after May 26, 1969; after the lapse of the 5-year period (or longer period approved by the Commissioner under section 4943(c)(7)) to dispose of holdings acquired by gift or bequest; after the lapse of the 10-year first phase holding period; or after the 15-year first phase holding period?			
Note: *You may use Schedule C, Form 4720, to determine if you had excess business holdings in 1986.*			
13 Taxes on investments that jeopardize charitable purposes (section 4944):			
a Did you invest during the year any amount in a manner that would jeopardize the carrying out of your charitable purposes?			
b Did you make any investment in a prior year (but after December 31, 1969) that could jeopardize your charitable purpose that you had not removed from jeopardy on the first day of your tax year beginning in 1986?			
14 Taxes on taxable expenditures (section 4945):			
a During the year did you pay or incur any amount to:			
(1) Carry on propaganda, or otherwise attempt to influence legislation by attempting to affect the opinion of the general public or any segment thereof, or by communicating with any member or employee of a legislative body, or by communicating with any other government official or employee who may participate in the formulation of legislation?			
(2) Influence the outcome of any specific public election, or to carry on, directly or indirectly, any voter registration drive?			
(3) Provide a grant to an individual for travel, study, or other similar purposes?			
(4) Provide a grant to an organization, other than a charitable, etc., organization described in section *509(a) (1), (2), or (3)*, or section 4940 (d)(2)?			
(5) Provide for any purpose other than religious, charitable, scientific, literary, or educational purposes, or for the prevention of cruelty to children or animals?			
b If you answered "Yes" to any of questions 14a(1) through 14a(5), were all such transactions excepted transactions as described in regulations section 53.4945?			
c If you answered "Yes" to question 14a(4), do you claim exemption from the tax because you maintained expenditure responsibility for the grant?			
If "Yes," attach the statement required.			
15 Did any persons become substantial contributors during the tax year? If "Yes," attach a schedule listing their names and addresses.			
16 During this tax year did you maintain any part of your accounting/tax records on a computerized system?			

Part VIII   Information About Officers, Directors, Trustees, Foundation Managers, Highly Paid Employees and Contractors

1 List all officers, directors, trustees, foundation managers and, if paid, their compensation for 1986 (see instructions):

Name and address	Title, and average hours per week devoted to position	Contributions to employee benefit plans	Expense account, other allowances	Compensation (if any)
Total . . . . ▶				

Part VIII   Information About Officers, Directors, Trustees, etc. (continued)

2   Compensation of five highest paid employees for 1986 (other than included in line 1—see instructions):

Name and address of employees paid more than $30,000	Title and time devoted to position	Contributions to employee benefit plans	Expense account, other allowances	Compensation

Total number of other employees paid over $30,000 ▶

3   Five highest paid persons for professional services for 1986 (see instructions):

Name and address of persons paid more than $30,000	Type of service	Compensation

Total number of others receiving over $30,000 for professional services ▶

Part IX   Minimum Investment Return

1 Fair market value of assets not used (or held for use) directly in carrying out charitable, etc., purposes:	
a Average monthly fair market value of securities	
b Average of monthly cash balances	
c Fair market value of all other assets (see instructions)	
d Total (add lines a, b, and c)	
2 Acquisition indebtedness applicable to line 1 assets	
3 Line 1d minus line 2	
4 Cash deemed held for charitable activities—enter 1½% of line 3 (for greater amount, see instructions)	
5 Line 3 minus line 4	
6 Enter 5% of line 5	

Part X   Computation of Distributable Amount (see instructions)

1 Minimum investment return from Part IX, line 6	
2 Total of:	
a Tax on investment income for 1986 from Part VI, line 5	
b Income tax under subtitle A, for 1986	
3 Distributable amount before adjustments (line 1 minus line 2)	
4 Additions to distributable amount:	
a Recoveries of amounts treated as qualifying distributions.	
b Income distributions from section 4947(a)(2) trusts	
5 Line 3 plus line 4	
6 Deduction from distributable amount (see instructions)	
7 Distributable amount as adjusted (line 5 minus line 6) (Also enter in Part XIV, line 1)	

Part XI — Limitation on Grant Administrative Expenses

Calendar year (or fiscal year) beginning in:	(a) 1986	(b) 1985	(c) 1984	(d) Total
1 Net value of noncharitable-use assets (see instructions)				
2 Multiply line 1 by .0065.				
3 Grant administrative expenses treated as qualifying distributions in the two preceding years	/////			/////
4 In the 1985 column, enter the amount from line 3. In the 1984 column, enter the smaller of line 2 or line 3	/////			
5 Grant administrative expenses for 1986 (from Part XII, line 13)		/////	/////	/////
6 Maximum amount of 1986 grant administrative expenses that may be treated as qualifying distributions (line 2, column (d), minus line 4, column (d))		/////	/////	/////
7 Excess grant administrative expenses for 1986 (line 5 minus line 6; if negative, enter -0-; enter result in Part XIII, line 5)		/////	/////	/////
8 Grant administrative expenses treated as qualifying distributions in 1986 (line 5 minus line 7)		/////	/////	/////

Note: *The amount on line 8 will be used in completing the schedule for 1987 and 1988.*

Part XII — Schedule of Grant Administrative Expenses (see instructions before making any entries)

1 Compensation of officers, directors, trustees, etc..	
2 Other employee salaries and wages	
3 Pension plans, employee benefits	
4 Legal fees.	
5 Accounting fees.	
6 Other professional fees	
7 Interest	
8 Taxes	
9 Occupancy	
10 Travel, conferences, and meetings.	
11 Printing and publications	
12 Other expenses	
13 Total	

Part XIII — Qualifying Distributions (see instructions)

1 Amounts paid (including administrative expenses) to accomplish charitable, etc., purposes:
  a Expenses, contributions, gifts, etc.—total from Part I, column (d), line 26 . . . .
  b Program-related investments
2 Amounts paid to acquire assets used (or held for use) directly in carrying out charitable, etc., purposes . . .
3 Amounts set aside for specific charitable projects that satisfy the:
  a Suitability test (prior IRS approval required) . . . .
  b Cash distribution test (attach the required schedule) . . . .
4 Total (add lines 1, 2, and 3) . . . .
5 Enter excess grant administrative expenses from Part XI, line 7
6 Total qualifying distributions (line 4 minus line 5). Enter this amount in Part XIV, line 4 . . . .
7 Organizations that qualify under section 4940(e) for the reduced rate of tax on net investment income — enter 1% of Part I, line 27b (see instructions) . . . .
8 Qualifying distributions (line 6 minus line 7). . . . .

Note: *The amount on line 8 will be used in Part V, column (b), when calculating the section 4940(e) reduction of tax in subsequent years.*

Part XIV Computation of Undistributed Income (see instructions)

	(a) Corpus	(b) Years prior to 1985	(c) 1985	(d) 1986
1 Distributable amount for 1986 from Part X . .				
2 Undistributed income, if any, as of the end of 1985:				
a Enter amount for 1985				
b Total for prior years: _____ , _____ , _____ .				
3 Excess distributions carryover, if any, to 1986:				
a From 1981				
b From 1982				
c From 1983				
d From 1984				
e From 1985				
f Total of 3a through e				
4 Qualifying distributions for 1986: _____				
a Applied to 1985, but not more than line 2a .				
b Applied to undistributed income of prior years (Election required)				
c Treated as distributions out of corpus (Election required)				
d Applied to 1986 distributable amount . . .				
e Remaining amount distributed out of corpus .				
5 Excess distributions carryover applied to 1986 *(If an amount appears in column (d), the same amount must be shown in column (a))*				
6 Enter the net total of each column as indicated below:				
a Corpus. Add lines 3f, 4c, and 4e. Subtract line 5				
b Prior years' undistributed income. Line 2b minus line 4b				
c Enter the amount of prior years' undistributed income for which a notice of deficiency has been issued, or on which the section 4942(a) tax has been previously assessed				
d Subtract line 6c from line 6b. Taxable amount— see instructions				
e Undistributed income for 1985. Line 2a minus line 4a. Taxable amount—see instructions . . .				
f Undistributed income for 1986. Line 1 minus lines 4d and 5. This amount must be distributed in 1987				
7 Amounts treated as distributions out of corpus to satisfy requirements imposed by section 170(b)(1)(E) or 4942(g)(3) (see instructions) .				
8 Excess distributions carryover from 1981 not applied on line 5 or line 7 (see instructions) . .				
9 Excess distributions carryover to 1987. (Line 6a minus lines 7 and 8.)				
10 Analysis of line 9:				
a Excess from 1982				
b Excess from 1983				
c Excess from 1984				
d Excess from 1985				
e Excess from 1986				

Part XV	**Private Operating Foundations (See instructions and Part VII, question 9)**

1 a If the foundation has received a ruling or determination letter that it is a private operating foundation, and the ruling is effective for 1986, enter the date of the ruling . . . . ▶

b Check box to indicate whether you are a private operating foundation described in section ☐ 4942(j)(3) or ☐ 4942(j)(5).

	Tax year	Prior 3 Years			(e) Total
	(a) 1986	**(b)** 1985	**(c)** 1984	**(d)** 1983	
2 a Enter the lesser of the adjusted net income from Part I or the minimum investment return from Part IX for 1986 and 1985 (Part VIII for prior years)					
b 85% of line 2a					
c Qualifying distributions from Part XIII, line 6, for 1986 and 1985 (Part X, line 4, for prior years)					
d Amounts included in line 2c not used directly for active conduct of exempt activities . .					
e Qualifying distributions made directly for active conduct of exempt activities (line 2c minus line 2d)					
3 Complete the alternative test in 3a, b, or c on which you rely:					
a "Assets" alternative test—enter:					
(1) Value of all assets					
(2) Value of assets qualifying under section 4942(j)(3)(B)(i)					
b "Endowment" alternative test—Enter ⅔ of minimum investment return shown in Part IX, line 6, for 1986 and 1985 (enter ⅔ of comparable amount (Part VIII, line 6) for prior years)					
c "Support" alternative test—enter:					
(1) Total support other than gross investment income (interest, dividends, rents, payments on securities loans (section 512(a)(5)), or royalties) .					
(2) Support from general public and 5 or more exempt organizations as provided in section 4942(j)(3)(B)(iii) . . .					
(3) Largest amount of support from an exempt organization					
(4) Gross investment income					

Part XVI	**Supplementary Information (see instructions)**

1   Information Regarding Foundation Managers

a List here any managers of the foundation who have contributed more than 2% of the total contributions received by the foundation before the close of any tax year (but only if they have contributed more than $5,000). (See section 507(d)(2).)

b List here any managers of the foundation who own 10% or more of the stock of a corporation (or an equally large portion of the ownership of a partnership or other entity) of which the foundation has a 10% or greater interest.

2   Information Regarding Contribution, Grant, Gift, Loan, Scholarship, etc., Programs

If you make gifts, grants, awards (see instructions), etc., to individuals or organizations, check here ☐ and complete these items:

a The name, address, and telephone number of the person to whom applications should be addressed

b The form in which applications should be submitted and information and materials they should include

c Any submission deadlines

d Any restrictions or limitations on awards, such as by geographical areas, charitable fields, kinds of institutions, or other factors

Part XVI	Supplementary Information (continued)

3   Grants and Contributions Paid During the Year or Approved for Future Payment

Recipient — Name and address (home or business)	If recipient is an individual, show any relationship to any foundation manager or substantial contributor	Foundation status of recipient	Purpose of grant or contribution	Amount
a *Paid during the year*				
Total ▶				
b *Approved for future payment*				
Total ▶				

Part XVII-A	Summary of Grant Programs and Other Activities	(a) Grants and program-related investments	(b) Administrative expenses	(c) Total
1	Gifts, contributions, scholarships and other grants			
2	Direct charitable activities (describe each):			
a	....			
b	....			
c	Direct technical and other assistance to grantees (see instructions)			
d	All other (attach schedule)			
e	Total—add lines 2a through d			
3	Program-related investments (describe each type)			
a	....			
b	....			
c	....			
d	All other (attach schedule)			
e	Total—see instructions			
4	Other qualifying distributions			
5	Other expenses not included in lines 1–4.			

Part XVII-B	Supporting Data

1   Describe on an attached schedule the bases (for example, time spent, salary expenses incurred, space utilized, etc.) used to allocate administrative expenses to the activities described in Part XVII-A.

2   For the foundation's principal direct charitable activities and program-related investments, provide a schedule of relevant statistical information, such as the number of organizations and other beneficiaries served, conferences convened, research papers produced, etc.

3   Attach a schedule for Part XVII-A, lines 2 and 3, setting forth for each activity or investment area the amount of any income produced by it.

Part XVIII	Public Inspection

1   Enter the date the notice of availability of the annual return appeared in a newspaper ▶

2   Enter the name of the newspaper ▶

3   Check here ▶ ☐ if you have attached a copy of the newspaper notice as required by the instructions. (If the notice is not attached, the return will be considered incomplete.)

Under penalties of perjury, I declare that I have examined this return, including accompanying schedules and statements, and to the best of my knowledge and belief, it is true, correct and complete. Declaration of preparer (other than taxpayer or fiduciary) is based on all information of which preparer has any knowledge.

Please Sign Here

Signature of officer or trustee — Date — Title

Paid Preparer's Use Only

Preparer's signature — Date — Check if self-employed ▶ ☐ — Preparer's social security no.

Firm's name (or yours, if self-employed) and address — E.I. No. ▶ — ZIP code ▶

SOURCES OF INFORMATION ON CORPORATIONS

Annual Survey of Corporate Contributions, 1987 edition, by L. C. Platzer. $15 for Associates, $75 non-Associates. The Conference Board, 845 Third Avenue, New York City, NY 10022.

> The latest (1985) data in this statistical survey of giving by the largest corporate donors documents that the rapid annual increases may be leveling off.

Banking on Leisure. 1985. $52 plus $4 shipping and handling. International Events Group, 213 W. Institute Place, Suite 303, Chicago, IL 60610.

> Proceedings from a seminar held to discuss how corporations decide to sponsor special events. Includes useful tips on how to snag a sponsor.

CFAE Corporate Handbook of Aid-to-Education Programs. 1984, $25. Council for Financial Aid to Education, 680 Fifth Avenue, New York, NY 10019.

> A description of 203 corporations with interests in education. For each, provides name, address, contact person, financial data on giving and a summary of their special education emphasis.

The Complete Guide to Corporate Fund Raising. 1982. $17.75. Public Service Materials Center, 111 N. Central Avenue, Hartsdale, NY 10530.

> Technical "how-to" of proposal writing to corporations, including useful section on research techniques.

Corporate 500: The Directory of Corporate Philanthropy, Fifth Edition, 1986. $290. Public Management Institute, 358 Brannan Street, San Francisco, CA 94107.

> Profiles 500 firms, of which sixty are firms not covered in the previous directory. Has twelve indexes.

Corporate Foundation Profiles, Fourth Edition, 1985. $55. The Foundation Center, 79 Fifth Avenue, New York, NY 10003.

> In-depth profiles of over 250 of the largest corporate foundations, including information on their parent company, giving trends, sample grants and other useful details. Also includes less extensive information (primarily financial data) on 470 other corporate foundations.

Corporate Philanthropy, The Business of Giving. 1982. $12. Council on Foundations, 1828 L Street, NW, Suite 1200, Washington, D.C. 20036.

> A compilation of articles by some of the nation's experts on the history, future and current operation of corporate philanthropy. Excellent background for the beginner.

Corporate Philanthropy Report. Monthly. $127/year. Public Management Institute, 358 Brannan Street, San Francisco, CA 94107.

> Very useful newsletter on the latest trends in corporate philanthropy, as well as references to new publications, changes in personnel and strategies for approaching firms. Recent issues contained some of the most in-depth information available anywhere on U.S. grantmaking by Japanese firms.

Directory of Corporate Affiliations. $140. National Register Publishing Company, Inc., 5201 Old Orchard Road, Skokie, IL 60077.

> This is a "who owns whom" of U.S. corporations and it comes out annually, with bimonthly updates. A very important resource for determining if a local firm in your community is actually owned by a larger one (who may have a private foundation and/or direct giving program).

Guide to Corporate Giving 3. 1985. $39.95. American Council for the Arts, 570 Seventh Avenue, New York, NY 10018.

> Describes the giving interests and policies of over 700 major companies in the fields of the arts, health, welfare, education and civic philanthropy.

How to Find Information about Companies. 1986. $95. Washington Researchers Publishing, 2612 P Street, NW, Washington, D.C. 20007.

> Originally designed for corporations who want to find out about other companies, but equally useful to those seeking corporate grants.

Key Company Directory. 1986. $540 to non-associates, $450 to associates, and $300 to educational institutions. The Conference Board, 845 Third Avenue, New York, NY 10022.

> A guide to the overseas and domestic operations of 2,000 U.S. manufacturing corporations. Includes sales, locations of facilities, types of products and number of U.S. plants. Published yearly.

Million Dollar Directory. $595. Dun's Marketing Services, 3 Century Drive, Parsippany, NJ 07054.

> This is a good place to get quick information on U.S. companies. Volume 1 lists about 49,000 companies each with a net worth of $1.2 million and over; Volumes 2 and 3 cover smaller firms. The arrangement of each volume is similar: The alphabetical listing of companies includes address, telephone number, names of officers and directors, products or services, Standard Industrial

Classification, approximate sales, number of employees, division names and functions. Indexes are also provided geographically.

The National Directory of Corporate Charity. 1984. $80. The Foundation Center, 79 Fifth Avenue, New York, NY 10003.

A description of the charitable activities of 1,600 major U.S. firms, including those with direct giving programs.

National Directory of Corporate Contributions. The Foundation Center, 79 Fifth Avenue, 16th Street, New York, N.Y. 10003. Expected publication date--late 1988. Price will reportedly be under $100.

The Foundation Center recently launched a new project to result in an annual directory that will reportedly be the most comprehensive and authoritative description yet of corporate philanthropy. Profiles of the direct giving programs as well as foundation activities of several thousand U.S. firms will be included, including information on many who do not normally publicize their activities. Contact the Center for information on how and when to order.

National Directory of Corporate Public Affairs. 1985. $50. Columbia Books, Inc., 1350 New York Avenue, NW, Suite 207, Washington, D.C. 20005.

Lists the names of individuals responsible for advertising and corporate contributions activity (plus other functions) in over 1,500 companies. Also provides general information on the firms' public involvement.

Resource Raising: The Role of Non-Cash Assistance in Corporate Philanthropy. 1986. $10. Independent Sector, 1828 L Street, NW, Washington, D.C. 20036.

An excellent discussion of a large number of examples of corporate gifts of products, human resources and services. Also gives guidelines on the legal and tax consequences of non-cash assistance.

Special Event Reports. Biweekly. $180/year. Special Events Report, 213 W. Institute Place, Suite 303, Chicago, IL 60610.

Useful means of monitoring which corporations are sponsoring which types of special events.

Standard & Poor's Register of Corporations, Directors and Executives. $245/year, lease basis. Standard & Poor's Corporation, 25 Broadway, New York, NY 10004.

Lists some 37,000 corporations alphabetically and for each gives name, address and telephone

number, names of officers and directors, products or services provided, SIC, annual sales, number of employees and sometimes their principal bank and law firm (useful for networking). This information is also available through an on-line computerized data system.

The Taft Corporate Giving Information System. Annual. $397 plus $15 for postage and handling. The Taft Group, 5130 MacArthur Blvd., NW, Washington, D.C. 20016.

Includes a *Directory* (with brief information on several thousand firms), *The Profiles,* which gives more in-depth information on the Fortune 1000 companies, and *Giving Watch*, a monthly newsletter. These products may also be ordered separately.

The Art of Winning Corporate Grants, by Howard Hillman. 1980. $14.95. Public Service Materials Center, 111 N. Central Avenue, Hartsdale, NY 10530.

Somewhat dated, but still useful and practical guide on writing proposals to foundations.

The Perfect Gift: Examples of Noncash Corporate Philanthropy, by Stephen Mittenthal. 1983. $4.75 plus $2.00 handling. The Grantsmanship Center, 650 S. Spring Street, Suite 507, Los Angeles, CA 90014.

Reprint from *The Grantsmanship NEWS* that provides a variety of examples of how resources, other than cash, can be obtained from firms.

Wall Street Journal Index. $365. Dow Jones & Company, Inc., 22 Cortlandt Street, New York, NY 10017.

This is the major newspaper covering business and thus one of the most up-to-the-minute sources on acquisitions, mergers and their implications, as well as major personnel changes. Also includes an increasing amount of coverage on trends in corporate philanthropy.

Who Owns Whom: North America. $225. Dun's Marketing Services, 3 Century Drive, Parsippany, NJ 07054.

Usually issued annually and provides a number of comprehensive indexes.

Who's Who in America, 1986-87, 44th revised edition. $243. Marquis Publisher, Front and Brown Streets, Riverside, NJ 08075.

This is a useful tool in looking up the background of donors, trustees, and sometimes key officers and staffs of foundations as well as corporations.

SOURCES OF INFORMATION ON ASSOCIATIONS

The Encyclopedia of Associations. $135. Gale Research Co., Book Tower, Detroit, MI 48226.
> Published in three volumes. The first volume is most useful as it gives the group's name and location, functions, number of members, number of employees, publications and conventions.

Membership Directory. Price unknown. American Society of Association Executives, 1575 Eye Street, NW, Washington, D.C. 20005.
> A professional association of those who head associations.

National Trade and Professional Associations of the United States and Canada and Labor Unions. $35. Columbia Books, Inc., 777 14th Street, NW, Washington, D.C. 20005.
> Describes over 6,500 organizations, with a subject index.

For **labor unions**, two beginning contact sources are the research offices at:

AFL-CIO
815 16th Street, NW
Washington, D.C. 20006
(202) 637-5000

International Ladies Garment Workers Union
1710 Broadway
New York, NY 10019
(212) 265-7000

REGIONAL ASSOCIATIONS OF GRANTMAKERS -1987

MULTI-STATE ASSOCIATIONS AND PRINCIPAL CONTACT

Conference of Southwest Foundations
(Serves primarily Arizona, Arkansas,
Colorado, Nevada, New Mexico,
Oklahoma and Texas)
Maud W. Keeling
Executive Secretary
Conference of Southwest
Foundations
Post Office Box 8832
Corpus Christi, TX 78412
(512) 850-5054

Pacific Northwest Grantmakers Forum
(Alaska, Idaho, Montana, Oregon and
Washington)
Catherine Anstett, Administrator
c/o The Seattle Foundation
425 Pike Street, Suite 510
Seattle, WA 98101
(206) 622-2294

Southeastern Council on Foundations
(Serves primarily Alabama, Arkansas,
Florida, Georgia, Kentucky, Louisiana,
Mississippi, North Carolina, South
Carolina, Tennessee and Virginia)
Robert H. Hull
Executive Director
Southeastern Council of
Foundations
134 Peachtree Street, N.W.
Atlanta, GA 30303
(404) 524-0911

ASSOCIATIONS CURRENTLY SERVING A STATE OR A MULTI-COUNTY AREA OF A STATE

Associated Grantmakers of Massa-
chusetts, Inc.
Miguel Satut
President
Associated Grantmakers of
Massachusetts, Inc.
294 Washington Street
Room 840
Boston, MA 02108
(617) 426-2606

Council of Michigan Foundations
Dorothy A. Johnson
President
Council of Michigan Foundations
P.O. Box 599
Grand Haven, MI 49417
(616) 842-7080

Council of New Jersey Grantmakers
Robert Corman
Chair
The Council of New Jersey
Grantmakers
57 Washington Street
East Orange, NJ 07107
(201) 676-5905

Donors Forum of Ohio
Carol A. Farquhar
Liaison Officer
Donors Forum of Ohio
c/o Kettering Foundation
5335 Far Hills Avenue
Dayton, OH 45423
(513) 434-7300

Foundation Forum of Wisconsin
Richard W. Yeo
Managing Director
Foundation Forum of Wisconsin
P.O. Box 11978
Milwaukee, WI 53211
(414) 962-6820

Grantmakers of Western New York
William L. Van Schoonhoven
President
Western New York Grantmakers
Association
c/o The Buffalo Foundation
237 Main Street
Buffalo, NY 14203
(716) 852-2857

Grantmakers of Western
Pennsylvania
Kate Dewey
Executive Director
Grantmakers of Western
Pennsylvania
368 One Mellon Bank Center
Pittsburgh, PA 15258

Indiana Donors Alliance
Kenneth Gladish
Secretary
Indiana Donors Alliance
c/o The Indiana Committee for
The Humanities
1500 North Delaware
Indianapolis, IN 46202
(317) 638-1500

Minnesota Council on Foundations
Jacqueline Reis
Executive Director
Minnesota Council on Founda-
tions
425 Peavey Building
Minneapolis, MN 55402
(612) 338-1989

Northern California Grantmakers
Caroline Tower
Executive Director
Northern California Grantmakers
334 Kearny Street
San Francisco, CA 94108
(415) 788-2982

Southern California Association
Lon M. Burns
President
Southern California Association
for Philanthropy
315 W. Ninth Street
Suite 1000
Los Angeles, CA 90015-4210

GREATER CITY ASSOCIATIONS

Association of Baltimore Area Grant-
makers
Martha Johnston
Program Officer
Community Foundation of
Greater Baltimore
6 East Hamilton Street
Baltimore, MD 21202

Clearinghouse of Midcontinent
Foundations
    Linda H. Talbot
    President
    Clearinghouse for Midcontinent
    Foundations
    Post Office Box 7215
    Kansas City, MO 64113
    (816) 276-1176

Co-ordinating Council for Foundations,
Inc.
    Bertina Williams
    Executive Director
    Co-ordinating Council for
    Foundations, Inc.
    999 Asylum Avenue
    Hartford, CT 06105
    (203) 525-5585

Donors Forum of Chicago
    Valerie Lies
    President
    Donors Forum of Chicago
    53 W. Jackson Boulevard
    Suite 430
    Chicago, IL 60604
    (312) 431-0260

Grantmakers Forum
    Marjorie M. Carlson
    Program Coordinator
    Grantmakers Forum
    1456 Hanna Building
    Cleveland, OH 44115
    (216) 861-3810

Metropolitan Association for Philanthropy
    Amy R. Rome
    Executive Director
    Metropolitan Association for
    Philanthropy
    5585 Pershing Avenue
    Suite 150
    St. Louis, MO 63112
    (314) 361-3900

New York Regional Association of
Grantmakers
    Barbara Bryan
    Executive Director
    New York Regional Association
    of Grantmakers
    505 Eighth Avenue
    18th Floor
    New York, NY 10018
    (212) 714-0699

Rochester Grantmakers Forum
    Pearl W. Rubin
    Rochester Grantmakers Forum
    c/o Daisy Marquis Jones
    Foundation
    620 Granite Building
    130 E. Main Street
    Rochester, NY 14604
    (716) 263-3331

San Diego Grantmakers Group
    Pamela Hall
    San Diego Grantmakers Group
    c/o San Diego Community
    Foundation
    525 B Street
    Suite 410
    San Diego, CA 92101
    (619) 239-8815

PART TWO

THE PROPOSAL PHASE

5

WRITING THE PROPOSAL

This chapter indicates some of the reasons why a well-written and well-planned proposal is necessary, identifies the major components of a proposal and discusses their purpose within the application, and suggests a timetable for proposal development.

REASONS FOR A GOOD PROPOSAL

Every book and manual dealing with proposal preparation emphasizes the importance of submitting a well-written application. They note that the proposal document itself is often the most significant factor in the approval or disapproval of a request for funds. Too often, however, the term *well-written* is interpreted only to mean clarity, conciseness, readability, appropriate literary style and the absence of jargon.

While these characteristics are important, it is even more crucial that the proposal demonstrate that:

● You have done your homework and are not duplicating what has already been done.

● This project is relevant to the funding source.

● The purpose of the project is really important and will address a critical need.

● You have done the best job of choosing an effective and feasible approach to solving this problem.

● Something tangible can be anticipated at the end of the project that justifies the resources requested.

● The project staff and its organization have the capability, credibility and experience needed to make the **project** succeed.

A colleague once noted that proposal writing is both an art and a science. There *are* specific techniques and processes of writing an application that can be acquired with practice and experience. But these, by themselves, are not substitutes for the authority which is evident in applications written by those knowledgeable in their field and excited at the opportunity to create something new.

Emphasizing writing style instead of content is a frequent mistake of beginning proposal writers. They are encouraged by some who boast of the ability to prepare a "quick and dirty application in twenty-four hours." In truth, such proposals sometimes do get funded. However, the boasters often omit the fact that they or their organization are already known to the funding source and have already reached informal agreements on the project through prior meetings or telephone calls.

It is wise to view the proposal document as the major means of communication with potential donors (even if this is not the case). The application thus bears the considerable burden of simultaneously creating a favorable impression and securing support for the proposed project.

In addition to content, the proposal's organization, readability, and effectiveness in providing all of the information requested by the funding source are all important. The following cautions will be useful:

Do read all forms and instructions provided by the funding source and follow them carefully. Recheck the proposal before it is sent to insure compliance.

Do maintain a balance between conciseness and sufficient detail to effectively explain the project. Admittedly, this is hard to do if a foundation limits the application to no more than two or four pages. However, there is method in their madness. You have to know a subject awfully well to describe it succinctly.

Do make certain that the reviewers are guided to the most important parts of the proposal. Use subheadings wherever necessary.

Do adapt the language of the proposal to the audience in the funding agency. All donors (including those in the research fields) now warn against the use of jargon. But, even technical phrases or words should be explained unless they are commonly used and easily understood. Remember that employees of funding agencies may not have had the opportunity to keep current with all aspects of their discipline. Assume they are intelligent, but give them the courtesy of being able to easily understand you.

Do make certain that the proposal flows logically from one section to another. In essence, you are telling a story about what needs to be done, why and how.

Do avoid abbreviations and acronyms (unless very common in your field).

Do have the proposal edited by someone else. Poor grammar, spelling or typing has doomed some otherwise excellent applications.

Do leave ample margins at the top, bottom and sides of each page. Also determine if the funding source wants proposals double or single spaced and if they prefer text guided by a particular style manual.

Don't bury your most important points behind unnecessary introductory phrases. Most proposals could benefit from the old writer's trick of eliminating the first two sentences in a draft, because number three is usually the heart of the matter.

Don't provide a slew of drawings, charts or statistical tables in the body of the proposal unless required by the application forms. Put them in an appendix if they are absolutely necessary.

Don't use citations to previous research without indicating how they apply to your own idea.

Don't be intimidated by the apparent lack of logic in application forms. After all, proposal format designers are human, too.

Don't be too concerned about using words that are "in" with particular funding sources. Most of these change so rapidly that they are "out" by the time the proposal reaches its destination.

Don't make commitments or propose approaches in the proposal that you have no means to implement. Most funding sources assume that actual project implementation may require some variation from the original proposal. But they are quick to spot and

seldom forgive those who have been deliberately misleading.

While the importance of a well-planned proposal may be obvious in terms of getting the money, you should not forget that an application can also serve other purposes. For example, a proposal:

● Allows you the opportunity to develop a useful work schedule for implementing the project. Many start-up problems can thus be avoided.

● Provides the framework for management of the project by establishing the rules of the game within your organization. For example, if participation of another group is essential to the success of the project, this can be negotiated at the time the proposal is written and evidence of this referenced in the application.

● Forces you into the discipline of making certain that adequate resources of time, money, personnel, facilities and so forth are anticipated.

● Serves as a vehicle for informing others, particularly new staff, of the goals and intended operation of the project.

● Tests the degree of real internal commitment to the project. More than one "good idea" has been dropped when it became necessary to do the hard work of describing and selling it through a proposal.

There are a number of other sources on proposal-writing. Some are oriented to applications to particular federal agencies, such as Reif-Lehrer (1982), Oetting (1986) and Williams (1988, copyright pending). Others focus on particular types of proposals, such as applications for research funding, as described by Niederhuber (1985) and Krathwohl (1977). Still others are aimed primarily at private foundations and corporate proposals, including Bauer (1984), Hillman and Chamberlain (1980), Dermer and Wetheimer (1982), and Kurzig (1980). Additional references can be found through the library.

MAJOR COMPONENTS OF A PROPOSAL

Two quick rules of thumb at the outset:

● There is no such thing as a standard proposal format. The type of information required by various funding sources and the sequence in which they want it provided varies widely.

● Almost always proposals to private funding sources should be shorter than those submitted to public agencies.

For the beginner, then, it is important to become familiar with the major types of information (or components) desired by the majority of funding sources and then tailor the actual organization of the proposal to the requirements of the particular donor to whom it will be sent.

PRIVATE FOUNDATIONS AND CORPORATIONS

Those who have not previously applied to private foundations and corporations find it hard to believe that these organizations seldom use forms and are explicit about wanting brief proposals. Two examples illustrate this point.

The Ford Foundation, whose grants exceeded $300 million in program year 1986-87, asks first for a brief letter of inquiry in order to determine whether the project is consistent with current interests and available funds. Their booklet, *Ford Foundation: Current Interests 1986 and 1987*, then directs completed proposals to include:

● Objectives.

● Detailed program for pursuing objectives.

● Qualifications of persons engaged in the work.

● A detailed budget.

● Present means of support and status of applications to other funding sources.

● Legal and tax status.

The Atlantic Richfield Foundation, one of the nation's largest corporate foundations, warns in its *General Requirements* that "elaborate and lengthy proposals should be discouraged." It then notes that a concisely written proposal, not more than two pages long, should cover:

● A brief description of the organization, including its purpose and proposed project.

● A statement of need for the project and a description of the methods chosen to meet its goals.

● The time it is expected to take to complete the project, as well as any major milestones.

● The total cost of the project, other sources and levels of funding, and the amount requested from the Foundation.

● A statement describing community support for and involvement in the project and the organization.

● Attachments including current budget, most recent audited financial statement, annual report, copy of IRS letter of determination, copy of the applicant's 990-AR submission to the Internal Revenue Service and a list of the organization's Board of Directors, including their outside affiliations.

Table 1 summarizes the informational elements most commonly expected in proposals to foundations and corporations.

PROPOSALS TO FEDERAL AND STATE AGENCIES

In some ways, proposals to state or federal agencies are easier to prepare than those to private sources. Not only do public agencies usually provide detailed forms and instructions, but they seldom have such stringent limitations on proposal length.

However, public agencies are seldom as forgiving if the proposal is not completed precisely as directed or if any required documentation is ommitted. Always double check such applications prior to their submission.

Table 2 describes the elements commonly found in applications to public agencies and lists the information normally contained in each section.

TIMETABLE FOR PROPOSAL DEVELOPMENT

Ideally, work on a proposal should begin at least a year in advance of when the project or program is expected to begin. This is particularly true for proposals to private foundations and corporations (who may require from ninety days to six months to make a final decision).

In practice, many individuals learn of a funding opportunity only days or weeks before a proposal

MAJOR COMPONENTS IN A PROPOSAL TO FOUNDATIONS AND CORPORATIONS

ELEMENT	INFORMATION NORMALLY PROVIDED
Title Page	Legal name of applicant organization; name of group to which check is to be made out (if different); address, name, title and telephone number of contact person; title of project; 25-word summary of project; amount requested; statement that project has been approved for submission by the Board of Directors; and, sometimes, statement of assurance of non-discrimination.
Purpose	Goals, objectives and/or expected results of project; description of whom it will serve, their geographic location and number; significance and need for project; comparison with other efforts in the same field and/or geographic area or other documentation of non-duplication of effort; and relevance to the donor's priorities and guidelines.
Approach	Plan of action or sequence of activities to be carried out; including staff responsibilities; staff and volunteer training; client selection procedures or policies; major milestones; beginning and ending of project; justification for the approach; specific outcomes anticipated; and method of evaluating and reporting results. This section also usually mentions plans for project dissemination and any recognition to be received by the donor.
Qualifications	General description of the organization's mission, history, major programs or activities and how these relate to the proposed project. Give names and backgrounds of those key to project, including consultants or cooperating agencies (evidence of their willingness to participate should be included). Mention special facilities, equipment or other capabilities to argue for your ability to complete the project.
Budget	Detailed budget for the project; amount to be contributed by applicant (usually distinguished between cash and in-kind); names (and amounts) of funds received from other donors; names (and sometimes amounts) of pending applications; description of how project will be funded after the grant expires; plans for additional fundraising (if needed); overall description of budget, expenses and revenues for the total organization. This last is usually only summarized if an audited financial statement and most recent 990 form are enclosed.
Attachments	Names of Board of Directors and their major affiliations; copy of IRS determination letter; organization's last annual report; brochure describing organization (optional); and letters of support (optional).

This handout taken from *Getting Funded: A Complete Guide to Proposal Writing* by Mary Hall, 1988.
Available from Continuing Education Publications, P.O. Box 1491, Portland, OR 97207.

TABLE 2   WRITING THE PROPOSAL

MAJOR COMPONENTS OF A PROPOSAL TO STATE AND FEDERAL AGENCIES

ELEMENT	INFORMATION TO BE PROVIDED
Title Page(s)	Title of project; name of project director; name, address and telephone number of submitting agency; name of program and organization to which submitted; inclusive dates of project; budget request; signatures of persons authorizing submission; and compliance certifications. A table of contents is usually also supplied.
Abstract	A self-contained, ready-for-publication description of the project covering objectives; need and significance; procedures; evaluation; and dissemination components. Should stress end products or project's advancement of knowledge. Usually 200 to 500 words long.
Purpose	Specific indication of the expected outcomes of the project, usually stated as goals and objectives, hypotheses and research questions. May explain how project relates to overall goals of a larger program. Should clearly identify both short-term and long-term results expected.
Statement of Need	Well-documented description of the problem to be addressed and why it is important. Should establish significance, timeliness, generalizability, and contribution to related existing knowledge or work in progress.
Procedures	A plan of action for how the purposes will be achieved. In non-research projects, this section usually starts with a description of the overall approach and its relevance or innovativeness and then provides details on methodology, participants, organization and timeline. In research projects, one usually describes the design, population and sample, instrumentation, data analysis and time schedule. This may also include a review of related research.
Evaluation*	Details the means by which the local agency and funding source will know that the project has accomplished its purposes. May also describe plans for collecting information or data to improve project operation. States purpose of evaluation; type of information to be collected; details on instruments, data collection, analysis, utilization and how results will be reported.
Dissemination*	Specifies how products and findings will be shared with others. This section may also detail reports to be provided to funding source.
Qualifications	Documents the ability of the sponsoring organization to successfully complete the project, including prior related experience. Outlines facilities and equipment required and how these will be provided. Lists specific personnel who will work on the project and what they will do. Includes resumes (and in research proposals, a list of prior publications). Describes rationale for any consultants to be involved, their role, and background and evidence of their commitment to participate.
Budget	The cost of the project annually and overall. Usually divided into categories such as personnel, supplies and materials, travel, data processing, facilities or equipment and indirect costs. Matching funds to be provided or other funds to be sought should also be specified. Most public sources provide specific budget forms.

* These categories may or may not be included in research proposals, or, if required, can be discussed as elements of the procedures component.

This handout taken from *Getting Funded: A Complete Guide To Proposal Writing* by Mary Hall, 1988.
Available from Continuing Education Publications, P.O. Box 1491, Portland, OR 97207.

must be submitted. They just have to do the best they can with the time that is available.

As with everything else in this field, there is no perfect or uniform model for the proposal development process. One model is presented in Table 3. It assumes that the idea for the project came first and then a needs assessment was conducted to determine if the idea really dealt with a significant problem and was not duplicated elsewhere. Conversely, the idea for the project may grow out of a more general needs assessment or an individual may first think of a particular approach he or she wants to try and then search out a problem to which it can be applied.

In writing any proposal, however, it is important to develop a detailed workplan specifying what steps need to be completed, their sequence, who will do them and who must be involved in various reviews. This will help in an organized approach to information-gathering. It will also insure that no important components are omitted which result in the proposal being rejected or missing the application deadline.

WRITING WITH COMMITTEES

The author has a personal bias against trying to write a proposal with a committee. However, others have done this very successfully and some claim it is the only way to develop a competitive application in a very short period. The following suggestions have been provided by a colleague who routinely involves groups in the preparation of proposals.

❑ Have an initial meeting with a few creative colleagues to brainstorm the project idea and assess its likelihood of being funded. If the application is to be submitted in response to an RFP, also critique this document using criteria similar to those provided in Chapter 2.

❑ Assign someone to check professional literature and informational sources on prior grants to insure that the proposed idea is not directly duplicative of prior work. If it is, begin thinking of a rationale to justify why the same effort should be made by your organization (perhaps the type of service is not available locally or there may be questions about the validity of the previous research).

❑ Select someone to be the "lead" for the proposal development. This person should specify the talent needed in the writing team, be responsible for getting all forms and instructions from potential funding sources, clarify deadlines and secure the necessary information on organizational compliance with federal and/or state requirements. The "lead" may not necessarily be the proposal's primary editor, but should be the person who is clearly in charge of seeing that the proposal is done properly.

❑ Hold a first meeting with everyone who will be asked to help write elements of the proposal. Discuss the project idea and be sure that there is sufficient internal commitment to go forth. Develop a detailed timeline for completion and submission of the document and make specific assignments. At this stage, it is critical to designate the "editor" who will be responsible for pulling draft language into some type of logical and coherent document.

❑ Hold as many brainstorming sessions as possible to critique the project idea and its various elements. Schedule opportunities for the various writers to see each other's drafts so that there is general awareness of the approaches being taken.

❑ Have one individual specifically assigned to conduct negotiations with the internal administrators. This is normally the project director. The project director should also have primary responsibility for discussions with potential funding sources.

❑ As soon as a draft of anticipated tasks is completed, secure help from an experienced individual in translating these into specific time and resource requirements. Cycle back to this person if major changes are made during the proposal's final preparation.

❑ When the proposal writer or editor has a final draft of the document, ask a colleague who is known for thorough and objective criticism to read the final draft and suggest modifications. Have another person read the document looking for grammar, consistent style, flow and readability. Make certain someone who is very careful gives the final proposal a check to ensure that the application complies with all requirements of the funding source.

TABLE 3   **WRITING THE PROPOSAL**

TIMETABLE FOR PROPOSAL DEVELOPMENT

MONTH	ACTIVITY
January	Idea is identified. Preliminary discussions held with colleagues locally and elsewhere to determine interest and significance.
February	Needs assessment instituted. Inquiries submitted to information sources (see Chapter 3) to determine if similar idea has been tried, to identify related research, and to see who is funding this type of project. Statistical data collection initiated if necessary.
March	Various approaches to implementing the idea discussed. Best approach chosen. Approval to proceed with development of proposal obtained from local administrators. Project director and other staff to be involved in proposal preparation identified. First draft of idea in project form developed and discussed with agency administrators, potential population to be served or studied, and other groups necessary to success of project. Status of organization's compliance with funding agency requirements determined.
April	Potential funding sources identified and preliminary outline or abstract sent to determine their interest and to acquire necessary application information.
May	Project idea modified by input received during previous months. Another inquiry to potential funding sources may be warranted. Project idea developed into completed proposal and reviewed by colleagues and local administrators. Copy also sent for preliminary review to any local or state group involved in a clearance procedure.
June	Funding source chosen. Final draft prepared based on source's forms or requirements. Official clearance received from local administrators. Review and clearance sought as necessary from other state or local agencies.
July	Proposal submitted to funding source. Receipt card with processing number received in return or some acknowledgement of receipt received.
August to October	Proposal reviewed. Approval or rejection received. In either case, comments of reviewers should be obtained.
November	Authorization to expend funds received. Project starts. Planning will begin in January for efforts to receive refunding.

This handout taken from *Developing Skills in Proposal Writing* by Mary Hall, 1988.
Available from Continuing Education Publications, P.O. Box 1491, Portland, OR 97207.

CHAPTER REFERENCES

Bauer, D. G.,*The "How -o" Grants Manual* (New York: Macmillan, 1984).

Dermer, J., and S. Wetheimer *The Complete Guide to Corporate Fund Raising* (Hartsdale, NY: Public Service Materials Center, 1982).

Hillman, H., and M. Chamberlain *The Art of Winning Corporate Grants* (Hartsdale, NY: Public Service Materials Center, 1980).

Krathwohl, D. R., *How to Prepare a Research Proposal* (Syracuse: Syracuse University Bookstore, 1977).

Kurzig, C., *Foundation Fundamentals: A Guide for Grantseekers* (New York : The Foundation Center, 1980).

Niederhuber, J. E., "Writing a Successful Grant Application," *Journal of Surgical Research* 39 (1985), 277-84.

Oetting, E. R., "Ten Fatal Mistakes in Grant Writing," *Professional Psychology Research and Practice*, vol. 17, no. 6 (1986), 570-3.

Reif-Lehrer, L., *Writing a Successful Grant Application*, (Boston: Science Books International, 1982).

Williams, C., *A Grantsmanship and Proposal Writing Manual* (Albuquerque: Development of Research and Human Services, 1988 [copyright pending]).

TITLE PAGES, ABSTRACTS AND ACCOMPANYING FORMS

This chapter outlines considerations in selecting a title and discusses the contents of a title page and abstract. It also provides examples of forms which frequently must accompany a proposal document.

CHOOSING THE TITLE

An experienced proposal writer once remarked, only partly facetiously, that the most important item in developing a successful project was the choosing of a good title. A title that aptly describes the primary goal of the project in words that will be easily remembered and often repeated is a definite asset. Here are several do's and don'ts:

Do suit the title to the potential funding source. For example, a highly technical sounding title might be appropriate for submission to the National Science Foundation or to one of the National Institutes of Health. It would be much less appropriate for a social service project submitted to a private foundation or a curriculum development project sent to a state education agency.

Do choose a title that describes the purpose of the project or that gives the casual reader some idea of what the project is about.

Do keep the title as short as possible. Remember that the project will normally be indexed or entered into some type of informational system. Brevity helps and, at least in the private sector, is mandatory.

Do research a foundation or company prior to proposing a project title that includes its name. Naming the project after a sole donor is usually mutually agreed upon after a decision has been made to fund a project, rather than at the initial application stage.

Do choose a title with some imagination and flair. While acronyms (words formed by the first letter or

first few letters in several words) are overused, they are an effective device for developing descriptive and memorable project titles.

Don't select a title that is likely to have been used frequently elsewhere. Imitation may be the sincerest form of flattery, but not in a project title. At last count, the author's own foundation had received 17 applications called "New Beginnings." Sixteen were not funded.

Don't choose a title which can be considered funny. Funding sources are sensitive to the fact that politicians have skimmed project titles listed in annual reports or government documents and have used the highly jargonized or flippant title as the basis for a critical speech.

Don't select a title which begins "A Project to...." Not only does this show lack of imagination, but it adds unnecessary length to the project label.

THE COVER AND TITLE PAGES

Increasingly, both private and public finding sources are encouraging applicants to *not* put a cover on a proposal. Since most federal agencies now prohibit applications from being bound (and in some cases, stapled), the utility of blank sheets of paper as covers is questionable.

Many federal programs now provide pre-printed cover sheets (some of which are several pages long) that double as title pages, as summaries and, occasionally, as guarantees of compliance with various federal regulations. An example of this approach is provided at the end of this chapter.

With private foundations or corporations, a decision on cover and binding is usually dictated by the preferences of the funding source (this is something you can determine by telephone). The size or complexity of the application, and possibly the amount requested, can also have a bearing. For example, universities that are presenting an elaborate case study in justification of an endowed chair usually enclose their material in some type of cover. Folders that have pockets into which different types of information can be slipped are another alternative.

Whatever the decision, never use a binding that makes it difficult to disassemble the proposal (something frequently done during the review process) and never select a cover that appears inappropriately elaborate or expensive.

There are no standard formats for a title page. Usually, directions on whether or not to include one are provided by the funding source. If not, title pages normally include:

● Title of the project.

● Name of the agency submitting the application.

● Name of the funding source to which the proposal is submitted.

● Beginning and ending dates of the project.

● Total funds requested from this source.

● Names, addresses, telephone numbers and signatures of the project director or principal investigator and the official authorized to indicate that the proposal has been approved by the submitting agency.

In most cases, federal agencies require from three to six copies of a proposal carrying original signatures in ink on the title page. Private foundations and corporations, however, normally want only one copy (unless specified otherwise).

THE ABSTRACT

Although this is one of the first pages in the proposal, it is usually the last page to be written (with the possible exception of a table of contents).

All aspects of the proposal must be clearly defined before they can be summarized, on one or two pages.

The abstract is intended to be a cogent summary of the proposed project and should be prepared with care. Many novices make the mistake of using the abstract as an introduction rather than as a precis of the proposal. The abstract plays several important roles:

● Private foundations and corporations frequently use it to make the basic determination of whether the project is eligible for, or even worthy of, further consideration. One experienced foundation executive says that, in nine out of ten cases, she never reads beyond the summary page before deciding whether to reject a project or retain it for further analysis.

● It is often circulated to key officials in the funding source (whether public or private) who have asked to see a precis of all incoming projects.

● Funding sources use it for the various national information systems that provide citations to sponsored projects.

● Donors may use it to secure input from others in their organization who serve in an advisory role. For example, many corporate foundations will consult their local manager in the community from which an application is submitted. The manager is often only provided with the summary unless the project is very extensive or complex.

● It can be used by the proposal writer to circulate to others in his or her organization who should know about the project, but who do not warrant receiving a copy of the complete proposal.

Most federal programs, many state sources and an increasing number of private donors now provide pre-printed summary or abstract pages that must preface the proposal. These forms often call for details on where the project is to be carried out, the number of project participants, the names of local Members of Congress, budget information on other sources of funds, and assurances that the applicant agency has complied with various regulations (more about this later). Examples of such forms from both public and private sources are provided in the attachments.

If no format is specified, the summary page should 1) give a quick overview of what the project proposes to do, and to whom, 2) provide a rapid understanding of the project's significance, generalizability and potential contribution, 3) highlight why the applicant organization and project staff are particularly qualified to conduct the project, and 4) in the case of foundations or corporations, provide references for how the project is consistent with their funding guidelines. The above list presumes that information such as the length of the project and the amount of funds requested has been provided earlier in the title page. Otherwise, these should also be worked into the summary.

Most abstracts are between 250 and 500 words and, unless a pre-printed form provides for this, should seldom be more than one page in length.

ACCOMPANYING FORMS AND INFORMATION

Up until a few years ago, most federal and state applications required the attachment of a plethora of originally signed forms which testified that the applicant agency was in compliance with an array of federal regulations on such issues as nondiscrimination, protection of human rights and intergovernmental review. Nowadays, compliance must usually be established *before* the proposal is submitted. Prior approval is normally documented through a checklist (see sample in the attachment) or through entering the number assigned to the organization for a specific compliance on the proposal's summary sheets. It is therefore increasingly important that the proposal writer be thoroughly familiar with requirements for various programs well in advance of the application deadline. Establishment of these compliance procedures or internal review processes are normally the responsibility of the project's sponsoring organization and not the director of the proposed project itself. Since these are institution-wide requirements, they frequently take considerable time to install and have approved.

A final word on compliances. Some public agencies will accept proposals from organizations whose compliance processes are still under review. The agencies signal this by indicating that you may enter the word "pending" in the space for the

organization's documentation number. It is normally assumed that these processes will be finished prior to a project's termination and renewal funds are seldom made available if they are not.

The most common attachment to proposals to foundations and corporations is a copy of the organization's letter of determination from the Internal Revenue Service indicating that the organization is a private, nonprofit agency qualifying under section 501(c)(3) of the Code and not a private foundation defined under section 509 (a) of the Code, since the latter cannot receive funds from another private foundation. A sample of such a letter follows this chapter. It should be included by all applicants unless they are public, such as a federal or state agency or a public school or university.

Be certain that the IRS letter's declaration period has not lapsed. This sometimes happens to relatively new organizations that have received a preliminary ruling of nonprofit eligibility. They must renew their status through refiling certain information by a specified date. Currently, re-establishing 501(c)(3) status is handled by the IRS's regional offices and may take several months to complete. Foundations may pledge a grant to an organization whose filing has lapsed, but they cannot disperse the funds until this status is reinstated.

Finally, it should be noted that most experienced proposal writers usually attach general information on their organization and a list of the names of their board of directors to all proposals to private foundations and corporate giving programs. For those who must frequently submit such proposals, it is well to have most of this information carefully crafted in a printed brochure. Not only does this save time for the individual proposal writer, but it insures that the organization's overall mission, history and management structure are presented consistently and effectively.

LETTERS OF ENDORSEMENT

Opinions vary as to whether an array of letters endorsing the proposal should be included as attachments. The author generally avoids these unless such letters are important in demonstrating that some commitment to, or cooperation by, the letter writer is essential to the project's success. If the applicant has determined that support from a particular individual or organization will "make the difference" in a decision by the funding source, it might by appropriate to have the proposal actually transmitted with a covering letter by that party.

A technique used effectively with one private foundation was an application sent by the president of another foundation that had recently made a decision to fund part of the project. This person obviously had the necessary credibility to recommend the importance of the project.

Letters of support can also be sent separately (but be timed to arrive simultaneously with the application). The authors of such letters should be selected with care. Most novice fundraisers tend to "overkill" and are sometimes downright insensitive (such as when securing a letter of support from a Member of Congress who also heads the appropriations subcommittee for the funding agency). Such expressions of interest are better handled by telephone.

SAMPLE OF A COVER PAGE REQUIRED BY THE NATIONAL SCIENCE FOUNDATION

APPENDIX III

IMPORTANT: Please Attach ONE Copy of this Form to the Signature Copy of the Proposal Cover Page.
Leave Back Side of Form Blank.

FORM APPROVED
OMB No. 3145-0058

Supplementary Information
PRINCIPAL INVESTIGATOR(S)/PROJECT DIRECTOR(S)

The National Science Foundation has an obligation to monitor the operation of its award process to assess patterns of gender, race, ethnicity, or handicap among proposed Principal Investigators/Project Directors.

To provide the NSF with the information it needs for this important task, Principal Investigators/Project Directors are requested to complete this form and attach a *single copy* to the cover page of the signature copy of the proposal.

This form will *NOT* be duplicated and will *NOT* be a part of the review process. Data will be confidential and will be maintained in secure data files in accordance with the Privacy Act of 1974. All analyses conducted on the data will report aggregate statistical findings only and will not identify individuals.

While submission of this information is not mandatory, NSF considers it an integral part of the complete proposal package.

Please check columns or enter information as appropriate for each PI/PD or Co-PI/PD
in the order as listed on the cover sheet.

PI/PD (Information for up to 5 PI(s)/PD(s))	1	2	3	4	5
Gender (M/F)					
Race and/or Ethnic Data					
American Indian or Alaskan Native					
Asian or Pacific Islander					
Black, not of Hispanic origin					
White, not of Hispanic origin					
Hispanic: Mexican American/Chicano					
Puerto Rican					
Cuban					
Hispanic, other					
Handicapped? (If No enter N. If Yes enter number from below.)					

  1. Visual   2. Auditory   3. Ambulatory   4. Learning

  5. Other/Multiple (Specify type(s) and PI/PD number(s) from above)

NOTE: The category that most closely reflects the individual's recognition in the community should be used for the purposes of reporting mixed racial and/or ethnic origins. Definitions follow.

American Indian or Alaskan Native: A person having origins in any of the original peoples of North America, and who maintains cultural identification through tribal affiliation or community recognition.

Asian or Pacific Islander: A person having origins in any of the original peoples of the Far East, Southeast Asia, the Indian sub-continent, or the Pacific Islands. This area includes, for example, China, India, Japan, Korea, the Philippine Islands and Samoa.

Black, not of Hispanic origin: A person having origins in any of the black racial groups of Africa.

White, not of Hispanic origin: A person having origins in any of the original peoples of Europe, North Africa, or the Middle East.

Hispanic: A person of Mexican, Puerto Rican, Cuban, Central or South American or other Spanish culture or origin, regardless of race.

NSF Form 1153 (Revised 5-84)   21

PROPOSAL TO THE NATIONAL SCIENCE FOUNDATION
Cover Page

FOR CONSIDERATION BY NSF ORGANIZATIONAL UNIT (Indicate the most specific unit known, i.e. program, division, etc.)	IS THIS PROPOSAL BEING SUBMITTED TO ANOTHER FEDERAL AGENCY? Yes ____ No ____ ; IF YES, LIST ACRONYM(S):

PROGRAM ANNOUNCEMENT/SOLICITATION NO.:	CLOSING DATE (IF ANY):

NAME OF SUBMITTING ORGANIZATION TO WHICH AWARD SHOULD BE MADE (INCLUDE BRANCH/CAMPUS/OTHER COMPONENTS)

ADDRESS OF ORGANIZATION (INCLUDE ZIP CODE)

TITLE OF PROPOSED PROJECT

REQUESTED AMOUNT	PROPOSED DURATION	DESIRED STARTING DATE

PI/PD DEPARTMENT	PI/PD ORGANIZATION	PI/PD PHONE NO.

PI/PD NAME	SOCIAL SECURITY NO.*	SIGNATURE	MALE*	FEMALE*
ADDITIONAL PI/PD				
ADDITIONAL PI/PD				
ADDITIONAL PI/PD				
ADDITIONAL PI/PD				

FOR RENEWAL OR CONTINUING AWARD REQUEST, LIST PREVIOUS AWARD NO.:	SUBMITTING ORGANIZATION IS: ☐ For-Profit Organization; ☐ Small Business; ☐ Minority Business; ☐ Women-Owned Business; (See cover page instructions, Page 3)

*Submission of social security numbers is voluntary and will not affect the organization's eligibility for an award. However, they are an integral part of the NSF information system and assist in processing the proposal. SSN solicited under NSF Act of 1950, as amended.

CHECK APPROPRIATE BOX(ES) IF THIS PROPOSAL INCLUDES ANY OF THE ITEMS LISTED BELOW:

☐ Animal Welfare ☐ Human Subjects ☐ National Environmental Policy Act

☐ Endangered Species ☐ Marine Mammal Protection ☐ Research Involving Recombinant DNA Molecules

☐ Historical Sites ☐ Pollution Control ☐ Proprietary and Privileged Information

PRINCIPAL INVESTIGATOR/ PROJECT DIRECTOR	AUTHORIZED ORGANIZATIONAL REP.	OTHER ENDORSEMENT (optional)
NAME	NAME	NAME
SIGNATURE	SIGNATURE	SIGNATURE
TITLE	TITLE	TITLE
DATE · TELEPHONE NO. Area Code:	DATE · TELEPHONE NO. Area Code:	DATE · TELEPHONE NO. Area Code:

SAMPLE OF A COVER PAGE AND SUMMARY FORM FROM THE PUBLIC HEALTH SERVICE

Form Approved Through 9/30/89
OMB No. 0925-0001

DEPARTMENT OF HEALTH AND HUMAN SERVICES
PUBLIC HEALTH SERVICE

GRANT APPLICATION

FOLLOW INSTRUCTIONS CAREFULLY

LEAVE BLANK		
TYPE	ACTIVITY	NUMBER
REVIEW GROUP		FORMERLY
COUNCIL/BOARD *(Month, year)*		DATE RECEIVED

1. TITLE OF PROJECT *(Up to 56 spaces)*

2. RESPONSE TO SPECIFIC PROGRAM ANNOUNCEMENT ☐ NO ☐ YES *(If "YES," state RFA number and/or announcement title)*

3. PRINCIPAL INVESTIGATOR/PROGRAM DIRECTOR   NEW INVESTIGATOR ☐

3a. NAME *(Last, first, middle)*	3b. DEGREE(S)	3c. SOCIAL SECURITY NUMBER

3d. POSITION TITLE

3e. MAILING ADDRESS *(Street, city, state, zip code)*

3f. DEPARTMENT, SERVICE, LABORATORY OR EQUIVALENT

3g. MAJOR SUBDIVISION

3h. TELEPHONE *(Area code, number and extension)*

4. HUMAN SUBJECTS

4a. ☐ No   ☐ Yes ⎰ ☐ Exemption # _____
                   ⎱ OR
                     ☐ IRB Approval Date _____

4b. Assurance of Compliance # _____

5. VERTEBRATE ANIMALS

5a. ☐ No ☐ Yes . . . IACUC Approval Date _____

5b. Animal Welfare Assurance # _____

6. DATES OF ENTIRE PROPOSED PROJECT PERIOD	7. COSTS REQUESTED FOR FIRST 12-MONTH BUDGET PERIOD		8. COSTS REQUESTED FOR ENTIRE PROPOSED PROJECT PERIOD	
	7a. Direct Costs	7b. Total Costs	8a. Direct Costs	8b. Total Costs
From:				
Through:	$	$	$	$

9. PERFORMANCE SITES *(Organizations and addresses)*

10. INVENTIONS *(Competing continuation application only)*

☐ NO   ☐ YES ⎰ ☐ Previously reported
              OR
               ⎱ ☐ Not previously reported

11. APPLICANT ORGANIZATION *(Name, address, and congressional district)*

12. TYPE OF ORGANIZATION

☐ Public, Specify ☐ Federal ☐ State ☐ Local
☐ Private Nonprofit
☐ For Profit *(General)*
☐ For Profit *(Small Business)*

13. ENTITY IDENTIFICATION NUMBER

14. ORGANIZATIONAL COMPONENT TO RECEIVE CREDIT TOWARDS A BIOMEDICAL RESEARCH SUPPORT GRANT

Code ☐☐   Identification _____

15. OFFICIAL IN BUSINESS OFFICE TO BE NOTIFIED IF AN AWARD IS MADE *(Name, title, address and telephone number)*

16. OFFICIAL SIGNING FOR APPLICANT ORGANIZATION *(Name, title, address and telephone number)*

17. PRINCIPAL INVESTIGATOR/PROGRAM DIRECTOR ASSURANCE: I agree to accept responsibility for the scientific conduct of the project and to provide the required progress reports if a grant is awarded as a result of this application. Willful provision of false information is a criminal offense *(U.S. Code, Title 18, Section 1001).*	SIGNATURE OF PERSON NAMED IN 3a *(In ink. "Per" signature not acceptable.)*	DATE
18. CERTIFICATION AND ACCEPTANCE: I certify that the statements herein are true and complete to the best of my knowledge, and accept the obligation to comply with Public Health Service terms and conditions if a grant is awarded as the result of this application. A willfully false certification is a criminal offense *(U.S. Code, Title 18, Section 1001).*	SIGNATURE OF PERSON NAMED IN 16 *(In ink. "Per" signature not acceptable.)*	DATE

PHS 398 (Rev. 9/86)

REMOVE AND USE FOR DRAFT COPY

DESCRIPTION: State the application's broad, long-term objectives and specific aims, making reference to the health relatedness of the project. Describe concisely the experimental design and methods for achieving these goals. Avoid summaries of past accomplishments and the use of the first person. This abstract is meant to serve as a succinct and accurate description of the proposed work when separated from the application. **DO NOT EXCEED THE SPACE PROVIDED.**

REMOVE AND USE FOR DRAFT COPY

KEY PERSONNEL ENGAGED ON PROJECT

NAME, DEGREE(S), SSN	POSITION TITLE AND ROLE IN PROJECT	DEPARTMENT AND ORGANIZATION

SAMPLE OF TITLE AND SUMMARY FORMS FROM TWO PRIVATE FOUNDATIONS

Fred Meyer
Charitable Trust

1515 SW Fifth Avenue Suite 500
Portland Oregon 97201
(508) 228-5512

GRANT APPLICATION SUMMARY

Organization _____   Founding Date _____

Address _____   Phone _____

_____

Contact Person's Name _____   Title _____

Purpose of Organization _____

_____

Major sources of operating funds (%) _____

_____   Total operating budget: $ _____

Description of project for
which funds are requested (no more than 25 words) _____

_____

_____

Specifically, how will funds be used? _____

_____

_____

What will project accomplish? _____

_____

_____

Anticipated project period _____   Geographical area to be served by project _____

Client group (and number) to be served by project _____

Amount and source of pledges/commitments to date _____

_____ Total: $ _____

Other funding sources
(and amounts) applied to for the project _____

_____ Total: $ _____

Amount requested from Meyer Trust _____ $ _____

Total project cost _____ $ _____

Type of request: Capital ☐   Operating support ☐   Special Project ☐

How will this project be financed in the future? _____

_____

BURLINGTON NORTHERN FOUNDATION GRANT APPLICATION

Organization Name _____

Organization Name shown on 501(c)(3) letter _____

Address _____
Street   City   State   Zip

Contact Person's Name _____ Phone _____

Contact Person's Title _____

Project Title and Brief Description (no more than twenty-two words) _____

_____

_____

Geographic Area to be served _____

Client Group to be served _____ Size of group _____

Anticipated Project Period: _____ to _____

Type of Request: ☐ Capital   ☐ Operating support   ☐ Special Project

Total Project Cost: $ _____

Amount Requested from Burlington Northern Foundation: $ _____

Amount and source of pledges/commitments to date: $ _____

_____

_____

Other funding sources (and amounts) applied to for this project: _____

_____

_____

Signature _____ Date _____

(Please answer fully all questions on following pages.)

Instructions

Please answer each question within the space provided.

Please attach the following additional required information:

☐ General financial information on your organization, including your total current budget and the principal sources and amounts of ongoing annual support.

☐ Copy of Treasury letter certifying your 501(c)(3) tax-exempt status, or evidence of government agency status under Section 170(c).

☐ Copy of latest IRS Report 990 or 990PF filed.

Additional attachments are not encouraged unless they are absolutely essential to our understanding of your project. The **original** form is required. Applications must be signed and dated. Do not mutilate or place in binders or other covers. All applications not prepared according to these instructions will be returned.

If an acknowledgement of the receipt of your application is desired, please self-address the attached card and return it with the application. Upon receipt, we will mail the card back to you.

1. Purpose   (What will this project specifically accomplish?)

2. Need   (What are the problems that this project will try to solve?)

3. Relevance   (Why should Burlington Northern Foundation support this project?)

EXAMPLES OF ASSURANCE OR COMPLIANCE CHECKLISTS FROM TWO FEDERAL PROGRAMS

*PRINCIPAL INVESTIGATOR/PROGRAM DIRECTOR: _____

CHECKLIST

Check the appropriate boxes and provide the information requested. Make this page the last page of the signed original of the application. *Do not attach copies of this page to the duplicated copies of the application.* Upon receipt and assignment of the application by the PHS, this page will be separated from the application. The page will *not* be duplicated, and it will *not* be a part of the review process. It will be reserved for PHS staff use only.

TYPE OF APPLICATION

☐ NEW application *(This application is being submitted to the PHS for the first time.)*

☐ REVISION of application number: _____
    (This application replaces a prior unfunded version of a new, competing continuation or supplemental application.)

☐ COMPETING CONTINUATION of grant number: _____
    (This application is to extend a funded grant beyond its current project period.)

☐ SUPPLEMENT to grant number: _____
    (This application is for additional funds to supplement a currently funded grant.)

☐ CHANGE of principal investigator/program director.
    Name of former principal investigator/program director: _____

☐ FOREIGN application. *(This information is required by the U.S. Department of State.)* City and country of
    birth and present citizenship of principal investigator/program director: _____

ASSURANCES *(See GENERAL INFORMATION section of instructions.)*

a. Civil Rights Form HHS 441	b. Handicapped Individuals Form HHS 641	c. Sex Discrimination Form 639-A	d. Scientific Fraud (Misconduct) Assurance
☐ Filed ☐ Not filed	☐ Filed ☐ Not filed	☐ Filed ☐ Not filed	☐ Administrative review process has been established. ☐ Reporting requirements of the published scientific misconduct regulations will be followed.

INDIRECT COSTS

Indicate the applicant organization's most recent indirect cost rate established with the appropriate DHHS Regional Office, or, in the case of for-profit organizations, the rate established with the appropriate PHS Agency Cost Advisory Office. If the applicant organization is in the process of initially developing or renegotiating a rate, or has established a rate with another Federal agency, it should, immediately upon notification that an award will be made, develop a tentative indirect cost rate proposal based on its most recently completed fiscal year in accordance with the principles set forth in the pertinent *DHHS Guide for Establishing Indirect Cost Rates*, and submit it to the appropriate DHHS Regional Office or PHS Agency Cost Advisory Office. Indirect costs will *not* be paid on foreign grants, construction grants, grants to Federal organizations, and grants to individuals, and usually not on conference grants. Follow any additional instructions provided for Research Career Development Awards, Institutional National Research Service Awards, and the specialized grant applications listed in the GENERAL INSTRUCTIONS section.

☐ DHHS Agreement Dated: _____   ☐ No Indirect Costs Requested.
☐ DHHS Agreement being negotiated with _____ Regional Office.
☐ No DHHS Agreement, but rate established with _____ Date _____

CALCULATION*

a. First 12-month budget period:
    Amount of base $_____ × Rate applied _____% = Indirect costs (a) $_____

b. Entire proposed project period:
    Amount of base $_____ × Rate applied _____% = Indirect costs (b) $_____

        (a) Add to total direct costs from page 4 and enter new total on FACE PAGE, Item 7b
        (b) Add to total direct costs from page 5 and enter new total on FACE PAGE, Item 8b

*Check appropriate box(es):
☐ Salary and wages base   ☐ Modified total direct costs base   ☐ Other base (Explain below)
☐ Off-site, other special rate, or more than one rate involved (Explain below)

Explanation *(Attach separate sheet, if necessary.):*

PHS 398 (Rev. 9/86)   Page ___*
*This is the required last page of the application. Number it appropriately.

REMOVE AND USE FOR DRAFT COPY

PART V
ASSURANCES

The Applicant hereby assures and certifies that it will comply with the regulations, policies, guidelines and requirements, as they relate to the application, acceptance and use of Federal funds for this federally-assisted project. Also the Applicant assures and certifies:

1. - It possesses legal authority to apply for the grant; that a resolution, motion or similar action has been duly adopted or passed as an official act of the applicant's governing body, authorizing the filing of the application, including all understandings and assurances contained therein, and directing and authorizing the person identified as the official representative of the applicant to act in connection with the application and to provide such additional information as may be required.

2. It will comply with Title VI of the Civil Rights Act of 1964 (P.L. 88-352) and in accordance with Title VI of that Act, no person in the United States shall, on the ground of race, color or national origin, be excluded from participation in, be denied the benefits of, or be otherwise subjected to discrimination under any program or activity for which the applicant receives Federal financial assistance and will immediately take any measures necessary to effectuate this agreement.

3. It will comply with Title VI of the Civil Rights Act of 1964 (42 U.S.C. 2000d) prohibiting employment discrimination where (1) the primary purpose of a grant is to provide employment or (2) discriminatory employment practices will result in unequal treatment of persons who are or should be benefiting from the grant-aided activity.

4. It will comply with Section 504 of the Rehabilitation Act of 1973, as amended, 29 U.S.C. 794, which prohibits discrimination on the basis of handicap in programs and activities receiving Federal financial assistance.

5. It will comply with Title IX of the Education Amendments of 1972, as amended, 20 U.S.C. 1681 *et seq.*, which prohibits discrimination on the basis of sex in education programs and activities receiving Federal financial assistance.

6. It will comply with the Age Discrimination Act of 1975, as amended, 42 U.S.C. 6101 *et seq.*, which prohibits discrimination on the basis of age in programs or activities receiving Federal financial assistance.

7. It will comply with requirements of the provisions of the Uniform Relocation Assistance and Real Property Acquisitions Act of 1970 (P.L. 91-646) which provides for fair and equitable treatment of persons displaced as a result of Federal and federally-assisted programs.

8. It will comply with the provisions of the Hatch Act which limit the political activity of employees.

9. It will comply with the minimum wage and maximum hours provisions of the Federal Fair Labor Standards Act, as they apply to hospital and educational institution employees of State and local governments.

10. It will establish safeguards to prohibit employees from using their positions for a purpose that is or gives the appearance of being motivated by a desire for private gain for themselves or others, particularly those with whom they have family, business, or other ties.

11. it will give the sponsoring agency or the Comptroller General through any authorized representative the access to and the right to examine all records, books, papers, or documents related to the grant.

12. It will comply with all requirements imposed by the Federal sponsoring agency concerning special requirements of law, program requirements, and other administrative requirements.

13. It will insure that the facilities under its ownership, lease or supervision which shall be utilized in the accomplishment of the project are not listed on the Environmental Protection Agency's (EPA) list of Violating Facilities and that it will notify the Federal grantor agency of the receipt of any communication from the Director of the EPA Office of Federal Activities indicating that a facility to be used in the project is under consideration for listing by the EPA.

14. It will comply with the flood insurance purchase requirements of Section 102(a) of the Flood Disaster Protection Act of 1973, P.L. 93-234, 87 Stat. 975, approved December 31, 1976. Section 102(a) requires, on or after March 2, 1975, the purchase of flood insurance in communities where such insurance is available as a condition for the receipt of any Federal financial assistance for construction or acquisition purposes for use in any area that has been identified by the Secretary of the Department of Housing and Urban Development as an area having special flood hazards. The phrase "Federal financial assistance" includes any form of loan, grant, guaranty, insurance payment, rebate, subsidy, disaster assistance loan or grant, or any other form of direct or indirect Federal assistance.

15. It will assist the Federal grantor agency in its compliance with Section 106 of the National Historic Preservation Act of 1966 as amended (16 U.S.C. 470), Executive Order 11593, and the Archeological and Historic Preservation Act of 1966 (16 U.S.C. 469a-1 *et seq.*) by (a) consulting with the State Historic Preservation Officer on the conduct of investigations, as necessary, to identify properties listed in or eligible for inclusion in the National Register of Historic Places that are subject to adverse effects (see 36 CFR Part 800.8) by the activity, and notifying the Federal grantor agency of the existence of any such properties, and by (b) complying with all requirements established by the Federal grantor agency to avoid or mitigate adverse effects upon such properties.

GPO 910-091

H14

EXAMPLE OF A 501(c)(3) DETERMINATION LETTER FROM THE INTERNAL REVENUE SERVICE

Internal Revenue Service
District Director

Department of the Treasury

P O Box 2350 Room 5137
Los Angeles, CA 90053

Employer Identification Number:
  91-1156099
Case Number:
  956350002

Date: DEC. 26, 1986

BUSINESS VOLUNTEERS FOR THE
 ARTS SEATTLE
1200 ONE UNION SQUARE
SEATTLE, WA 98101

Contact Person:
  THORNTON, B.
Contact Telephone Number:
  (213) 894-4170

Our Letter Dated:
  2/12/82
Caveat Applies:
  no

Dear Applicant:

This modifies our letter of the above date in which we stated that you would be treated as an organization which is not a private foundation until the expiration of your advance ruling period.

Based on the information you submitted, we have determined that you are not a private foundation within the meaning of section 509(a) of the Internal Revenue Code, because you are an organization of the type described in section 509(a)(1) and 170(b)(1)(A)(vi). Your exempt status under section 501(c)(3) of the code is still in effect.

Grantors and contributors may rely on this determination until the Internal Revenue Service publishes a notice to the contrary. However, a grantor or a contributor may not rely on this determination if he or she was in part responsible for, or was aware of, the act or failure to act that resulted in your loss of section 509(a)(1) status, or acquired knowledge that the Internal Revenue Service had given notice that you would be removed from classification as a section 509(a)(1) organization.

Because this letter could help resolve any questions about your private foundation status, please keep it in your permanent records.

If the heading of this letter indicates that a caveat applies, the caveat below or on the enclosure is an integral part of this letter.

If you have any questions, please contact the person whose name and telephone number are shown above.

Sincerely yours,

Frederick C. Nielsen

Frederick C. Nielsen
District Director

THE PURPOSE

This chapter discusses the purpose statement in the proposal, distinguishes between goals, objectives, hypothesis and research questions, and describes samples of outcome statements in applications to private and public funding sources.

All components in a proposal are important, but the purpose section is perhaps one of the most critical: it tells the funding agency what you intend to accomplish and, hopefully, is in language sufficiently precise and measurable to assure donors that the project is well conceived.

Before discussing how purpose statements may vary in different types of projects and for different categories of potential funders, it is useful to review some of the basic problems normally found in this section of the proposal.

PROBLEM ONE: *The purpose statement is confused with the procedures section.*

Norton Kiritz (1975 reprint) speaks to this eloquently when he describes how many proposals fail to distinguish between *means* and *ends*. He quotes two sample objectives that purport to be aimed at establishing services for particular populations. He then goes on, "What is wrong with these objectives?" and answers himself, "They don't speak about outcomes."

"If I support your project for a year, or for two years, and come back at that time and say, 'I want to see what you have done—what have you accomplished?' What can you tell me? The fact that you have established a service, or conducted some activities, doesn't tell me whether you have helped to solve the problem you defined. I want to know the outcome of your activities....Knowing that you worked at it is not enough."

Albert Einstein memorialized this problem when he said, "Our age is characterized by the perfection of means...and the confusion of goals...."

PROBLEM TWO: *The purpose of the project is confused with the overall goals of the organization.*

The author once received a proposal from a national youth organization whose proposal started out: "The purpose of this program is to help our members become healthy, self-sufficient and contributing members of society." Several pages later, the proposal said: "This project then, will solve the problem of attrition among volunteer leaders by providing a year round, hands-on learning laboratory to excite them about our mission and provide them with the necessary skills to carry it out."

One may quibble with the precision and measurability of either statement, but it was obvious that the real purpose of the project had to do with the latter statement and only incidentally with the first.

PROBLEM THREE: *The proposal does not distinguish between purpose statements, goals, objectives, hypothesis and research questions or it uses these terms inappropriately.*

Unfortunately, the novice proposal writer who commits this error has plenty of company because much of the literature on proposal writing does the same thing. There are some common reasons for this:

● Particularly in educational literature, funding to develop the "best" goals and objectives has underwritten several people's careers. Incentives (such as promotion, publications, national recognition and even salary) push towards a lack of consensus, rather than widespread agreement, on such terms.

● The format for writing and displaying outcomes in research applications usually differs from those included for demonstration, service, training or other types of projects. Many authors do not acknowledge these differences and provide a recommended approach that is not suitable for all types of funding requests. The problem is compounded because many funding sources also use these terms interchangeably.

● The use of measurable objectives is much more common and valued in some academic disciplines than in others. Objectives (for example) are found more readily in applications from educational applications, than in proposals from arts organizations.

● The necessity to push a proposal's development may limit the amount of pre-planning, thought, review and refinement necessary for the preparation of well-stated and non-superficial objectives.

● Some projects, while lending themselves to a clear cut statement of aims, do not require measurable objectives. This is particularly true in requests to private foundations or corporations for small sums to underwrite general operating support or in proposals for facilities and equipment.

● For various reasons, the proposal writer may be reluctant to commit a project to measurable outcomes. Generally, it is best to be as precise about your aims as possible and to state clearly in the proposal if decisions on measurability must wait until after the effort is under way. Most funding sources, whether public or private, will automatically permit minor deviations from proposal objectives and will even consider major modifications as long as they are included in the decision.

The remainder of this chapter addresses some of these problems.

GOALS AND OBJECTIVES: AN OVERVIEW

Proposal writers may want to include both statements of *goals* and statements of *objectives*. The two are frequently confused because both describe a desired condition or outcome. However, these two types of statements usually differ in dimensions of specificity, accountability and time. *Goals* are included in proposals to provide an overall conceptual orientation to the ultimate purpose of the project.

They are usually more abstract in content, broader in scope, less subject to direct measurement and focused on more long-term perspectives. Goals should, however, describe aims that can reasonably be achieved by the completion of the project (unless the writer is directed to do otherwise by the funding source).

Most projects have only one or two goal statements. The writer who begins to draft a lengthy list of goals should consider whether the project has been sufficiently well thought out or whether some of the statements are better presented as objectives.

An *objective*, on the other hand, should be specific and concrete, more likely to be measurable and more likely to address short-term or intermediate accomplishments. A proposal may have several objectives and, depending on the complexity of the project, these may be of several different types.

Definitions for some of these alternative kinds of objectives, such as *product, process, performance* and *behavioral objectives,* are discussed with appropriate examples later in the chapter.

The following example of a goal and one objective (which has several subparts) was taken from a demonstration project submitted for funding to the U.S. Office of Education.

[GOAL] *This program is designed to prepare parents to function independently and effectively in helping their children develop to their own potentials.*

[OBJECTIVE] *The parents who participate in the program will be able to: 1) identify the educational content in events that occur in the home; 2) structure sequential and cumulative instructional tasks in the home for the child; 3) observe the child and use checklists to monitor progress; 4) use available equipment and processes in the home to teach children specific skills; and 5) use packaged materials prepared by the project or other agencies in teaching specific skills.*

In reviewing this example, one can see that the goal conveys the overall intent of the entire program. The objective, however, is written to identify several specific accomplishments for which information can later be collected to judge whether these were achieved. It is simply a matter of stylistic preference that all of these outcomes were included in a single objective as opposed to being displayed as five separate statements.

HYPOTHESIS AND RESEARCH QUESTIONS: AN OVERVIEW

In research proposals, intended outcomes are more commonly stated as *hypotheses* or *questions*. It depends on personal preference or the instructions of the funding source whether these are preceded by some general *goal* statements. It is also a matter of choice as to how much elaboration is provided in the *purpose* section. Some authors simply summarize their hypotheses or questions here in order to assist the reviewer to gain a general understanding of the project's aims. They then describe these much more fully in the *procedures* component along with the information on design and methodology.

Hypotheses, should be stated in such a way that they can be tested by securing information to judge their truth or falsity. Krathwohl (1977) advises that hypotheses should not be stated in the null form and should always be included wherever there is a basis for prediction.

One example of such a statement was included in a proposal recently approved by the National Institute of Education. It was as follows:

[HYPOTHESIS] *There will be an increase in formalization of procedures for identifying competencies, developing competency measures, measuring competencies and incorporating competencies into instruction.*

In this proposal, the objectives section was limited to a few short statements outlining the scope and focus of the project. The specific research hypotheses were then discussed in the procedures component. The writers decided that the meaning of the hypotheses were dependent on a discussion of research variables which, in turn, needed to be identified through a presentation of the research's theoretical base. They included all of this information under the label of "research design."

Research proposals also frequently include *questions*. These are used in lieu of hypotheses in exploratory studies or in projects of a survey research nature. *Questions* should be phrased very specifically to indicate the exact nature of the proposed inquiry. The care with which the questions are selected and written will also demonstrate whether the researcher has really thought through a particular problem and has identified the most important issues to investigate.

The following example of research questions also comes from a proposal submitted to the National Institute of Education. This proposal included a three-part approach to stating outcomes. First, the author listed a general objective. Following each objective, he listed a series of general research questions, each of which was followed by more precise sub-questions presented in narrative form. Each objective had from two to six paragraphs of research questions attached.

Part of the text (here bold) was italicized in the original proposal in order to improve readability and to help call the attention of the reviewer to the most significant points.

[OBJECTIVE] *To hypothesize a model for implementing accountability systems by analyzing previous experience and research.*

[QUESTION] **What procedures and phases typify accountability system implementation?** *What formal and informal forces are relevant, and how do they interact? What are the roles of administrators, committees, governmental bodies, outside consultants, educational researchers, and business officials? How do the tensions between self-perception and external perception of these roles affect the linkage among implementation procedures and phases? What criteria are relevant for assessing the success of implementation and its components, and can this success be systematically related to role tensions and perceptions? To what extent is the nature of implementation symptomatic of underlying organizational pathologies? How does implementation design and execution incorporate behavioral concerns?*

Developing research *hypotheses* or *questions* for a grant application differ little from preparing them for journal articles or even dissertations. The novice proposal writer thus has a wealth of resources and samples to consult in any university library. There is one caveat, however: These statements in proposals must be written succinctly and clearly so that they are easily understood by the typical, intelligent reader. This point is included in Chapter 14 in the various criteria used by funders in selecting grantees.

DIFFERENT KINDS OF OBJECTIVES: A MORE PRECISE DESCRIPTION

The following discussion explains and provides examples of four types of objectives commonly found in projects that focus on utilization and application of knowledge (i.e. demonstration, development, training and service proposals) and contrast these with examples of objectives in projects whose primary purpose is to develop new knowledge (i.e. research proposals). However, writers should compare their own expectations for objectives with the definitions, examples and instructions for such statements provided by specific funding sources.

BEHAVIORAL OBJECTIVES

Outcome statements that deal with human performance in one of the three behavioral domains (cognitive, affective or psychomotor) are usually classified as behavioral objectives. Most authors agree that to be complete, a behavioral objective should include information that answers the four questions:

❏ Who is going to perform the specified behavior?

❏ What behavior is expected to occur?

❏ Under what circumstances will the behavior be observed?

❏ How is the behavior going to be measured?

An example of a project that meets these criteria follows:

[BEHAVIORAL OBJECTIVE] *During an inservice workshop, high school mathematics teachers will demonstrate their comprehension of diagnostic and prescriptive techniques as measured on a staff-developed test.*

PERFORMANCE OBJECTIVES

In order to make objectives more specific and measurable, types of outcome statements called *performance objectives* are frequently requested. These statements must include information that addresses the same four questions specified for behavioral

objectives; but, in addition, a performance objective must also answer:

❏ What amount of time is necessary to bring about the specified behavior?

❏ What is the expected proficiency level?

To be classified as a performance objective, the previous example might be reworded as follows:

[PERFORMANCE OBJECTIVE] *At the end of a four-day inservice workshop, the participating high school mathematics teachers will demonstrate their comprehension of diagnostic and prescriptive techniques as measured by a minimum gain of ten raw score points on a staff-developed pre- and post-test.*

This type of objective is frequently considered more desirable than the behavioral objective because it brings a specific element of time to the outcome (which aids in structuring the necessary procedures and resource requirements) and adds a performance criterion (which aids in evaluating whether the objective has really been achieved).

In writing either behavioral or performance objectives, two guidelines should be given special attention.

● **Care should be exercised to describe the behavior that is to be demonstrated as precisely and specifically as possible.** Although the previous example about high school mathematics teachers was taken from a funded project, the objective is not as effectively written as it might be because of the use of the somewhat vague phrase "demonstrate comprehension." The objective might have been strengthened by using a phrase less subject to several possible interpretations. Examples of other imprecise words that should be avoided include:

> knowing
> appreciating
> thinking
> enjoying
> grasping the value of

In contrast, words like the following are much less vague:

> writing
> listing
> constructing
> reading

● **Special effort should be made to establish expected performance levels that are realistic.** In projects that are clearly experimental or exploratory, most funding sources are tolerant if the specific level of proficiency following treatment or participation cannot be realistically predicted at the time the proposal is written. There are several ways to handle this problem through an effective evaluation design or through a phased set of procedures that provide for some initial data gathering prior to the specification of anticipated performance criteria. Horst, Tallmadge and Wood (1975) provide some useful suggestions on this issue. A related problem is the setting of specific performance levels in projects where some continuing change or sustained performance is expected over time. In these cases, the objective should probably focus on terminal expectations.

An example of both a goal and a performance objective is shown in Table 1, which also indicates how a clear objective can help map out procedures and evaluation.

PRODUCT OBJECTIVES

The term *product objective* may be used by funding sources in one of two ways: either to refer to the behavior expected of project participants (thus making this type of objective synonymous with behavioral or performance objectives) or, more commonly, to refer to a concrete item to be produced by the project (such as a book, training materials, a film, a report and so forth). Frequently, *product objectives* are used interchangeably with the term *deliverables*. The writer should seek further clarification from any funding source that asks for this type of objective but does not provide either a clear definition or content criteria.

Whether required or not, most proposal writers will want to include behavioral or performance objectives. But they sometimes omit objectives for major items or materials that will result from the project. This is a mistake if the production of these products will require any significant amount of resources or are a major outcome of the project. Unless these products are referenced, there may be no justification for describing the procedures that will lead to their development. And unless these procedures are included, there will be no basis for

justifying the requested level of staff, equipment, time, facilities or dollars.

While there are no common content criteria for product objective, the proposal writer may find it useful to make certain that each statement answers the following questions:

❑ **Who will produce the product?**

❑ **What product will be developed?**

❑ **When will the product be available?**

❑ **Who will evaluate the product?**

❑ **How will the product be evaluated?**

An example of the objective that meets these criteria follows:

[**PRODUCT OBJECTIVE**] *Within sixty days of receipt of a signed contract, the product staff shall provide five copies for a career education evaluation model which shall be judged at least 90 percent effective by five of the participating schools on a staff-development checklist covering the criteria specified by the Office of Career Education.*

Some writers argue that *products* or *deliverables* should be included at the end of the proposal's procedure section. However, the author prefers that they be included in the outcome statement, or, next best, be listed immediately after the outcome section with a separate heading.

● Products are frequently the most important way that the project can demonstrate it will have tangible results.

● Many reviewers (in both public and private sources) receive far more proposals that they have time to read carefully. They may thus miss these crucial project results if buried at the end of a discussion of procedures.

An example of how to present such products in a model proposal is provided in Worthen and White (1987). Only a portion of the example is presented here.

[**PROJECT DELIVERABLES**] *During the second year, the project anticipates the production of four separate deliverables.*

*1. **The Revised Notetakers Handbook.** It is anticipated that this handbook will be approximately*

TABLE 1   **THE PURPOSE**

PROPOSAL DESIGN CHART FOR A PERFORMANCE OBJECTIVE

Goal

To help selected high school students acquire independent study skills in mathematics.

Objective

Forty students selected from the tenth grade will be able to demonstrate newly acquired independent study skills by successfully completing a test on a major segment of the mathematics curriculum every two months. Success will be determined by the students achieving a score of 80 percent or more. The test will be devised by an independent consultant.

Need

To provide alternative learning opportunities for students who do not benefit from the regular mathematics program.

Procedure

A mathematics teacher will provide one hour of orientation instruction each week, pointing out the major areas of information to be covered. Supplementary reading material will be distributed following each session. Students will also be given a set of self-tests for each curriculum component. A tutor will be available during the week to answer questions.

Evaluation

A mathematics teacher will administer the test every two months, grade the examinations, and report the results to the project director. The director and an independent study consultant will meet with each student to discuss test results and assist in designing additional independent study to remedy any deficiencies.

This handout taken from *Getting Funded: A Complete Guide to Proposal Writing* by Mary Hall, 1988.
Available from Continuing Education Publications, P.O. Box 1491, Portland, OR 97207.

seventy-five pages long and will include additional examples and illustrations of quality notes for hearing-impaired students. Each of the revisions will be based on the data gathered during the first year pilot test of notetaking services.

*2. **Tutoring Handbook. The Tutoring Handbook** will be the first edition of training materials for paraprofessional adults and student peer tutors. While critical reviews will be obtained on the tutoring materials, it is anticipated that the guide will require substantial revisions during the third year of the project.*

PROCESS OBJECTIVES

In many cases, you may feel that processes which will significantly impact on project success are just as important as product outcomes, particularly in projects where the concern is for the effectiveness of innovative or experimental procedures as well as the actual results of these efforts. You or the funding source may thus want process objectives included.

Process objectives can be of many different types, covering such areas as teaching, training, learning, materials development, administration, counseling, evaluating, advisory group participation and so forth. As noted earlier, the writer should probably limit process objectives to those areas of most concern to the funding source, to innovative or experimental activities, or to processes that will require an unusual or significant level of resources.

In deciding whether process objectives are necessary, the writer should ask:

❏ Is the inclusion of this process as an objective essential for explaining the benefits of the project?

❏ Will the funding source not understand why procedures and resources are included for this process unless it is mentioned as an objective?

❏ Will it be necessary to address this process as a significant element in the evaluation component of the proposal?

If the answer to these questions is "yes," then a process objective should probably be prepared.

In structuring the content of such statements, the following questions may be answered.

❏ Who is the group or individual who will perform the process?

❏ What is the activity or performance that will result from the process?

❏ How will the process be evaluated?

The writer may also choose to include information on timing, expected performance levels and additional details on evaluation of the process. Examples of two process objectives from proposals financed by the U.S. Office of Education follow:

[PROCESS OBJECTIVE] *1. In discussion of social issues, student interaction with the teacher and with other students will show a statistically significant increase indicated by the number of comments or questions directed to the teacher and other students. Using an interaction analysis technique, observers will record the number of interactions in a sampling of experimental and regular social studies classrooms.*

2. Community representatives will participate actively as council members, as determined by the degree to which they fulfill their established project roles in the planning and operational stages of the program. Active participation will be judged on a majority of positive responses to a structured interview with all council members, selected project staff, and a random sample of target area parents.

RESEARCH OBJECTIVES

Some researchers prefer to state their project's intended outcomes as *research objectives*, rather than as *hypotheses* or *research questions*. This approach is frequently found in research applications to private foundations or corporations.

Krathwohl (1977) provides useful guidance for either approach, as paraphrased here.

❏ Make the objectives specific and concrete so that they provide clean-cut criteria against which the rest of the project can be judged.

❏ Keep them short.

❏ Make them explicit rather than implicit and don't imbed them in a running narrative.

❏ Make them achievable.

❏ List them in priority order (unless another display format makes better sense given the structure of the rest of the proposal).

The recommendations included earlier in this chapter for the development of all types of objectives should also be observed.

Because of the variability of research objectives, examples from previously approved projects may have limited use. However, a few are included (with their funding source identified) so that the beginning writer will have some visual understanding of what these might look like.

From an application to the National Science Foundation:

> **[RESEARCH OBJECTIVES]** *The purposes of this project are:*
>
> *To determine the existence and characteristics of features we hypothesize to exist in all major coastal upwelling regions;*
>
> *To identify the time and space scales of the upwelling process off Peru;*
>
> *To investigate the response of the velocity field to variations in the wind, sea level and density structure.*

An objective from an application to the National Institutes of Health:

> *This project will develop a general model of the process of population policy formation in developing countries. The model will integrate the impact of socio-economic determinants and situational political variables.*

An example from the U.S. Department of Agriculture:

> *The objectives of this study are:*
>
> *To determine the extent of in-migration and out-migration and characteristics of migrants in selected counties;*
>
> *To identify the expected and actual outcomes of migration, especially with reference to a) household income, b) level of satisfaction with publicly-provided goods and services, and c) level of satisfaction with environmental amenities;*
>
> *To better understand the determinants of migration, and thus the likely extent of future net migration in the counties;*

> *To identify the impact of migration on various affected groups of residents within such counties.*

Because of the extensive literature on writing objectives, the novice could well benefit from a trip to the local library for a quick review of some of the major works in this field, such as Bloom (1956), Mager (1962), Smith (1964), Ammerman and Melching (1966), Popham et al. (1969), Popham and Baker (1970), and Broudy (1970).

Perhaps the most logical argument for this kind of investment and care in writing clear and appropriate kinds of objectives was provided by Batten (1965), who wrote, "The correct statement of an objective is the first step in its attainment."

PURPOSE STATEMENTS IN PROPOSALS TO PRIVATE FUNDING SOURCES

The statement of purpose in applications to corporations and private foundations should normally be much shorter and more direct than those in government applications. When dealing with private sources, it is important to focus on *the results that you expect to obtain with their funding*, rather than to worry too much about the niceties of whether these are stated as goals, objectives or hypotheses.

Consider the following examples, all from proposals that were actually submitted to a foundation.

> **EXAMPLE 1:** *This program's goal is to use low-income loans to improve housing stock in your X, Y, Z communities for low income homeowners at or below the poverty level.*

> **EXAMPLE 2:** *Our organization plans to educate key policymakers on the options for addressing the problem of _____, by sponsoring the first international conference on _____, a topic in which we know you have a vital interest.*

> **EXAMPLE 3:** *The long-standing partnership between the University of A and your Company has been founded on shared goals. Both the College and the Company are committed to excellence. Both depend upon the creation and application of sophisticated technologies. Both must maintain an international leadership position...and both must remain competitive. We therefore ask you to strengthen this*

alliance by establishing an endowed lectureship to bring outstanding scholars from other countries, thus reinforcing our economic and technological ties.

All three examples did two things fairly well: They described the purpose of their request while also indicating its relevancy to the funding source.

Let's consider another example, this one from an application to a corporation that has supported the organization in the past. The request is for unrestricted funding.

EXAMPLE 4: *As one of our corporate friends, you know that (name of organization) has had an enormous impact on policy—in such areas as public lands management, water resource allocation, and siting and cleanup of waste treatment plants. Further, our mediation work over the last decade has helped establish a cost effective alternative to the courts for resolving environmental disputes. In short...no other organization matches our record of success at conservation problem-solving...we intend to maintain and develop further the strong domestic environmental policy programs on which we built our reputation...but we would also like to expand our work to help the environmentally and economically troubled Third World address development policy issues.*

One might conclude from these four examples that private donors do not care about the measurability of outcome states. *Wrong!*

● Many realize that they are supporting programs that simply do not lend themselves to the type of quasi-experimental evaluation designs found in large or more complex projects financed by federal agencies (particularly in the research fields);

● Those that want real precision and definite measurement criteria will normally signal this in their guidelines or by the types of projects they have funded in the past;

● A significant number of foundations or corporations will negotiate written "memorandums of understanding" with an applicant once they have made the decision to support a project. The tightly-crafted objectives will be reflected in these administrative agreements as opposed to being expected in the original proposal.

And, foundations and corporations are as concerned as federal donors about the types of issues described in the following discussion on the importance of well-written purpose statements.

IMPORTANCE OF WELL-WRITTEN OUTCOMES

The project outcomes may very likely be the most critical portion of a proposal. Because they serve the purpose of stating what the project intends to accomplish, objectives or other similar statements form the basis on which reviewers will answer such questions as:

❏ Is the project relevant to the funding source?

❏ Will the project accomplish something that is significant, important, timely, innovative and worthy of support?

❏ Will the proposed outcomes really help solve an identified problem or need?

❏ Are the intended outcomes of the project achievable?

❏ Can the project be expected to result in data or information that will tell whether the award was a success?

❏ Are the suggested procedures appropriate to carry out the intended outcomes?

❏ Is the budget reasonable for what will be achieved?

❏ Is the experience and training of key staff appropriate to the purposes of the project?

The entire fate of the proposal may rest on judgments made about the outcomes. In the long run, however, it is the funded project which suffers most if these are poorly defined.

● Unclear outcomes must be clarified before the program can be implemented. The staff may flounder through several months of operation and actually lose some personnel while arguing points that should have been settled when the proposal was developed.

● Evaluation cannot be performed until the outcomes are defined. The project may thus enter competition for renewal with no supporting data on previous accomplishments.

● Effective and appropriate procedures cannot be designed, implemented or priced until the outcomes are clear. The project may run halfway into its first year only to find that the budget is totally inadequate or that there is just not enough time to achieve what has been promised.

● Important audiences for the project may become hostile at the confusion and withdraw from future participation.

● Quarrels or acrimonious debate with the funding source may develop because the purposes of the project were misunderstood.

Every proposal has to be submitted with the thought that it might actually be financed. Projects with poorly written outcomes are best lost on the way to the mailbox.

CHAPTER REFERENCES

Ammerman, Harry L., and William A.Melching, *The Derivation, Analysis and Classification of Instructional Objectives* (Alexandria, VA: Human Resources Research Office, George Washington University, May 1966).

Batten, J.D., *Beyond Management by Objective* (New York: American Management Association, 1965).

Bloom, Benjamin S., ed. *Taxonomy of Educational Objectives, Handbook I: Cognitive Domain.* (New York: Longmans, Green, 1956).

Broudy, H.S., "Philosophical Foundations of Educational Objectives," *Education Theory* 20 (Winter, 1970), 3-21.

Horst, Donald T., G. Kasten Tallmadge, and Christine T. Wood, *A Practical Guide to Measuring Project Impact on Student Achievement*, Monograph Series on Evaluation in Education, no. 1. (Los Altos, CA: RMC Research Corporation, 1975).

Kiritz, N.J., *Program Planning and Professional Writing* (Los Angeles: The Grantsmanship Center, 1975), xvii.

Krathwohl, D.R., et al., *Taxonomy of Educational Objectives, Handbook II: Affective Domain* (New York: Longmans, Green 1964).

Krathwohl, David R., *How to Prepare a Research Proposal.* 2nd ed. (Syracuse: Syracuse University Bookstore, January, 1977).

Mager, R.F., *Preparing Instructional Objectives.* (Palo Alto, CA: Fearon Publishers, 1962).

Popham, James, and Eva Baker, *Establishing Instructional Goals* (Englewood Cliffs, NJ: Prentice-Hall, 1970).

Popham, James, et al., *Instructional Objectives.* AERA Monograph Series on Curriculum Evaluation (Chicago: Rand McNally, 1969).

Smith, Robert G., Jr., *An Annotated Bibliography on the Determination of Training Objectives* (Alexandria, VA: Human Resources Research Office, George Washington University, 1967).

_____ ,*The Development of Training Objectives* Research Bulletin II. (Alexandria, VA : Human Resources Research Office, George Washington University, 1964).

Worthen, B.R., and K.R.White, *Evaluating Educational and Social Programs: Guidelines for Proposal Review, Onsite Evaluation, Evaluation Contracts and Technical Assistance* (Boston: Kluwer-Nijhoff Publishing, 1987), 49.

8

STATEMENT OF NEED

This chapter discusses the preparation of the statement of need and its role in the proposal, and provides examples from successful applications.

Most proposals, particularly those submitted to state and federal agencies, contain a section called the *Statement of Need* or *Statement of the Problem*. The former designation is usually found in applications for service, training or capital projects, with the latter term more commonly used in research or demonstration projects.

In applications to private sources, the writer may already have touched on some of the issues discussed in this chapter. For example, you may previously have signalled that you are not "reinventing the wheel." However, it is wise to document that claim more thoroughly now. You may also have cleverly tied the outcome statement to language indicating why the purpose of the proposal is relevant to the donor's priorities and guidelines. If you have not, this is an important topic to introduce at this time or to address in more depth.

PURPOSE OF THE NEEDS STATEMENT

Normally, this section of the proposal demonstrates:

● A thorough understanding of the issues that the project is attempting to explore or resolve.

● The importance of these issues, not only to the project participants, but to the larger society.

● A critical analysis of the literature in the field and how this project will fill some significant gap.

● The timeliness of the project and why it should be funded now.

● The innovativeness of the effort, if not at the national level, at least locally. If the project is, in fact,

a duplication, then rationale should be provided as to why additional resources should be allocated to the problem.

● The potential generalizability and contribution of the project to the resolution of other problems of importance.

● The relationship of the problem and its proposed solution to the interests and capabilities of you and your organization. Research proposals, particularly, are expected to describe how the current project will build on and extend your previous investigations.

● The beginning rationale for the procedures, approach and plan of action to be discussed in the next section of the proposal.

● How the need you want to resolve fits the guidelines or "enlightened self-interest" of the potential funding source.

There are several considerations to keep in mind when writing this section of the proposal:

❑ Even if you have already shown that the project relates to the general interests of the funding source, you must demonstrate that the *specific* problem or need you are addresssing is of special importance. All agencies, whether public or private, receive far more worthy applications than they can possibly support. A compelling rationale for why your issues are most significant may make the difference.

❑ You must emphasize why this specific need is of unique or direct importance to the particular funding source to which you are applying. By solving this need, will you: Help them resolve a legislative mandate? Initiate a critical service in a community in which they already have major operations? Allow them to use their funds to lever support from others?

❏ The discussion of related research or prior experience (with both the problem and your proposed solution) bears the major burden for establishing your overall scholarship in, and knowledge of the field. Meador (1985) quoted proposal reviewers in the Department of Defense as saying that fully one-third of the proposals they received indicated that the writers had never bothered to check what work had already been done.

❏ The needs identified must be consistent with the project objectives and procedures. A frequent mistake is to describe a massive and complex need but propose a project which addresses only a very small part of the problem. A colleague once labeled this the "elephant-mouse obstetrics syndrome," pointing out that many needs statements describe a huge problem, but eventually give birth to weak and timid remedies. While the purpose behind the project can be tied to some overwhelming national concern, project limitations should be clearly explained and a rationale provided as to why only part of the need is being addressed.

❏ The statement of problem must be sufficiently focused and delimited to assure the reader that there is hope for a solution, given the time and resources requested in the proposal. Reducing the scope of the project to a manageable level demonstrates the experience and sincerity of the applicant. Proposing resolution of a problem that is obviously too complex or expensive is either the sign of a novice or the footprints of someone willing to promise anything in order to get funded.

❏ Be wary of claiming to be the "first" in the field or to be addressing a need that is "more important than anything else." At best, such statements suggest lack of a historical perspective, at worst, egomania.

❏ Read application instructions carefully to see how the funder wants you to demonstrate familiarity with related research or other work. Some ask that this be covered in depth in an attachment. Others want you to discuss the literature in justification of your statement of need. Do not make the mistake of doing too little with whatever references you include. The potential donor is interested in your critical analysis of the literature, not a simple bibliography. It is what the writer does with these citations that establishes professional competence rather than the fact that he or she is aware of them at all.

❏ Include sufficient statistical data to substantiate the need, describe the importance of the population to be served or studied, and predict the contribution of the project's outcomes. But, do not overwhelm the reader. Extensive charts, tables or graphs should be put in an appendix and only referenced in the narrative.

❏ Citations to prior work and sources for statistical data should always be footnoted (the actual bibliography may be an appendix). Determine in advance if the funding source prefers a particular footnote style.

❏ If the problem you have identified is the result of a needs assessment conducted by you or others, be certain to mention this. Also determine if the funding source wants information on how the needs assessment was done and what other problems were identified by it. If the report on the needs assessment is lengthy, include a precis as an attachment to your proposal (unless directed otherwise by the donor). Private funding sources are particularly likely to be overwhelmed with a bulky initial application. You can always send them additional material if they request it.

❏ As with other sections of the proposal, use subheadings and ample paragraphing to assist in communication.

❏ Even if not instructed to do so on the application form, whenever possible, underscore your competence and prior experience in this section. You might: a) cite relevant research or projects previously conducted by you or others in your organization, or b) refer to your roles in other programs which led you to understand the importance of the problem you are currently addressing.

EXAMPLES OF SUCCESSFUL STATEMENTS OF NEED

CASE STUDY 1

The following example is provided to show how the proposal can:

● Quickly summarize the problem being addressed and thus orient the reader to a more elaborate discussion.

● Demonstrate familiarity with prior research.

● Give credibility to the problem by indicating that prior work on it has been documented.

● Include statistical data without interrupting the flow of the narrative.

● Give legitimacy to the procedures that will subsequently be proposed by showing that their lack of availability has been recognized as part of the problem.

● Establish the experience of the applicant by citing prior research of the principal investigator and other project staff.

The example represents a page in a proposal submitted by a university in Oregon to create a demonstration project providing services and training to potential women school administrators.

Women have always been under-represented in school administration although they have predominated as teachers since the Civil War. This has been documented nationally and in Oregon.[1] Furthermore, women's status in educational administration has declined.[2] Three major reasons for women's under-representation in Oregon school management have been documented: a) because it is a male sex-typed occupational role, women have not aspired to be administrators and men believe it is inappropriate for women to enter these roles; b) employed women certificated personnel have less advanced training than employed men certificated personnel,[3] and when women enter graduate programs in education they typically do not enter programs in administration,[4] and, finally; c) there are formal and informal processes of grooming, recruitment and administrative selection at the local school level perpetuating sex inequity and sex-segregated jobs.[5]

Limited sex role definitions, lack of advanced training, and discriminatory recruitment and selection processes interact in perpetuating women's under-representation in administration. To actually achieve sex equity in school management it will be necessary to find simultaneous solutions to these problems.

1. See (name of project director), 1975, 1976 for reports of a study of school administrators in Oregon and (name of a project staff member) et al., 1975 for theoretical discussion of sex segregation and sex role socialization.

2. See Table 1, Appendix A.

3. See Table 2, Appendix A.

4. During 1961-74, 181 males and 8 females received degrees in educational administration from (name of university that is submitting current proposal).

5. See Table 3, Appendix A.

CASE STUDY 2

The second example is taken from an application for a research proposal submitted by a state agency to a federal funding source to evaluate the comparative effectiveness of different types of service and income maintenance programs. The short excerpt from the justification section of the application is included to show an approach for tying the statement of need at the local level to an interest of the funding agency itself.

The national investment in social welfare demonstration projects continues to expand, yet the consequences these projects have on the level of client and family functioning have been only partially evaluated. Without careful assessment, the relative merits of any given project will be lost or incorrectly estimated, while errors may be repeated if the project serves as a prototype.

A favorable set of conditions allowing a careful assessment has arisen in a demonstration project jointly sponsored by the 1115 Demonstration Project Section of the Bureau of Family Services, the Office of Special Services (Title V) of the Bureau of Family Services, and the Mississippi Department of Public Welfare.

The Mississippi Department of Public Welfare has agreed to the creation of four groups of AFDC clients who will receive various combinations of increased services and/or increased financial assistance.

CASE STUDY 3

As noted earlier, most projects address problems that are a subset of a much broader area of concern. The following example provides an illustration of:

● How to briefly describe the scope and significance of the larger area of interest.

● How to delimit the specific topic that is to be the focus of the project and show its possible contributions.

This excerpt was taken from an application for entomological research submitted to the National Science Foundation.

The economic cost and environmental destructiveness of scolytid bark beetle outbreaks in the coniferous forests of the western and southern United States are too well known to need documentation here and the consequent importance of bark beetle control is clear. For over a decade the major effort has been in pheromone research.

The proposal then goes on to discuss some important prior research on bark beetle pheromones and the potential economic impact of this line of inquiry. The proposal continues:

However, there are still basic questions about the natural release of bark beetle pheromones which must be answered.

Following this, the writer identifies several problems that remain unsolved and quickly focuses on the specific set of issues that will be addressed in the proposed research. The section ends with a summary of how this project may impact on future developmental efforts aimed at control of the bark beetle. Throughout the section, frequent references are made to the researcher's prior study in this field and to new products and control methodology that have resulted.

CASE STUDY 4

A more lengthy example is now shown of a proposal which effectively uses both prior research and extant statistical data to document the importance and seriousness of a need. This example comes from a project to develop an exemplary home-based preschool program for children who potentially will enter the first grade without adequate preparation.

Although it was included in a demonstration proposal, it may well serve as a model for a research application.

Note particularly how this approach:

● Establishes the competence of the staff by initially citing several studies and then explores more fully the relevant findings in the most important works.

● Makes use of an apparent weakness in the project's site (i.e. its socio-economic characteristics) to actually strengthen the reason why the project should be tried in this locale.

● Demonstrates the capability of the applicant to adequately evaluate the project by indicating the ongoing and extensive nature of its prior assessments of student performance.

● Makes use of research and statistics to justify the importance of both the need (i.e. preschool services for certain types of children) and the approach (i.e. a home-based model involving parents in the delivery of services).

A growing body of research literature is conclusive regarding what Rosseau and Froebel knew intuitively, that a major influence on a student's pattern of achievement and motives for achievement as well as his personality structure, is the home in which he grows up (Ausubel, 1966; Boratz, 1970; Bing, 1963; Coleman, 1966; Crandall, 1960; D'Amoto, 1962; Deutsch, 1965 and 1967; Hertzig, 1968; Hess, 1968; Jensen, 1969; Levenstein, 1969; Marans, 1967; Schaefer, 1969; and numerous others). The behavior and attitudes of the parents, as well as the physical setting and materials provided, have a direct impact on a child's behavior before and during the school years. Gordon (1968) categorizes three elements of the home in particular: demographic factors, cognitive factors, and emotional factors.

The proposal then goes on to discuss the more relevant findings of this author and a few others.

To begin to enrich the home environment and contribute to children's successful performance in school (according to deHirsch, 1970, who summarizes the findings of many researchers), providing assistance to the home cannot start early enough.

A few more citations and discussions of prior work on the importance of the child's home follow. The proposal then shifts to the need for early childhood programs generally and the problems in the applicant's school district specifically.

The need for early childhood educational programs based on sound research evidence, careful planning, the best thinking about children, and high quality evaluation has again been stated forcefully by one of its proponents, Zigler (1971). The need is most striking in areas like (county of applicant), *areas where lumbering, mining, farming, and similar wage-earning occupations form the economic base. Specifically, in* (county of applicant), *public nursery schools or kindergartens are unknown and private kindergartens serve less than 9 percent of the preschool population. (In the entire* (state of applicant), *public kindergartens have never served more than 29 percent of the five-year-old preschool children.)*

The Inventory of Readiness Skills (a test locally normed) administered to 154 preschool children in April, 1970, along with a School District Readiness Test and checklist, revealed that almost 50 percent of pupils entering first grade score lower than is necessary or desirable. Similarly, the Stanford Reading Achievement Test, administered to a relatively large sample of pupils in May, 1970, revealed that 40 percent of pupils in grades 1-12 scored in the first quartile. With a sample of 159 first grade children on the same test administered at the same time, 62 percent scored in the first quartile.

The numbers of children who score low vary from grade to grade, but in every grade in (school district of applicant) *the numbers scoring below the 25th percentile are greater than the national norm.*

The entire statement of need in this proposal is only slightly more than eight double-spaced pages. Before ending, the writers have amply proven the importance of preschool programs, the significance and potential contribution of a cost-effective model of home-based early childhood education, the importance of this program to the local applicant's community, the capability and scholarly experience of the project staff and the relevancy of this problem to other regional and national problems (i.e. reducing dropout rates in later grades and increasing the effectiveness of school-age enrichment or remedial programs for children of low-socio-economic backgrounds). The discussion has shown that a plausible rationale exists for assuming that the project is timely, innovative, transportable to other communities and schools and capable of being implemented. Needless to say, the proposal was funded for several years at a significant level of support.

CASE STUDY 5

In particularly fortuitous circumstances, an applicant can use the calamities facing other organizations as the rationale for expanding its own services. The following example is from a proposal to a private foundation. The request for funds followed hard on the heels of extensive media coverage of the terrible financial plight of major arts organizations in the area, problems which had been documented by a task force appointed by a local big city mayor. Communities in the area had subsequently been mobilized to create a pool of funds, called the Arts Stabilization Program, for which organizations could qualify through better management and partial elimination of deficits.

The short proposal started off by reminding the foundation that the mission of the applicant was to recruit volunteer business consultants to help organizations resolve management problems, improve administrative procedures, plan for the future, and get maximum use from limited financial resources.

The application then explained:

Our organization is now taking on an expanded role by providing technical assistance to arts organizations which will participate in the Arts Stabilization Program, an outgrowth of Mayor X's task force on the arts.

After describing the types of new services to be provided, the proposal continued:

This added responsibility, along with increased demand for our services from smaller arts groups, necessitated that we increase the director position from half-time to full-time. Obviously, this has increased the budget and therefore the need for annual operating support.

Had the foundation not already been familiar with the local arts crisis, the applicant would undoubtedly have included as attachments (and briefly referenced in the needs statement) the most compelling of the newspaper stories.

SUMMARY

It may be helpful to conceptualize the **outcome** portion of the proposal as answering the question of *"what* should be done?" Logically, the **statement of**

need or **statement of the problem** then answers the question of *why*?" It thus lays the groundwork for the next question, *"how?"* which will be described in the proposal's next section, the **procedures** or **approach**.

CHAPTER REFERENCE

Meador, R., *Guidelines for Preparing Proposals* (Chelsea, MI: Lewis Publishers, 1985).

THE PROCEDURES

This chapter discusses elements typically found in the procedures component of proposals. It discusses how these vary in different kinds of applications and provides some general guidelines on writing and format.

The *procedures* section (also called the *approach* or *plan of action*) is typically the longest part of a proposal. It bears the major burden of telling *how* the project will be carried out and the rationale for the majority of the budget. It must convince the funding source that you really know how to achieve the outcomes and solve the problems that have been described earlier. And, while a proposal may sometimes get by with fuzzy or imprecise objectives, it is very hard to obfuscate inexperience or incompetence when designing and describing methodology.

SOME IMPORTANT GUIDELINES

There are a number of problems commonly found in the procedures section of the proposal.

PROBLEM 1: The procedures do not match the outcomes.

This is the most commonly made mistake in preparing this proposal component. There are sometimes sins of omission as well as of commission, that is, the proposal may include objectives for which there are no procedures; but it may also include procedures that appear irrelevant and unrelated to any objectives.

In research applications, for example, project outcomes frequently call for producing results that will be generalized to other situations or audiences. Yet, the proposed procedures provide no realistic plan for the control of important variables. The resulting data may thus have little or no predictive value.

Research projects are not the only place where inappropriate procedures are sometimes found. As an example, one university proposed a program to encourage public school personnel to become self-sufficient in conducting classroom evaluations. Yet, the suggested procedures called for producing courses, materials and models that would always require the involvement of university faculty as trainers or consultants. The funding source pointed out that the outcomes and the procedures were mutually contradictory: One proposed to create independence, but the other simply called for a new form of long term dependency. The project was not funded.

PROBLEM 2: The proposal does not actually include procedures or a plan of action.

This omission is most commonly found in applications that have described the initiation of some new type of service in the outcomes section of the proposal, rather than stated outcomes that tell what the intended results of the service are to be.

A recent application to a private foundation, for example, said that the purpose of the project was to open a new food bank. The rest of the proposal was then devoted to justifying why hunger is a particular social problem and why more food banks are needed. It provided: no clues on where the food bank would be sited, how the facility would be provided, what population it would try to serve, how the availability of the food would be publicized, how the actual food to be distributed would be obtained, how many people would be needed to operate the food bank and so forth. This request was also not supported.

PROBLEM 3: The procedures do not match the objectives and needs on the dimensions of innovativeness and scope.

In another example, a corporation received an application from a large national group to underwrite a conference aimed at solving the problem of the lack of communication among scientists involved in acid rain research. The group devoted several pages to justifying why acid rain was such a significant issue. But it provided no justification as to why communications between scientists was the most important aspect of this problem, nor why a conference could be expected to make any lasting impact on the problem's resolution. This proposal was also rejected.

PROBLEM 4: The procedures have no sound rationale.

Increasingly, funding sources expect the applicant to explain why it has selected the particular approach found in the procedures. This is because donors know that a problem can reasonably be addressed through many different solutions. You must convince them that you have selected the best one and justify your choice over other possible approaches. One method for doing this is to cite other projects that have successfully used similar procedures. Another is to cite "expert testimony" such as research findings or articles by authoritative figures, which suggest that your approach is both effective and significant.

PROBLEM 5: The procedures are not demonstrated to be feasible.

A number of studies have looked at reasons why proposals are not approved (see Chapter 14) and many have found that the criterion of "feasibility" is one of the most important. Clues that reviewers look for when judging this include:

● Evidence that you know of other studies or projects where similar procedures have been used and are able to cite examples suggesting that the procedures will likely achieve the intended results.

● The care with which the procedures are separated into distinct and manageable activities.

● Documentation that the writer has thought through an effective time schedule and has sequenced the activities into logical and complementary phases.

● Evidence that the writer is aware of any potential problem areas with the suggested procedures and

has some plan in mind for either correcting or dealing with these eventualities.

CONTENT OF THE PROCEDURES COMPONENT

The kind of information that private funding sources want about procedure is similar to that desired by governmental grantmakers, except that the private sector usually wants it in much less detail. However, both types of donors expect that the procedures section for training, service, demonstration or development projects will likely differ from elements included in most research proposals.

Tables 1 and 2 indicate some of the sections commonly found in these two types of projects. These charts should only be used as general guidelines. Specific content and the order in which the narrative is arranged should be dictated by directions from the anticipated funding source.

SOME GUIDELINES ON CONTENT

Because procedures vary so widely from project to project, it is difficult to provide a definitive discussion of what to avoid or include in every application. However, the following suggestions will cover some of the issues of typical concern to novice writers when they attempt to present their project's procedures.

THE INTRODUCTION

The writer of a proposal is essentially telling a story and, like any good author, should pay attention to both the flow of the narrative and the plot construction. However, unlike the storyteller, the proposal writer does not want to leave the reader guessing about what will come next. Therefore, experienced writers frequently suggest that you begin this component with an introductory section to "set the stage." They note that the procedures component is likely to be the longest portion of an application, to include many separate kinds of information and to involve technical and sometimes complex material. It is important that the reviewer know how this component is to be structured.

ELEMENTS FOR PROCEDURES IN DEMONSTRATION, DEVELOPMENT, SERVICE AND TRAINING PROPOSALS

INFORMATION TO BE INCLUDED IN EACH SECTION

Introduction	This section should briefly summarize the project's approach and indicate why it was selected. The significance, innovativeness, appropriateness and feasibility of the approach should be demonstrated. This section may also discuss how this approach will build on prior work and it may also explain the conceptual or theoretical base for the project.
Approach or Plan of Action	The narrative describes the plan for how you will achieve the objectives and solve the problem mentioned earlier. It should cover services to be provided, products to be produced and so forth. The individuals or groups who will participate and/or receive services should be described along with how they will be selected. If not covered in an introduction, this section will also describe the dissemination of project results (unless these are in separate components). Private funding sources also expect evidence of community and participant support for the approach. The narrative may be presented in sequential phases or organized by broad task categories (such as site selection, participant selection, material development, field testing). It should also contain a specific timeline for the project, including major milestones. Displaying the timeline visually is recommended. Some funding sources also ask that this selection include a detailed work plan, laying out discrete activities and identifying who will do them.
Administration and Personnel	You should provide a description of the roles and responsibilities of project staff, consultants, advisory groups and cooperating agencies. Unless covered in the proposal component on organizational capability, you may also want to document their experience and any unique qualifications. Tell the funding source how the project will be managed and governed and how it relates to the administrative structure of your organization.
Deliverables (optional)	Some authors argue that it is a good idea to close the procedures section of the proposal with a section that outlines the specific products and benefits expected from the project. If you have summarized these earlier in the outcomes component, you may want to describe them in more depth here.

This handout taken from *Getting Funded: A Complete Guide to Proposal Writing* by Mary Hall, 1988. Available from Continuing Education Publications, P.O. Box 1491, Portland OR 97207.

TABLE 2   **THE PROCEDURES**

ELEMENTS FOR PROCEDURES IN A RESEARCH PROPOSAL

INFORMATION TO BE INCLUDED IN EACH SECTION

Introduction

This section should prepare the reviewer for the type of methodology to be used in the project (i.e. survey, experimental, longitudinal, formulative, case studies) and explain why this approach was chosen. It should call attention to any innovative or unique aspects of the design and methods and how they improve on previous approaches. This section may also summarize prior related work of the principal investigator and indicate how the current project will build on or extend these efforts.

Population

If appropriate, provide a description of the population that is to be studied and include relevant details on sampling procedures, subject or site selection, and securing participation. Any potential hazards to the population or staff should be identified along with methods of coping with these. Requirements of government agencies for a description of processes to protect human subjects and vertebrate animals may also be covered.

Design and Method

The narrative should describe the specific research to be conducted and the way in which it will be carried out. Usually, this includes a discussion of the theoretical base for the research (with appropriate citations to other studies), identification of research variables, elaboration of research questions and hypotheses, and the specific activities to test these. You may also want to identify any problems anticipated with the design or methods and describe what you intend to do to treat them. Unless they are mentioned elsewhere, this section should also discuss planned evaluation and intended dissemination of project results.

Instrumentation, Data Collection and Analysis

A presentation of the specific measures and procedures chosen to collect necessary data should be furnished. Details on establishing validity and reliability should be dealt with, particularly for new instruments. Either here or in the design you should speak to the extent that the results are expected to be generalizable. Also define the methodology and criteria to be used in analyzing and judging the resulting data. Justification for these choices should be provided, along with any indication of innovativeness.

Work Plan or Timeline

Some funding agencies want a very detailed work plan laying out the project activities in sequence, along with identification of who will do what. Others will accept a timeline with key events, functions or chronological phases.

Administration and Personnel

Describe the intended management of the project unless this is addressed as a separate component. Discuss roles and responsibilities of project staff, consultants and any other groups or agencies involved. Justification should be provided for the relevant expertise of proposed staff and consultants, as well as for the amounts of time they will devote to the project.

Accomplishments to Date (optional)

As noted earlier, some funding sources want a summary of results on all work they have funded during the previous five years for the project's principal investigator. It may also be helpful here to describe related research by you or your organization in order to justify your experience and expertise and show how the current project will make a contribution.

This handout taken from *Getting Funded: A Complete Guide to Proposal Writing* by Mary Hall, 1988. Available from Continuing Education Publications, P.O. Box 1491, Portland, OR 97207.

In addition to providing a type of "table of contents," the introduction can play the following roles:

● It can introduce the reviewer to the overall type of approach to be used in the project and provide a brief justification for its appropriateness.

● In research applications, it can also alert the reader to the specific type of methodology to be followed. It is important to provide this kind of clue early in the procedures section. Otherwise, the reader may gain an initially negative or inaccurate reaction (which is difficult to overcome) because a superficial reading did not clearly signal the type of research involved.

● It can call attention to any innovative material or methodology to be employed.

● It can summarize the theoretical base for the procedures and demonstrate how these will result in products or knowledge of utility and significance to others.

THE APPROACH OR DESIGN

This is probably the most important part of the discussion on procedures because it is where you describe the specific program or research to be implemented, the methodology to be employed, the population to be studied or served, the specific activities to be completed and a rationale which justifies these choices.

The content for this section should be adapted as appropriate to fit the type of project proposed. For example, a research application may open this discussion with the conceptual base for the project, the research hypotheses or questions to be addressed, and the specific variables to be considered. Demonstration or training projects, on the other hand, may begin by describing the specific services to be provided or the materials to be developed. Both will then probably proceed to a description of the techniques to be used to accomplish the work.

In preparing this narrative, it is important that you describe how unexpected events or results will be treated. One paradox of project development is the necessity for trying to plan for the unanticipated. It may be that your initial participants will unexpectedly withdraw from the project; a variable that was expected to be important to the research may prove to have limited utility; or materials that are developed may not have the intended results.

Unless the writer has tried to predict each point in the project's procedures where a major problem might occur, insufficient time or resources may be requested to correct the difficulty. And unless the writer flags potential difficulties and includes at least a recognition of the need for corrective action, the reviewer may gain an impression of inexperience or sloppy planning.

Finally, unless you include statements about intentions to revise the procedures (and perhaps even portions of the objectives) based on the results of certain project activities, the funded program may be committed to continuing activities that are no longer appropriate or are clearly unworkable.

To avoid having to repeatedly seek approval from the funding source for modifications in project operation, you should straightforwardly address these possibilities in the application itself wherever possible. Techniques which are useful include:

● The use of field-tests for all unproven procedures and materials, and activities providing for necessary revision or refinement.

● The design of activities in sequential phases with a period at the end of each element allowed for necessary modifications in the remaining plan of action.

● The planning of periodic consultation with the funding source to discuss necessary changes. The funders will probably insist on this anyway. Sometimes a project can avoid unnecessary interferences by including such check points in the application and indicating that consultations will generally be limited to this schedule.

● The flagging of checkpoints when the project staff intends to review evaluative data and make decisions about necessary modifications.

PARTICIPANTS

The proposal should describe any groups to be involved in the project, should identify the basis on which they will be chosen and should detail the procedures to be followed in their selection (including assignment to treatment group, if appropriate). The method you will use to secure cooperation and participation should be specified, plus the fact of whether or not such groups will be paid for their involvement.

Nowadays, it is very important that you provide some evidence that such groups are likely to cooperate with your project. Private foundations and corporations particularly want evidence of community involvement and support for projects. Using education as an example, funding sources are well aware that many public school personnel will no longer voluntarily serve as unpaid subjects for university-based research efforts—particularly those which are likely to interfere with classroom instruction or will require extensive time after normal school hours. These funding agencies are no longer willing to gamble that you will be able to locate desirable subjects after the award is made. Documentation that such individuals have already been contacted and have agreed to assume the necessary roles is a prerequisite in the proposal itself. This same point applies to other groups who feel that they have either been "over studied" in the past or have been exploited by unsympathetic or irresponsible investigators. The same is true for participation in the project by other agencies.

Writers of proposals dealing with animal subjects should be certain to conform to all professional and federal requirements for their acquisition, breeding, care, feeding, disease control and so forth. Compliance with requirements governing the qualifications of personnel dealing with animals should also be documented. Your administrative officers should be consulted on the amount of detail necessary to demonstrate that your organization has met federal requirements on registration and/or accreditation to use laboratory animals.

Finally, you should be aware of federal and state regulations governing privacy and protection of human subjects and those involving the use of minor children as research subjects. Evidence that you intend to comply with such requirements and the procedures you will use for doing so should be included in the application.

INSTRUMENTATION, DATA COLLECTION AND ANALYSIS

Depending on the length and complexity of your description of these topics, they may be addressed in a single section or may be discussed separately. However presented, you should include an appropriate level of detail in issues such as:

● Variables to be addressed or types of specific information to be obtained (unless this has been adequately covered elsewhere).

● The specific instrumentation to be used to collect the necessary data and a description of the background and content of any measures which are not well known to typical reviewers.

● Supporting psychometric data on each measure and other evidence justifying suitability, technical soundness and comprehensiveness.

● Sources from which specific information will be obtained.

● Methods of data collection.

● Data collection schedules.

● Data preparation and storage.

● Data retrieval.

● Data analysis (including discussion of the units of analysis, data analysis models and justification of these choices).

● Data reporting (including report audiences, types of reports and reporting schedule).

● Data utilization and application.

Another suggestion that might be of help is:

Use appropriate charts or tables for summarizing this narrative if the discussion is at all complex. Tables 3 and 4 provide some examples of how another proposal has handled this.

Identify any audience which must review and approve your data collection instruments or procedures. Identify the amount of time estimated for this review and describe procedures for how modifications will be made, if necessary. Remember that all federally funded projects involving the administration of instruments to large groups of subjects must have prior clearance. Further details on this should be sought from the appropriate federal agency.

WORK PLAN

In many proposals, the specific activities needed to implement the procedures and their planned sequence will have been included in the discussion of the approach or design. Even so, it is a good idea to summarize these in a separate section clearly

TABLE 3

THE PROCEDURES

EXAMPLE OF TABLE DISPLAYING DATA COLLECTION DESIGN

Instrumentation for Implementation: School Staff Reactions

Construct	Variable	Instrument Type	Source
Commitment	1. Self-reported level of personal commitment to the implementation process	Questionnaire	Principal
	2. Staff-reported level of commitment of the staff in general to implementation	Questionnaire	Principal
Resistance/Support	1. Self-reported level of resistance/support	Questionnaire	Principal
	2. Locus of resistance/support	Questionnaire/Interview	Principal District Liaison
Influence/Power	3. Perceived level of personal influence upon the implementation system and process	Questionnaire	Principal Teacher
	4. Perceived level of referent group influence upon the implementation system and process	Questionnaire	Principal Teacher
Satisfaction with Process	5. Self-reported level of satisfaction with the implementation system	Questionnaire	Principal Teacher
	6. Self-reported level of satisfaction with the implementation process	Questionnaire	Principal Teacher

This handout taken from *Getting Funded: A Complete Guide to Proposal Writing* by Mary Hall, 1988.
Available from Continuing Education Publications, P.O. Box 1491, Portland, OR 97207.

121

TABLE 4

THE PROCEDURES

EXAMPLE OF DISPLAY ON DATA ANALYSIS

Types of Hypotheses and Related Data Analysis Procedures

Type of Hypothesis	Type of Analysis	Unit of Analysis	Data Analysis Model
Relationships between variables (e.g., task orientation is positively related to achievement)	Cross-sectional analysis Cross- lagged panel analysis	Generally corresponding to unit of observation for the related variables (see Instrumentation Section)	Correlational techniques (e.g., zero-order correlation, canonical correlations)
Comparison of states of affairs (e.g., student involvement will increase)	Longitudinal analysis	Generally corresponding to unit of observation for the related variables (see Instrumentation Section)	Descriptive statistics, time series, f and t tests
Path/amount of influence among variables (e.g., student achievement is influenced by programmatic functions, climate, and student backgrounds)	Cross-sectional analysis Cross-lagged analysis	Generally corresponding to unit of observation for the related variables (see Instrumentation Section)	Generalized regression analysis

This handout taken from *Getting Funded: A Complete Guide to Proposal Writing* by Mary Hall, 1988. Available from Continuing Education Publications, P.O. Box 1491, Portland, OR 97207

identified by the label of "work plan" or "project timelines." The major purpose of this section is to indicate the appropriate dates on which major accomplishments and products will be completed and to show the reviewer how the activities will be spread throughout the project period.

Most proposal writers recommend that you use charts, graphs or other types of diagrams to present your project timelines for key activities. Unless the project is very short or has only a few activities, the reviewer may become lost if this discussion is only presented in narrative form.

There are many techniques to choose from in presenting your work plan, including Gantt Charts, PERT (Program Evaluation Review Technique), The Critical Path Method (CPM) or simple time charts. Examples of three of these methods are displayed in Figures 1, 2 and 3.

You should adapt these to your particular need. Those such as Gantt Charts are most useful for depicting dates in relation to activities. PERT and CPM are most useful for showing the intended interrelationships among events.

Most experienced project planners use some type of work sheet to develop the information they then summarize in a timeline included in the proposal. In doing this, they consider information such as: a) the specific activities that must be carried out and the amount of time each will take; b) the order in which the activities must be accomplished; c) the amount of staff and consultant help that can reasonably be expected for each activity; and d) the amount of "down time" that can be anticipated (such as holidays, vacations, sick leave and so forth).

If after considering all of these issues you feel that the projected timeline will exceed the anticipated grant period, you should consider modifying your procedures. If this seems impossible, you may want to go back and scale down the entire project — starting with a further delimitation of outcomes.

Remember, because the activities are committed to paper doesn't mean they will get done. It is a good idea to have your estimates checked by someone else. Typically, the originator of a project idea is unrealistic about the amount of work that can be accomplished in any given period of time. You need a less involved colleague to help make your estimates more realistic.

ADMINISTRATION

This section of the procedures may include information such as:

● How will the project be administered?

● What are the key project positions? What are their roles?

● How are other project personnel to be utilized?

● How will project personnel be selected? What criteria will be used?

● How does the project relate to other units in your organization? What is the chain of command?

● Are other agencies involved in the project and, if so, what are their roles?

● What are the roles of any consultants and advisory bodies? How will these individuals be selected? What criteria will be used? How will participation be secured?

In many proposals, this discussion is combined with the section on personnel. In others, the personnel section may be used solely to include the resumes of staff who are known at the time the proposal is submitted.

Wherever presented, the information should serve four purposes:

● To lay out the administrative rules of the game for the project and thus avoid confusion and later misunderstandings.

● To explain clearly to the funding source who will be responsible for the project and its various activities.

● To document that you have competent people in charge of the project. To build necessary justification for your budget requests. This last point is very important. For example, if funds are to be included for a significant number of consultants, their roles in the project and their contributions to its success must be documented. Money may also be needed to pay travel and per diem expenses of advisory board members or to cover the cost of staff services to such groups. The importance of these individuals to the project must be explained.

FIGURE 1   THE PROCEDURES

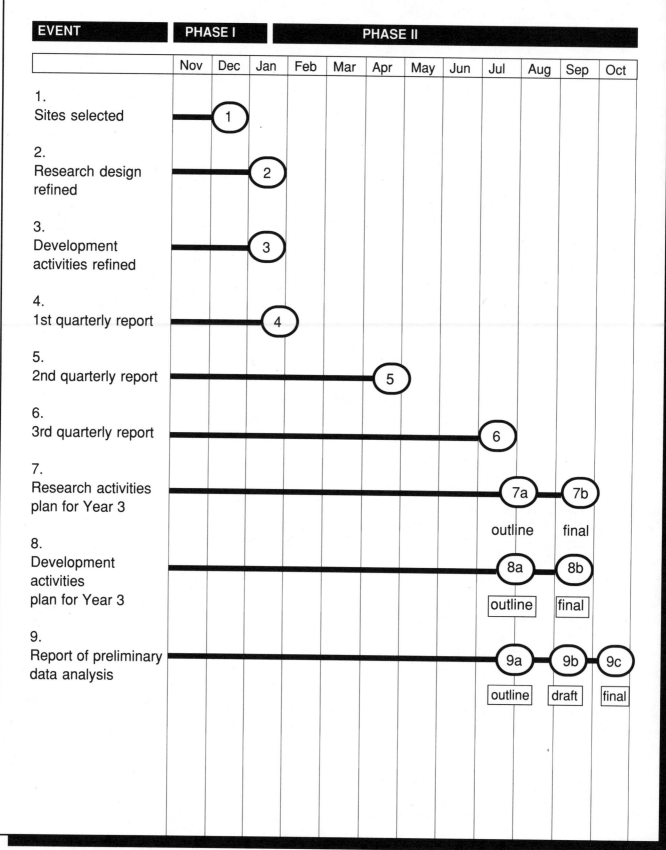

EXAMPLE OF A GANTT CHART

EVENT	PHASE I		PHASE II									
	Nov	Dec	Jan	Feb	Mar	Apr	May	Jun	Jul	Aug	Sep	Oct
1. Sites selected		①										
2. Research design refined		②										
3. Development activities refined		③										
4. 1st quarterly report			④									
5. 2nd quarterly report						⑤						
6. 3rd quarterly report								⑥				
7. Research activities plan for Year 3									7a outline		7b final	
8. Development activities plan for Year 3									8a outline		8b final	
9. Report of preliminary data analysis									9a outline		9b draft	9c final

This handout taken from *Getting Funded: A Complete Guide to Proposal Writing* by Mary Hall, 1988.
Available from Continuing Education Publications, P.O. Box 1491, Portland, OR 97207

FIGURE 2 AND FIGURE 3   THE PROCEDURES

EXAMPLE OF A PERT CHART

Program Schedule (dates will be adjusted according to project start date)

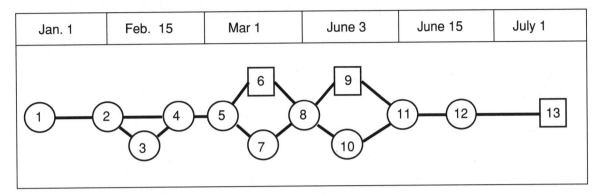

| Jan. 1 | Feb. 15 | Mar 1 | June 3 | June 15 | July 1 |

Activity

1-2	Hire Staff	6-8	Synthesize findings/paper
2-3	Secure Consultants	8-9	Review with funding source
2-4	Outline paper content	8-10	Validate paper with forum members
4-5	Draft position paper	9-11	Revise paper
5-6	Forum review of paper	11-12	Edit final paper
5-7	Conduct literature search	11-13	Production of final paper

Symbol Code

◯ Begin or end activity

▢ Milestone

This chart was adapted from a much more elaborate PERT diagram included in a project whose purpose was to prepare position papers outlining needed research in a field. The writers included a diagram of this type for each major phase of the project. This example deals with one such phase.

EXAMPLE OF A SIMPLE TIME SCHEDULE

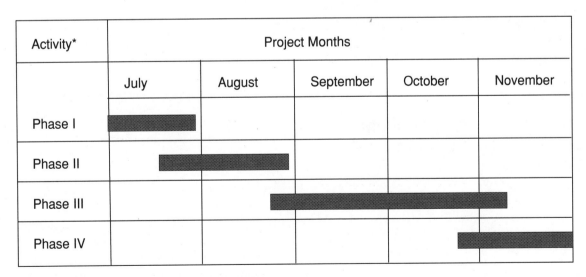

Activity*	Project Months				
	July	August	September	October	November
Phase I	▓▓▓▓				
Phase II		▓▓▓▓			
Phase III			▓▓▓▓▓▓▓▓		
Phase IV					▓▓▓▓

* The activities which constitute each phase were described earlier in the proposal. This type of chart is suitable only for providing a quick overview of major project elements.

This handout taken from *Getting Funded: A Complete Guide to Proposal Writing* by Mary Hall, 1988. Available from Continuing Education Publications, P.O.Box 1491, Portland, OR 97207.

ACCOMPLISHMENT TO DATE

For any proposal which builds on your earlier work or on related projects undertaken by your organization, it is a good idea to mention this somewhere in the application in a clearly labeled section. The purpose of this is to: a) show how the current project will build on past efforts; b) demonstrate your prior experience and capability; and c) provide the funding sources with details on other external funds which you've received to solve this same or a similar problem. The latter is very important to many funding sources who, without this detail, may feel that they are being asked to support work that has already been paid for by another public or tax-exempt source. This discussion may have taken place earlier when you prepared the statement of need. If not, you can tack it on to the procedure component.

DELIVERABLES

Information on the anticipated results of the project will already have been covered in the objective section. But it may be useful to summarize these in a special section at the end of the procedures component to quickly remind the reviewers and the funding source of the actual and potential outcomes that will result from this award. It is also appropriate at this point to speculate on the potential utilization and application of project results.

THE PROCEDURE COMPONENT IN APPLICATIONS TO PRIVATE SOURCES

As mentioned earlier, private foundations and corporations want about the same type of procedural information as governmental funders; they just want less of it. Most federal applications, for example, suggest that the narrative in the procedures section not exceed 20 pages; foundations and corporations usually ask for no more than two pages.

The writer thus needs to be creative in getting a great deal of information across concisely. The following example was taken from an application to a foundation for a capital grant. After an opening section which explained the nature of the applicant's services and why a new facility was needed for their expansion, the organization included the following chart:

PROBLEM - old facility

1. *old building*

2. *not near highway*

3. *poor general visibility*

4. *inadequate parking*

5. *mechanical and electrical system outdated*

6. *no inside van loading or parking*

7. *small, poorly divided office space*

8. *lack of good meeting space for training and volunteers*

SOLUTION - new facility

1. *newer building*

2. *central to county, near freeway access*

3. *good corner visibility*

4. *40-car parking lot*

5. *new or improved system part of the remodel*

6. *space for eight vans and for van loading*

7. *office division based on program requirements*

8. *spaces designed for small or large groups for volunteers and classes*

They then included a one-page chart outlining the major milestones for completing their fundraising, site selection, design, construction, moving, and a celebratory event. This was followed by a very short description of what staff would be involved (and to what degree) during each of these phases. Their grant was approved and the building brought in below budget.

EVALUATION

This chapter discusses the purpose of evaluation in funded projects, describes ways to present the evaluation component in the proposal, identifies some steps commonly followed in designing evaluation and suggests criteria for judging the effectiveness of an evaluation plan.

SOME QUESTIONS ABOUT EVALUATION

One of the first questions asked when anyone raises this topic is: *"What do you mean by the word evaluation?"* This issue is not simply a matter of semantics. For behind the fog of rhetoric, there are differing opinions along dimensions of motivation, philosophy, purpose, scope, methodology, utilization and audience. For those who want to further pursue the history and implications of these various approaches, a good beginning point is *Systematic Evaluation* by Stufflebeam and Shrinkfield.

The issues are too complex and space is too limited to restate that discussion here. But the reader should be left with a simple message: **it is important to clarify how the term will be used in the proposal and to test this use against the perceptions of the applicant's organization, the project staff and the funding source.** All three are important audiences for a project's evaluation: The organization because it may want to continue a project after the external funds are depleted; the staff because they are the individuals who need information to improve the project's operation and will ultimately have to defend its success or failure; and the funding source because it will not only want to know if the project achieved its objectives but will likely want some insights on the probable impact of these results on others.

A second question frequently asked is: *"How does evaluation differ from research?"* Worthen and Sanders (1973) differentiated these two terms as follows:

Evaluation is the determination of the worth of a thing. It includes obtaining information for use in judging the worth of a program, product, procedure, or objective, and the potential utility of alternative approaches designed to attain specified objectives.

Research is the activity aimed at obtaining generalizable knowledge by contriving and testing claims about relationships among variables or describing generalizable phenomena. This knowledge, which may result in theoretical models, functional relationships, or descriptions, may be obtained by empirical or other sympathetic methods and may or may not have immediate application.

For our purposes, the following general definition will serve as the basis for subsequent discussion:

Evaluation is any systematic process which is designed to reduce uncertainty about the effectiveness of a particular project and its results.

A third question of concern is: *"How do I decide whether to include anything about evaluation in the proposal?"* There are really two major ways to answer this. First, the writer may have no choice because the funding source specifically asks for details on the planned evaluation. And even if this expectation is not explicit, the writer may find during the pre-proposal phase that the funding source has only supported projects that have included an evaluation component. Second, the writer may decide that, irrespective of the demands of the funding source, evaluation should be included for the good of the project. A quick way to make this decision is to answer the following questions:

❑ Is it important that, during the project's operation, the staff have some way of determining whether materials and processes are effective?

❏ Is it important that the project be able to demonstrate whether or not it achieved its desired outcomes?

❏ Will a new proposal have to be submitted to receive continuing funding for the project?

It is impossible to conceive of a case these days where the answer will not be "yes" to at least one of these questions. Thus, like it or not, the average proposal writer will need to include some type of plan and some amount of time and money to conduct necessary evaluation. Decisions about the type and extent of the needed evaluation can be guided by the later discussion on the purpose of evaluation.

A fourth question asked by some is: *"What do I do if I want to include an evaluation component but I know nothing about the subject?"* Again, there are several tacks one can take.

● **One can borrow ideas from the evaluation plans developed for other programs.** There are several manuals around that provide simple step-by-step approaches to developing a general evaluation strategy. The evaluation components in previously funded projects are another useful source of possible models. However, the writer should seek the guidance of someone who has knowledge of the field in order to choose which strategy to adopt.

● **A colleague or consultant can be asked to review the rest of the proposal and to develop an appropriate evaluation strategy.** Almost all organizations employ someone who has had appropriate training and experience in evaluation. These individuals can be a useful resource for the novice proposal developer. And, if this is not the case, using a consultant to secure a detailed evaluation design (which may only be summarized in the proposal itself) is a worthwhile investment—particularly if this is a component that is important to the competitiveness of the overall proposal.

● **The issue can be avoided in the application by indicating that a staff member or consultant will be hired after the project is funded to develop appropriate evaluation methodology.** Unfortunately, many funding sources will buy this approach. But in the long run, its use may cause real problems for the funded project. Without any idea of the type or scope of evaluation needed, it is almost impossible to accurately estimate the amount of funds to include in

the proposal's budget. Consequently, the project staff may later be forced to divert significant resources to this function and thus weaken the rest of the project. Also, a lack of pre-planning for evaluation may result in the loss of important data. If this approach is chosen, however, the writer is well advised to at least consult some knowledgeable person when estimating the amount of funds to allocate to evaluation activities. More information on the use of evaluation consultants is provided later in the chapter.

Decisions about evaluation have been somewhat easier since the completion of work by the Joint Committee on Standards for Educational Evaluation. Project developers in all fields can benefit from consulting the Committee's *Standards for Evaluation of Educational Programs, Projects and Materials* (1981). Another useful resource, this one aimed specifically at community non-profit agencies is Van Maanen's, *The Process of Program Evaluation.*

A fifth question may be: *"What can I do if I know that some type of evaluation should be included but the nature of my project neither warrants nor lends itself to the more sophisticated and expensive designs seen elsewhere?"* This is a frequent issue in applications to private foundations and corporations, particularly when the grant amount requested is not very large to begin with. Some of the approaches that have been used by others include:

● Indicating in the proposal that the donor (or the donor's representative) will be asked to participate in a site visit during or after the project's operation to see that the promised results are being achieved.

● Forming a local advisory committee for the project, one of their responsibilities being to judge the effectiveness of the effort and to report back to the donor.

● In the case of equipment or facility grants, noting that the donor will be provided with photographs as well as a final statement on project costs (to prove the outcomes were achieved within the original promised amount).

● Selecting a local individual known to be expert in the field to periodically visit the project and furnish reports to the donor.

Remember, the definition of evaluation has to do with "judging the worth" of something. There are many creative ways, other than actual testing or experimental field designs, to do this.

PURPOSES OF EVALUATION

There are almost as many purposes for evaluation as there are definitions. If you want to pursue this topic in more depth, you may find the Worthen and Sanders (1973) tables summarizing a comparative description of evaluation approaches particularly useful. In most cases, however, you are faced with choosing from among purposes that fall into four commonly-used categories.

Formative evaluation, a term coined by Scriven (1958, 1967), produces information used to improve a project during its operation. The primary audience for this information is the project staff, the administration of the project's sponsoring organization, and, occasionally, the careful monitor of the funding agency. Many funding sources do not require formative-type evaluation; yet, it is probably the most important aspect of evaluation. It helps determine whether processes and procedures are working; whether project materials are sound and effective; and whether participants and clients are satisfied with services. It may also produce information that is appropriate for use in requests for project renewal—particularly if such applications have to be submitted soon after the project's initiation.

Some authors now argue that **all** evaluation is *formative* in that the majority of projects involve some activities that are ongoing, irrespective of when external funding begins and ends. However defined, formative evaluation is essential to good management. Its inclusion, in some form, is definitely recommended for most proposals and it should be allocated specific resources.

Summative evaluation, on the other hand, involves the collection of data necessary for judging the ultimate success of the completed project. Its audience is only incidentally the project staff (who at this point can do little to correct already-made mistakes). Summative evaluation's major purpose is to document the extent to which the project's outcomes were achieved. Its primary users are the funding source and other audiences interested in the project's results. This is the type of evaluation most commonly requested in proposals.

Pay-off or *impact evaluation* is designed primarily to help judge the overall worth and utility of a project's results. Unlike summative evaluation, it is not particularly concerned with finding out whether the project did what it promised. But it is very much concerned with whether these achievements have any value. This type of evaluation can occur both during a project's operation (i.e. in the formative stages) or at a project's termination (i.e. summative stages). But regardless of when it occurs, it focuses on the value of the project's effects and the ends to which the project's means were directed. Its audience may thus be both the project staff and the funding sources, plus other types of policy makers who are concerned about the ultimate value of externally funded activities.

The fourth category of evaluation purposes are those usually associated with *context* or *antecedent evaluation*. This type of evaluation tries to answer the question of what factors exist in the project's environment or its history that may influence project conduct and outcomes. As with pay-off evaluation, this type of information gathering may influence both a project's operation and the value of its outcomes. It is thus useful to a wide range of audiences. Unfortunately, few funding sources actually request that context evaluation be provided—yet its omission may diminish the value of any other type of information gathering.

The necessity to at least consider this type of evaluation purpose is perhaps best illustrated by a now forgotten project of several years past. The project purported to have substantially increased the reading scores of disadvantaged children. After all of the results were in, however, it was discovered that the children's families had received a significant pay increase soon after the project started. The resulting change in family life style was sufficient to cast doubt on the project's entire results. It was also later discovered that many of the children were simultaneously participating in several other reading improvement projects. Since none of the projects were monitoring their participants' environment, none had been aware of the potential contamination of each other's services. Context evaluation can help avoid such project myopia.

In summary, then, it has been suggested that there are at least three essential steps for the writer to take prior to actually constructing the discussion of evaluation in a proposal:

● To decide if any evaluation is warranted and, if so, who is going to construct its design.

● To arrive at a definition of the desired evaluation and check this with other significant project audiences.

● To determine the broad purposes and audiences for the proposed evaluation.

DISPLAY OF EVALUATION IN A PROPOSAL

To some, it may seem backwards to start with a discussion of how the evaluation will be displayed in the proposal. But unless you have some visual model of what this component will look like, it is difficult to structure the necessary planning and make certain the appropriate information is provided.

There are many outlines that one can follow, but the two suggested in Tables 1 and 2 will be sufficient for most proposals.

These two tables can be adapted to fit the informational needs of your specific project. A brief coverage of the major elements common to both outlines follows.

STEP ONE: Identify What Is Going to Be Evaluated

There are several way to approach this step. They can be used separately or together.

● The writer may supply a list of questions that the evaluation will attempt to answer.

● The discussion may simply include a few sentences indicating what the focus and purpose of the evaluation will be (i.e. distinguishing whether efforts well be made to gather formative as well as summative data, for example).

● The writer may refer to or restate the objectives on which the evaluation will focus. Chapter 8 may be of some use in determining appropriate content for such objectives.

If this last approach is used (and it is one of the most common formats), you will want to be certain that appropriate process objectives as well as product and/or performance objectives are identified. Typically, the types of instruments used to measure processes are quite different from those used to measure a product. Tables 3 and 4 are useful in understanding this difference.

If not already done in an introduction to the evaluation component, at this point you should also provide a rationale for the limitations of the evaluation (such as the need for unobtrusive data gathering or the participation necessary by other organizations), especially if these will affect several other aspects of the evaluation's design.

STEP TWO: Describe What Information Will Be Needed

Simply stated, this is where you describe the kind and content of the information that is needed to meet the purposes for the evaluation. This step is especially critical if the preceding discussion of what is going to be evaluated has been only general in nature. Some authors call this selecting the "indicators" for the evaluation. It really means specifying the type of evidence that one is going to accept in determining whether an objective is met or a question has been answered. It may not be necessary to describe all of the information that will probably be collected, but at least some illustrations for each major question or objective should be provided. An example of a commonly used "indicator" is participant results on various tests. Another may be the number and characteristics of people who complete the project. It is important in completing this step that the focus be on *what* evidence will be collected or used, rather than *how* it will be obtained.

STEP THREE: Describe Where the Information Will Be Obtained

The intended sources for the desired information should be mentioned, at least briefly. Examples of possible sources include project participants, project staff records, historical files on the participants, data banks of other organizations and so forth. It may also be helpful to include a few words about the appropriateness of these sources, keeping in mind issues such as availability, cost, potential bias and so forth.

TABLE 1   EVALUATION

EXAMPLE OF OUTLINE FOR AN EVALUATION PLAN*

Step	Question
1. Objectives/Issues	What questions are being asked?
2. Information Requirements	What information is needed to answer the questions?
3. Information Source	From whom can the necessary information be secured?
4. Instruments	What can be used to find the answer?
5. Design	Who will complete the instruments and what comparisons may be made?
6. Time Schedule	When will the information be collected, analyzed and reported?
7. Analysis	What do we do with the data?
8. Report	Who needs to know about it?

*Adapted from a discussion by Owens and Evans (1978).

TABLE 2   **EVALUATION**

ALTERNATE EXAMPLE OF OUTLINE FOR AN EVALUATION PLAN*

I. Rationale (Why is this evaluation being done?)

II. Objectives of the Evaluation Study

    A. What will be the product(s) of the evaluation study?

    B. What audiences will be served by the evaluation study?

III. Description of the Program Being Evaluated

    A. Philosophy behind the program

    B. Content of the program

    C. Objectives of the program, implicit and explicit

    D. Program procedures (strategies, media, etc.)

    E. Students

    F. Community (federal, state, local) and instructional context of program

IV. Evaluation Design

    A. Constraints on evaluation design

    B. General organizational plan (or model) for program evaluation

    C. Evaluative questions

    D. Information required to answer the questions

    E. Sources of information; methods for collecting information

    F. Data collection schedule

    G. Techniques for analysis of collected information

    H. Standards; bases for judging quality

    I. Reporting procedures

    J. Proposed budget

V. Description of Final Report

    A. Outline of report(s) to be produced by evaluator

    B. Usefulness of the products of the study

    C. Conscious biases of evaluator that may be inadvertently injected into the final report

TABLE 3

EVALUATION

EXAMPLE OF A WORKSHEET DEVELOPED TO EVALUATE A PROCESS OBJECTIVE*

Objective	Teachers in the Webster reading program will participate in a four-day training workshop to learn the purposes of the curriculum and how to effectively implement it.
Information Require- ments	1. A copy of the training workshop design (including purposes, expected outcomes and teaching strategies). 2. Names of the workshop staff and of the teachers scheduled to attend.
Information Source	1. Workshop staff. 3. Workshop observer. 2. Workshop participants.
Instruments	1. Observation schedule. 3. Workshop participant questionnaire. 2. Pretest and posttest for participants. 4. Attendance sheet.
Design	1. Pre- and post-administration of the knowledge test. 2. The evaluator will attend the session and complete the observation schedule. 3. Participants will complete the questionnaire and the daily attendance sheets. 4. Workshop staff will be interviewed after the workshop.
Time Schedule	1. Pretest to be administered as the first activity. 2. Posttest to be administered as the last activity. 3. The evaluator will complete the observation schedule on the first and third mornings, and the second and fourth afternoons. 4. The questionnaire will be given the last afternoon before the posttest.
Analysis	1. A pretest analysis will be done indicating the participants' general level of knowledge about reading instruction prior to the workshop. 2. A "t" test will be used to determine if a significant growth in participants' knowledge occurred. 3. A tabulation of observations will be made to determine the level of involvement of workshop participants and the degree of congruency between the workshop plan and its implementation. 4. The questionnaire will be tabulated to determine the participants' view of how well they understand the purposes of the new curriculum and how to effectively implement it. 5. Participants' attendance will be summarized to indicate the average daily attendance in relation to the number of teachers scheduled to attend the workshop. 6. Workshop staff interviews will be summarized in narrative fashion.
Report	1. An oral report by the morning of the second day indicating the general areas of strengths and weaknesses of the participants based on their pretest results. 2. An oral debriefing by the evaluator based on observation notes on the day after the workshop. 3. A written report to the project director, superintendent and school board reporting the complete evaluation findings regarding the workshop and the participants' suggestions for future training.

*Quoted from Owens and Evans (1977).

TABLE 4

EVALUATION

EXAMPLE OF A WORKSHEET DEVELOPED FOR A PRODUCT OBJECTIVE*

Objective	By the end of the school year, the fourth grade program students will have made significant growth in reading as measured by the Woodcock Reading Test.
Information Requirements	The reading scores for the fourth grade students administered at the beginning and end of the school year and the test norms.
Information Source	The fourth grade students.
Instrument	Woodcock Reading Test.
Design	Pretest/posttest.
Time Schedule	Pretest—September 15 -18. Posttest—May 12-16.
Analysis	Compute a "t" test to determine if a significant growth occurred. The test publisher's norms may also be useful to provide a descriptive level, in terms of grade equivalent scores, of the group's pretest and posttest means.
Report	Final report submitted to superintendent and funding agency.

*Quoted from Owens and Evans (1977).

STEP FOUR: What Instruments Will Be Used to Get the Information

If the evaluation intends to build from carefully constructed objectives, then the methods or instruments to be used for evaluation will already be imbedded in such statements. Often, though, the measurement technique concocted when the objectives were written are not subjected to careful analysis.

It will by useful, perhaps essential, to review the fundamental issues of measurement when developing this element of the evaluation component. A basic text of particular value is *Quasi-Experimentation: Design and Analysis Issues for Field Settings* (Cook and Campbell, 1979). For those structuring evaluation of educational projects, two documents that will assist in this review are *A Procedural Guide for Validating Achievement Gains in Educational Projects* (Horst and Tallmadge, 1976) and *A Practical Guide to Measuring Project Impact on Student Achievement* (Horst, Tallmadge and Wood, 1976).

It is also important to recognize that evaluation methodology is currently shifting towards techniques that are essentially descriptive as opposed to the traditional quantitative, experimental-design approaches. A useful discussion of these newer approaches can be found in *Qualitative Evaluation Methods* (Patton, 1980).

The following narrative discusses some of the problems commonly experienced in choosing instrumentation. It is deliberately general because of the variety of issues that must be considered in selecting from among methodologies.

1) What sorts of things should an evaluation try to measure? Measurement is, in its simplest form, a deliberate sampling of behavior. Programs dealing with humans are typically analyzed from three perspectives: cognitive (thought) processes, affective (feeling) processes, and psychomotor (movement) processes. All of these processes can be measured by sampling what people say or do, that is, by sampling behavior.

2) Isn't it more difficult to sample affective behavior than physical or cognitive behavior? Not really. Actually, no measurement is a direct and perfect assessment of what is taking place in a person. There is no way of knowing whether physi-

cal or paper-pencil test behavior is entirely representative of the behavior of the person studied. Measurements of values, attitudes, and preferences are sometimes controversial; but affective changes are no more "unmeasurable" than physical or cognitive changes. Any form of measurement that is well conceived and well performed adds accuracy and precision to our observations and intuitions. It is sometimes difficult to find existing instruments to measure affective changes, but that is not a suitable rationale for ignoring this aspect of behavior.

3) How can one find out what instruments already exist? Almost every discipline has catalogs, reference documents, bibliographies, annual directories or even computerized information systems which will provide clues to instruments, whether quantitative or descriptive, that have been used by others in the past. A local university or college library is probably the best place to start looking for such materials. Journals and other periodicals also frequently contain articles describing results obtained from more recently developed instruments.

4) What if an existing instrument is not available? This is often a serious problem, since the advantages of proven techniques (particularly if they are standardized or have been subjected to extensive field-testing) are often overshadowed by their disadvantages (cost and inapplicability to the project's objectives). Anxious project developers are often guilty, however, of committing one of two serious errors when existing instruments are unavailable.

● They revise their objectives and procedures, usually by narrowing the focus, to make them more conveniently measured by existing tests; or

● They propose the construction or use of new instruments without consideration of the time and money that may be needed to test the appropriateness and technical soundness of such devices.

Both errors should be avoided. The basic rule to follow when an existing technique or instrument is not available is: proceed with caution to construct a locally validated and reliable method of measurement or documentation and make certain its development and use are guided by professionally qualified staff.

5) What is meant by "technical soundness" of an instrument? The terms *validity* and *reliability* are commonly used when describing the technical adequacy of a test or measurement device. Both concepts are rather complex and the novice should definitely do some additional reading if these terms are unfamiliar. But a few observations are provided to give a flavor of why these issues are important.

Validity refers to the degree to which an instrument measures what it is supposed to measure and not something else. Supposing that the project is developing material that is designed to teach the student some new information in science, an instrument would be said to have "face validity" if it were determined that it actually tested the intended skills, knowledge or behavior they were designed to be taught through the project's materials.

In some cases, tests that are apparently valid, or even standardized, may be entirely inappropriate. Consider the impact several years ago when multi-linguistic children were inappropriately classified for instruction based on the outcomes of "valid," but culturally insensitive intelligence tests. Common sense and logic, therefore, are indispensable tools in constructing a valid measuring instrument.

Reliability refers to the accuracy of an instrument and the degree to which it is free from random or capricious errors. If a reading test were administered to a group on two consecutive days, for example, and the results showed a one-year average increase in reading ability, one would question the reliability of the instrument. Detailed analysis of the test would probably reveal a number of questions that were ambiguous, irrelevant or misleading; students undoubtedly guessed at the answers and, by sheer chance, did better on the second test, or they may have learned how to "take the test" the first time it was administered and naturally improved their performance. Most measurement books provide several techniques for determining the reliability of instruments. But again, if locally developed instruments are to be constructed and used, these techniques should be chosen and administered by individuals who know what they are doing.

Individuals who are working with instruments other than tests sometimes forget that reliability and validity are important constructs for any information gathering device that purports to accurately measure or describe a particular phenomenon or behavior. A good discussion of technical considerations when developing and/or using instruments such as attitudinal scales or questionnaires is provided by Dawes (1972).

Another aspect of technical adequacy which writers sometimes overlook is the importance of the conditions under which instruments are used. A perfectly valid and reliable device can produce totally inaccurate and misleading results if it is either used incorrectly or if contamination factors are not identified and controlled. Examples of issues which are commonly addressed include ways in which the project's evaluation will guard against: a) results obtained through the normal maturation of participants, or exposure to experiences other than those provided in the project; b) the impact of a decrease or increase in the number of participants; c) learning that occurs when participants take a pre-test, translated into higher scores when they take a post-test; d) particular characteristics of the participants (such as high or low intelligence or varying socio-economic characteristics) that will influence the ability to generalize results to a larger population; and e) results obtained simply because the participant or phenomenon are under study. Called the "Hawthorne Effect," this last problem is one which frequently crops up in externally funded projects.

6) *What kind of instruments are appropriate for which uses?* There is no well established list of instruments that are recommended for each type of objective, since methodology is so dependent on the logic and purpose of the type of information desired. Looking at the kinds of instruments that have been used in similar projects or talking to an individual with more in-depth skills in measurement are two sources you can consult to answer this question. It is recommended, however, that you consider the inclusion of at least two or more forms of measurement for the critical objectives or evaluative questions of the project.

The need for considering the use of several types of instruments is caused both by the imprecision which exists in the measurement field (remember, most instruments only provide estimates of what is taking place) and the need to make certain that significant types of behavior are adequately documented. As noted before, most measurement is simply a sampling of behavior. The more samples obtained, the more useful the results.

7) *What can one do if it is impossible to determine reliability or validity of an instrument?* One common response to this problem is to indicate that such evaluation findings are intended to be "exploratory" or "tentative." While such admissions may salve the writer's conscience, they don't address the basic problem of how much confidence anyone can have in the resulting data.

Another, more preferred, approach is to select means of measurement more appropriate to the local capability. For example, there are a number of measurement techniques that are widely accepted in educational and social programs but that are not subjected to the same rigorous tests of validity and reliability. Many of these are "unobtrusive measures"—observations of behavior (e.g. seating arrangements, conversational patterns, frequency of attendance and so forth) made without the subject's awareness that they are being documented. Other "measurements" that are widely used are analyses of historical and file data, minutes of meetings, correspondence, budget reports and so forth. One of the most powerful measuring techniques is the interview. As many foundation executives will tell you, a probing, perceptive questioner can often obtain more "facts" about a project than a dozen tests.

STEP FIVE: Describe the Intended Analysis

Most evaluative results will be subjected to some type of statistical and/or theoretical analysis and the general techniques to be used should be briefly described in the proposal. Again, most funding sources do not expect an exhaustive listing of the intended treatments because they assume that some of this will have to be determined after the project is in place. But it is important that the evaluation component contain some discussion on this point both to a) demonstrate the technical competence of the applicant, and b) indicate the types of information which are liable to result from the analysis.

STEP SIX: Complete the Evaluation Design

As shown in Table 2, most of the elements to be included in the evaluation's design have already been addressed in preceding steps. But there may be some additional factors that have not yet been considered. If so, they should by addressed at this point. Examples include: a description of the timeline for conducting the evaluation (this can be modeled on the techniques described in Chapter 9);

a discussion of standards to be used in judging the results of the evaluation (such as how much deviation from the project's intended outcomes will be tolerated before a modification in procedures and/or materials is undertaken); what kinds of comparisons will be made among different results obtained during the evaluation; how matters of participant privacy will be handled; and, finally, who will be responsible for administering and/or carrying out the necessary evaluation.

This last point is especially significant because most funding sources want to know whether the evaluation will be conducted solely by project staff, by consultants or by a mix of both. This detail is also important in justifying the necessary resource requests.

Table 5 provides an example of how one school district displayed its intended distribution of responsibility among project staff and consultants.

STEP SEVEN: Describe the Intended Reporting and Utilization

Either within the overall evaluation design or as a separate element, you should provide some information on how findings will be reported and how they will be used. In preparing this discussion, it is useful to:

● Separate out the various audiences which the evaluation will serve (i.e. project staff vs. funding source).

● Distinguish between the reporting process and its intended products.

In talking about formative evaluation, for example, you might indicate that the primary audience of these findings will be the project staff and they they will be given an oral briefing every week on the status of evaluation findings. Once a month, they will be given a written report that describes the effectiveness of key processes or project materials. It might be suggested then, that the staff and the external evaluator will periodically meet to develop recommendations to the project director about necessary modifications and changes.

In the case of summative evaluation, the audience will mainly be the funding source. The proposal might indicate that the funders will be given both an annual report and an end-of-the-project report. The annual report will be used to help make judgments

TABLE 5   **EVALUATION**

EVALUATION RESPONSIBILITIES OF THE PROJECT STAFF AND OF AN EXTERNAL EVALUATOR*

Task	Project Staff	External Evaluator
Coordination	Designate a person to coordinate the evaluation responsibilities for the program.	Designate an evaluation person as a primary contact for working with this program.
Evaluation Plan	Review the general evaluation plan and revise as necessary to fit the project. Return the revised plan to the external evaluator.	1. Prepare a general evaluation plan in cooperation with the project staff. 2. Revise and approve the project's revised evaluation plan.
Instrumentation	1. Reproduce required copies of all evaluation instruments. 2. Order required copies of standardized instruments and answer sheets. 3. Develop any local monitoring or evaluation instruments. 4. Obtain a review and approval for use of each proposed evaluation instrument.	1. Prepare a draft copy of all instruments to be used. 2. Provide the project with a specimen set of standardized instruments to be used together with cost information and an order blank. 3. Review any project-developed instruments if requested by the staff.
Data Collection	1. Schedule and administer all evaluation instruments identified in the evaluation plan. 2. Collect and code file data specified in the plan. 3. Code responses to all instruments where needed. 4. Mail a duplicate copy of all code sheets to the external evaluator for computer processing.	1. Provide the project with a schedule and design for data collection. 2. Provide written directions for administering nonstandardized evaluation instruments. 3. Prepare common codes and coding directions for all answer sheets and data collection forms.
Data Analysis	Identify if there is any special data analysis the staff would like to have run that has not already been included in the evaluation plan.	1. Verify the correct scoring and/or coding of all instruments. 2. Keypunch the data. 3. Provide scoring services. 4. Analyze the data.
Reporting	1. Identify the information needs of the people in the project if they have changed since the evaluation plan was prepared. 2. Review the draft evaluation report for any factual errors or misrepresentations. 3. Print the required number of evaluation reports and abstracts.	1. Prepare a draft copy of the evaluation report and give it to the project evaluation coordinator for review. 2. Prepare a final camera-ready copy of the evaluation report. 3. Prepare a camera-ready copy of an evaluation report abstract.

*Adapted from Owens & Evans (1977).

about project refunding, with the final report used to judge the overall effectiveness and impact of the program. Some writers feel it is a good idea to briefly outline the intended format for these reports in the proposal so that there is no basis for later misunderstandings on the type and amount of information to be shared.

Other audiences to be mentioned might include a project's advisory council, the applicant's organization, and the project's participants. It is important that any significant users of the evaluation be identified and their reporting needs at least described in general terms so that adequate justification is given for budgetary requests to serve these purposes.

STEP EIGHT: Putting It All Together

Tables 3 and 4 provide examples of a worksheet that can be used to capture decisions as each of the preceding steps is completed. While such worksheets may not actually be displayed in the proposal itself, they are a useful way to structure the planning process and to make certain that a plan of action is developed for each major objective or evaluative question.

The results of these sheets can then be summarized in the proposal using the formats suggested earlier.

SOME FINAL COMMENTS

Requirements for extensive documentation of evaluation plans are most commonly found in experimental education and social service projects or proposals to governmental sources. Increasingly, though, private foundations ask questions such as: "How will you know if this project is successful?" or, "What plans do you have for monitoring project performance?" Even proposals for new business ventures typically ask for a description of anticipated methods of quality control or project development feedback.

As noted earlier, evaluation requires people, time and dollar resources. If these are not identified and secured at the outset, they will undoubtedly have to be "contributed" by the project staff's own organization. Given that the costs of project evaluation typically range between 10 and 20 percent of the entire budget, their omission can be an expensive lesson.

However, the best reason for doing a careful job of planning evaluation during the proposal stage is that evaluation is an essential element of competent management. Earlier in the book, reference was made to Alice's famous remark: "If you don't know where you are going, any road will take you there." Likewise, if you haven't planned evaluation, you may never know if you arrived.

CHAPTER REFERENCES

Cook, T., and D. Campbell, *Quasi-Experimentation: Design and Analysis Issues for Field Settings* (New York: Rand McNally, 1979).

Dawes, R., *Fundamentals of Attitude Measurement* (New York: Wiley, 1972).

Horst, D.P., and G.K. Tallmadge, *A Procedural Guide for Validating Achievement Gains in Educational Projects*, Monograph Series on Evaluation in Education, no. 2 (Washington, D.C.: Government Printing Office, 1976).

Horst, D.P., G.K. Tallmadge, and C.T. Wood, *A Practical Guide to Measuring Project Impact on Student Achievement*, Monograph Series on Evaluation in Education, no. 1 (Washington, D.C.: Government Printing Office, 1976).

Joint Committee on Standards for Educational Evaluation, *Standards for Evaluation of Educational Programs, Projects and Materials* (New York: McGraw-Hill, 1981).

Owens, T.R., and W.D.Evans, *Program Evaluation Skills for Busy Administrators* (Portland, OR: Northwest Regional Educational Laboratory, 1977), 39 and 40.

Patton, M., *Qualitative Evaluation Methods* (Beverly Hills CA: Sage, 1980).

Scriven, M., "Definitions, Explanations, and Theories," in *Minnesota Studies in the Philosophy of Science*, vol. 11, ed. H. Feigl, M. Scriven and G. Maxwell (Minneapolis, MN: University of Minnesota Press, 1958).

_____, "The Methodology of Evaluation,"in *Curriculum Evaluation*, ed. R.E. Stake, American Educational Research Association Monograph Series on Evaluation, no.1. (Chicago: Rand McNally, 1967).

Stufflebeam, D.L., and A.J.Shrinkfield, *Systematic Evaluation: A Self-Instructional Guide to Theory and Practice* (Hingham, MA: Kluwer Academic Publishers, 1985).

Van Maanen, J., *The Process of Program Evaluation, Reprint Series on Management* (Los Angeles: The Grantsmanship Center, 1979).

Worthen, B.R., and J.R.Sanders, *Educational Evaluation: Theory and Practice.* (Worthington, OH: Charles A. Jones Publishing Company, 1973).

A CHECKLIST FOR JUDGING THE ADEQUACY OF AN EVALUATION DESIGN

Directions: For each question below, check whether the evaluation design has clearly met the criterion (Yes), has clearly not met the criterion (No), or cannot be clearly determined (?). Check NA if the criterion does not apply to the evaluation design being reviewed. Use the Elaboration column to provide further explanation for criterion where a <u>No</u> or a <u>?</u> has been checked. The word "program" will be used to mean the program, project or product being evaluated.

Criterion	Criterion Met				Elaboration
	Yes	No	?	N/A	

I. CRITERIA REGARDING THE ADEQUACY OF THE EVALUATION CONCEPTUALIZATION

A. Conceptual Clarity and Adequacy

	Yes	No	?	N/A
1. Is an adequate description of the whole program presented?	❑	❑	❑	❑
2. Is a clear description given of the part of the program being evaluated?	❑	❑	❑	❑
3. Is a clear description of the evaluation approach given? (e.g., comparison group study, single group study, goal-free evaluation, formative, summative, etc.)	❑	❑	❑	❑
4. Is the evaluation approach adequate and appropriate for evaluating the program?	❑	❑	❑	❑
Based on the above, do you feel the evaluation is clearly and adequately conceived?	❑	❑	❑	❑

B. Scope

	Yes	No	?	N/A
1. Are the intended outcomes or goals of the program clearly specified?	❑	❑	❑	❑
2. Is the scope of the evaluation broad enough to gather information concerning all specified program outcomes?	❑	❑	❑	❑
3. Are any likely unintended effects from the program described?	❑	❑	❑	❑
4. Is the approach of the evaluation broad enough to include measuring these unintended effects?	❑	❑	❑	❑
5. Is adequate cost information about the program included in the scope of the evaluation?	❑	❑	❑	❑
Based on the above, do you feel the evaluation is adequate in scope?	❑	❑	❑	❑

C. Relevance

	Yes	No	?	N/A
1. Are the audiences for the evaluation identified?	❑	❑	❑	❑
2. Are the objectives of the evaluation explained?	❑	❑	❑	❑
3. Are the objectives of the evaluation congruent with the information needs of the intended audiences?	❑	❑	❑	❑

Note: This checklist has been reproduced without citation in a variety of documents.
Apologies are given in advance to whomever was the original author.

	Criterion Met				Elaboration
	Yes	No	?	N/A	
4. Does the information to be provided allow necessary decisions about the program or product to be made?	❏	❏	❏	❏	
Based on the above, do you feel the information provided is relevant to and adequately serves the needs of the intended audience?	❏	❏	❏	❏	

D. Flexibility

	Yes	No	?	N/A	
1. Can the design be adapted easily to accommodate changes in plans?	❏	❏	❏	❏	
2. Are known constraints or parameters on the evaluation discussed thoroughly?	❏	❏	❏	❏	
3. Can useful information be obtained in the face of unforeseen constraints, e.g., non-cooperation of control groups?	❏	❏	❏	❏	
Based on the above, do you feel the evaluation study allows for new information needs to be met as they arise?	❏	❏	❏	❏	

E. Feasibility

	Yes	No	?	N/A	
1. Are the evaluation resources (time, money and personnel) adequate to carry out the projected activities?	❏	❏	❏	❏	
2. Are management plans specified for conducting the evaluation?	❏	❏	❏	❏	
3. Has adequate planning been done to support the feasibility of conducting complex activities?	❏	❏	❏	❏	
Based on the above, do you feel the evaluation can be carried out as planned?	❏	❏	❏	❏	

II. CRITERIA CONCERNING THE ADEQUACY OF THE COLLECTION AND PROCESSING OF INFORMATION

A. Reliability

	Yes	No	?	N/A	
1. Are data collection procedures described well and was care taken to assure minimal error?	❏	❏	❏	❏	
2. Are scoring or coding procedures objective?	❏	❏	❏	❏	
3. Are the evaluation instruments reliable? (i.e., is reliability information included?)	❏	❏	❏	❏	
Based on the above, do you feel that if the evaluation were conducted again the results would turn out the same?	❏	❏	❏	❏	

B. Objectivity

	Yes	No	?	N/A	
1. Have attempts to control for bias in data collection and processing been described?	❏	❏	❏	❏	

	Criterion Met				Elaboration
	Yes	No	?	N/A	
2. Are sources of information clearly specified?	❏	❏	❏	❏	
3. Do the biases of the evaluators preclude an objective evaluation?	❏	❏	❏	❏	
Based on the above, do you feel adequate steps have been taken to ensure objectivity in the various aspects of the evaluation?	❏	❏	❏	❏	

C. Representativeness

	Yes	No	?	N/A	
1. Are the data collection instruments valid?	❏	❏	❏	❏	
2. Are the data collection instruments appropriate for the purposes of this evaluation?	❏	❏	❏	❏	
3. Does the evaluation adequately address the questions it was intended to answer?	❏	❏	❏	❏	
Based on the above, do you feel the information collection and processing procedures ensure that the results accurately represent the program?	❏	❏	❏	❏	

D. Generalizability

	Yes	No	?	N/A	
1. Are sampling techniques adequate to permit generalizations to the population of interest?	❏	❏	❏	❏	
2. Does the cultural context of data collection techniques affect generalization?	❏	❏	❏	❏	
3. Are the inferential statistics employed appropriate for the sample, data and the questions to be answered?	❏	❏	❏	❏	
Based on the above, do you feel the information collected can be generalized when necessary?	❏	❏	❏	❏	

III. CRITERIA CONCERNING THE ADEQUACY OF THE PRESENTATION AND REPORTING OF INFORMATION

A. Timeliness

	Yes	No	?	N/A	
1. Have efficient reporting techniques been used to meet the needs of the clients?	❏	❏	❏	❏	
2. Does the time schedule for reporting meet the needs of the audience?	❏	❏	❏	❏	
Based on the above, do you feel the information is timely enough to be of use to the client?	❏	❏	❏	❏	

B. Pervasiveness

	Yes	No	?	N/A	
1. Is information disseminated to all intended audiences?	❏	❏	❏	❏	
2. Are contractual constraints on dissemination of evaluation information observed?	❏	❏	❏	❏	

	Criterion Met				Elaboration
	Yes	**No**	**?**	**N/A**	

3. Are attempts being made to make the evaluation information available to relevant audiences beyond those specified in the contract? ❏ ❏ ❏ ❏

Based on the above, do you feel that information is being provided to all who need it? ❏ ❏ ❏ ❏

IV. GENERAL CRITERIA

A. Ethical Considerations

1. Do test administration procedures follow professional standards of ethics? ❏ ❏ ❏ ❏

2. Have protection of human subjects guidelines been followed? ❏ ❏ ❏ ❏

3. Has confidentiality of data been guaranteed? ❏ ❏ ❏ ❏

Based on the above, do you feel the evaluation study strictly follows professional standards of ethics? ❏ ❏ ❏ ❏

B. Protocol

1. Are appropriate persons contacted in the appropriate sequence? ❏ ❏ ❏ ❏

2. Are departmental policies and procedures to be followed? ❏ ❏ ❏ ❏

Based on the above, do you feel appropriate protocol steps were planned? ❏ ❏ ❏ ❏

DISSEMINATION

This chapter describes the need for dissemination activities, discusses their inclusion in the proposal document, provides examples of dissemination techniques and lists some guidelines for planning dissemination. It also discusses the issue of references to planned publicity in applications to private sources.

The cynic sometimes feels that the relative emphasis on dissemination activities can be predicted by assessing the amount of criticism funding sources are receiving from legislative bodies or the public: during periods of complaint, there is a great demand for dissemination efforts; in more tranquil times, dissemination is afforded little attention.

This comment points out that there are sound political as well as professional and programmatic reasons behind requests from funding agencies to include dissemination activities in proposals. Funding sources, faced with increasing pressure to justify their expenditures, insist in turn that the recipients of their largess do their share in demonstrating that changes occurred, impacts happened, and new knowledge was produced.

Dissemination activities thus become one of the products of a project. This product magnifies the results of the project by sharing it with a wider audience and maximizes its use to society.

THE NEED FOR DISSEMINATION

None of these remarks should be construed as an attempt to slight what indeed are very serious problems: How do we decrease the gap between research and utilization? How do we share the results of a project with others who are dealing with the same problem? How do we avoid using up scarce resources to either discover the same knowledge or repeat the same mistakes? How do we try to reduce problems of concern by making more effective use of new insights, technology, products or other results from funded studies?

That these problems have assumed increasing importance is seen by the nationwide trend in recent years of devoting larger percentages of project budgets to this function, and in many cases, of supporting proposals whose sole purpose is to conduct dissemination or information-exchange activities. As noted earlier, it is obvious that one trend in the grants and contract field is a major shift from primary preoccupation with the *production* of new knowledge to a much greater emphasis on knowledge *dissemination* and *utilization*. This trend has affected what must be included in research proposals as well as in applications for other types of projects.

HOW MUCH DISSEMINATION?

The extent of dissemination will, of course, be dictated by the nature of the project.

Projects that are intended to produce well-tested products of regional or national significance should have an extensive dissemination plan. In fact, writers of proposals for these types of projects might well consider asking the funding source whether it would be possible to add a year or two to the proposed project. This additional time would be used to not only do an effective job of dissemination, but conduct appropriate training for potential users of the information.

Workaday programs which develop a service in one community which is similar to efforts already under way in many other settings may need less post-project information-sharing.

Research projects that are intended to produce highly exploratory or tentative results might be described only to select academic or technical audiences. But studies which produce more significant or general findings might, in addition, be shared with potential users such as policymakers, development/ demonstration organizations or practitioners in the field.

CONSTRAINTS ON DISSEMINATION

As one of the final steps in preparing the project application, you must develop an appropriate and effective dissemination approach. The strategy should be influenced by the importance of the expected results, the instructions of the funding source, the nature of intended users and limitations such as available resources or capabilities of the anticipated project staff.

This last point is frequently overlooked, yet it can have a profound impact. Effective dissemination is just as specialized a field as other aspects of project management or operation. It requires its own unique sets of knowledge, skills, experiences and predispositions. We are all familiar with the case of individuals who obviously know their disciplines well but are simply incapable of transmitting this knowledge to others. It may be necessary to hire a consultant for this aspect of the project. In fact, if the dissemination activities are expected to be an important part of the project, you should seriously consider involving other organizations who specialize in dissemination-type activities. This involvement should be sought in the preparation of the proposal as well as in later project operation.

IMPACT ON THE PROPOSAL

After thinking through an appropriate dissemination strategy, you should consider where this approach should be reflected in the proposal document itself. There are at least three possible ways of handling this:

● A separate section of the proposal, labeled "dissemination," can be prepared to include information on the need for dissemination, appropriate objec-

tives, procedures, evaluation and staffing. Budget information would, of course, be included with the regular fiscal component of the application.

● The necessary information on dissemination can be inserted, where appropriate, in other components of the proposal. Using this approach, for example, the dissemination methodology might simply be an element in the description of the project's procedures.

● A combination of the two above approaches can be developed. For example, objectives dealing with dissemination would be included in the discussion of project outcomes. However, details on the need for information-sharing, the proposed dissemination and its approach, and necessary evaluation would be presented in a separate component.

The format selected for presenting the dissemination plan is normally a matter of personal preference. However, if the funding source has shown a special interest in knowledge utilization or dissemination in the past or includes a specific request in its application for details on dissemination, you should make certain that this function is described in some detail and presented in a section that is distinct and clearly labeled.

Some other guidelines include:

● If the dissemination activities are of an innovative nature or will result in specific products (such as a film or training package), these should be identified as expected project outcomes and given specific visibility as planned objectives.

● If the dissemination involves an extensive set of activities (using considerable time and resources) or involves the use of unproven or exemplary strategies, some method of monitoring the results of this investment and approach should be included in the project's evaluation plan.

● The specific staff, consultants or sub-contractors who will be responsible for dissemination should always be identified.

● Major events in the dissemination process should be flagged on the project's timeline. If these activities are complex, then a separate diagram showing their flow and interaction with other project activities might be included.

SOME EXAMPLES OF DISSEMINATION TECHNIQUES

The specific techniques chosen for dissemination should match the types of impact or outcomes desired. For example, if the purpose of the dissemination plan is simply to *inform* others about the project's operation and its results, then techniques such as newsletters, articles, reports, conferences and so forth may be appropriate.

On the other hand, if the purpose of dissemination is to encourage audiences to actually *use* project results, then more extensive and dramatic strategies may be warranted, such as on-site demonstrations, press conferences, multi-media presentations showing products in use, briefings for policymakers, training sessions or workshops teaching others to adapt or adopt project materials.

The following descriptions of alternative dissemination techniques are presented purely as a shopping list of possible approaches. The list includes examples of the types of things that have been found in proposals in the past.

● A project newsletter that is circulated to selected organizations and individuals in the field.

● Conferences or seminars hosted for individuals and groups that might be interested in project results.

● Site visits arranged for representatives of key professional associations, members of the media or other agencies involved with similar problems.

● Interim working papers to describe those portions of project findings of most immediate interest to other audiences.

● Papers delivered at national conferences.

● Articles prepared for scholarly journals or periodicals or, if appropriate, for publications of more general circulation.

● Pamphlets describing available project products and their potential use which are mailed to appropriate recipients throughout the country.

● Books or manuals issued by the applicant organization, the funding source or commercial publishers.

● Demonstrations of techniques or materials developed by the project at meetings, conferences or sites of potential adopters.

● Agreements with other agencies or commercial firms to produce and market project results or to undertake further development and refinement.

● Production of audiovisual materials such as films, slide shows, filmstrips, video-tapes or television programs.

● Special briefings for key national or state officials, or other policymakers.

● Project staff appearances as speakers at local, state, regional or national meetings.

● Press conferences or the preparation of press releases for use with the mass media.

● Filing of project documents with national information sources and services of the type described in Chapter 3.

● The development of a model course or seminar which shows how the information resulting from the project can be explained to others in a formal instructional setting. (Sometimes this approach also includes the development of a special textbook, collection of readings or other materials to be utilized in the course.)

● The development of "traveling exhibits" to showcase the materials in other similar organizations around the country.

● The training of individuals in other organizations to conduct in-service workshops or provide consultative services on project materials to practitioners.

● The development of self-instructional modules that will allow others to learn how to use project results without attendance at formal training sessions.

Examples of possible approaches are almost endless and limited only by the creativity and resources available to the proposal writer. The necessity for thinking through the best approach cannot be overemphasized, however. Frequently, a particularly innovative and exciting dissemination strategy will be the deciding factor in securing funds for a project which in all other respects is similar to other applications received on the same topic.

SOME OTHER CONSIDERATIONS

Thus far, the discussion has dealt with dissemination needed to publicize the program to a wider external audience. But there is also a need to consider what dissemination or communication activities will be needed for the project staff internally and for the community in which the project is taking place. These are both important audiences. They must be kept informed about what is happening within the project, and their support, backing and involvement should be consistently encouraged. Again, the approach taken and the amount of resources devoted will depend on the nature and scope of the project. Once this is identified, it should be appropriately displayed within the proposal and sufficient detail provided to justify requested resources.

There are many other questions which must be considered in the design of the dissemination strategy. This discussion cannot be exhaustive, but is illustrative of the types of issues which should not be overlooked.

❑ Is it important to involve the potential information users or receivers in the planning of the dissemination program?

❑ Have provisions been made to collect information necessary to help potential users assess the applicability of project results to their own situations?

❑ Is there a theoretical or conceptual base for the dissemination plan?

❑ Should this be described in the proposal and, if so, have sufficient references to prior research or experience been provided to justify this base?

❑ Do the dissemination activities of the project need to be coordinated with those of another organization or group?

❑ Will the dissemination activities stimulate a significant number of inquiries or contacts from other individuals and groups? How will these be handled, and are sufficient resources available?

❑ Are the values and objectives of the project liable to be viewed as offensive or upsetting by other individuals and groups? Have techniques for preventing opposition or dealing with complaints been devised?

❑ Does the dissemination strategy reflect a recognition of the adoption stages (i.e. awareness, interest, evaluation, trial and adoption/adaption) and of the characteristics of the potential adopters (i.e. innovators, early adopters, early majority adopters, late majority adopters, and laggards)?

❑ Is the proposed strategy flexible so that it can be modified during the project's operation if necessary? What phases of the approach are most subject to possible change and should these be flagged in the application?

❑ Have provisions been made to determine and record the relative effectiveness of various strategies and communications in order to alter strategies as the situation changes?

❑ Should techniques be included to verify the informational needs and preferences of those for whom dissemination is planned?

❑ Does the technique provide for soliciting feedback and, if so, how will this information be used?

❑ Have the decision-making timelines of potential users been considered?

❑ Will the dissemination plan get the necessary information to those who want it when they can use it?

❑ Have alternative dissemination techniques been included if diverse audiences are to be reached?

In summary, the dissemination component of a proposal can be an important element in the success of an application. Because it may be one of the last elements of the project to be planned, the tendency may be to minimize or ignore its significance. But because of recent trends in funding, you should avoid a hasty or ill-designed description. An approach should be chosen which is appropriate to the outcomes and scope of the project, responsive to the interests of the funding source, considerate of staff capabilities and other limitations, suitable to available resources and, above all, effective in achieving its intended impact.

PUBLICITY FOR THE FUNDING SOURCE

A related issue is the degree to which it is important to signal in an application that some type of effort will be made to give public recognition to the grantor. This question is most frequently raised by those applying for the first time to private foundations and corporations.

There are a variety of opinions in the private sector on both the importance and tastefulness of such publicity. Corporate donors, who after all are frequently using their stockholders' resources for grantmaking, believe that some attention to project publicity by the applicant is a reasonable expectation. Many of them tend to look on their grants as "investments," with at least one expected result being appropriate public recognition of the firm's community citizenship.

Others, especially small family foundations, sometimes make their grants anonymously and would be offended by an extensive description in an application of plans to publicize their gifts.

Since attitudes vary so much about this sensitive issue, it is best to try to determine the funding source's, expectations for publicity during the preproposal phase. Handle this tactfully. Most donors will naturally say "no," if you ask: "Will the extent of the publicity you receive influence your decision on giving us a grant?" A better approach might be to say: "We are thinking of holding a press conference to recognize all of our project donors. Do you think this is a good idea?" If they say "yes," you can go on to explore other ways in which the project might secure recognition. Remember, public awareness of what you are doing is as much in your own agency's self-interest as it is a benefit for those who provide you with the funds.

Many organizations do not know how to secure publicity. Increasingly, major daily newspapers and television stations have handouts available describing how to secure news coverage of such projects. An example is the *Media Access Guide* developed jointly by the *Seattle Times* and Metrocenter YMCA. Some have persons on their staff who will meet with you to discuss the best means of arranging media attention. Some local chapters of professional media associations also provide technical assistance to small nonprofits. Smith (1987) reported on a new organization, called ADNET, which is being formed in several cities to secure voluntary services for nonprofits from professional advertising personnel.

Finally, it is important to recognize that the issue of whether to publicize or not may be a moot question for projects such as exhibits or artistic performances that will require the attraction of large audiences in order to be a success. The same is true for projects aimed at marshalling public support for a particular cause. In these cases, a careful plan should be included in the proposal for how the public will be told about the project, attendance encouraged, or other actions generated. It may even be appropriate to ask the prospective donor if its organization has special talent and expertise in this field that can be consulted in the public relations design.

CHAPTER REFERENCES

Anderson, R., and S. Silha, *Media Access Guide* (Seattle, WA: Metrocenter YMCA, 1986).

Smith, S., "ADNET Puts Heart into Madison Avenue," *Corporate Philanthropy Report*, vol. 2, no. 12 (June 1987), 3.

12

QUALIFICATIONS

This chapter discusses presentation of organizational capability to complete the project, including details on personnel, facilities, contractors, consortiums and other unique or special resources or organizational issues.

Information documenting the capability of the organization submitting the application and the individuals to be involved in the project's operation may be presented in several different sections of a proposal. Sometimes, the funding source asks that these be included as a separately labeled component.

Whichever the case, sufficient detail should be included somewhere in the application to explain:

● How your organization's history, mission and prior experience uniquely qualify it to be selected for this project.

● What personnel (permanent, temporary or consultants) will be needed for the project, their roles, relevant experience and professional backgrounds. If not all staff has yet been chosen, also describe your planned selection process.

● Whether any services or activities will be subcontracted, why and to whom. Again, a planned selection process should be included if subcontractors have not yet been identified.

● The facilities and equipment needed for the project, those already possessed by the organization and plans for securing the remainder.

● Any organizational issues important to the project (such as consortia arrangements, plans to have a special advisory board and so forth).

● Unique or special administrative issues (such as who will retain copyright, patent or ownership of items produced or purchased with grant funds).

● How the donor can be assured that the project has appropriate support in the community. This issue is of particular importance to private foundations and

corporations. It can be dealt with through reference to appropriately constituted advisory boards, by some project funds being provided by community sources or through letters of endorsement.

The remainder of the chapter will be devoted to two of these issues most frequently dealt with as separate proposal components: personnel and facilities/equipment.

PERSONNEL

The writer should carefully read the instructions of the funding source to see what information is requested about personnel. Usually, these instructions are fairly general, so the following guidelines may be helpful.

Do include the title, responsibilities, number and percentage of time assigned to the project for each type of staff person. Sometimes this information can best be displayed in a table or organization chart.

Do give the names and biographical sketches for key staff. Proposals for large or complex projects or research funding usually should include a full biography for the project director or principal investigator.

Do tailor the biography to emphasize experiences relevant to the project. Oetting (1986) and Eaves (1972) provide useful guidance on preparing biographies for principal investigators.

Do briefly describe the selection process and criteria for key project positions unfilled at the time of application. This issue is discussed in more detail later.

Do include ample justification for the use of consultants. Their number and responsibilities should be mentioned as well as an explanation as to why these roles will not be filled through regular appointments. A background sketch should be included for consultants known at the time of application.

Do mention the source of other salary support for key positions that will not be assigned full time to the project. Donors are wary of projects headed by part-time individuals whose other sources of compensation are unknown.

Do provide information on the sex, race and ethnicity of key staff. Some federal funding sources also require the ages of project directors.

Do give a brief overview of the organizational and management structure of the project, if this has not already been provided in the procedures component.

Do include a description of the role and membership of advisory boards.

Do include or be prepared to furnish letters agreeing to participation from any consultants or significant advisors mentioned by name in the proposal.

Don't include the names of well-known experts in the field and indicate "they will be asked to participate once the project is funded."

Don't pad biographies by multiple references to "manuscript in progress." This is an unfortunate but frequent ploy by young researchers. There are other techniques helpful to those applying for their first research grants which are discussed later.

Don't include salary for project directors that, when added to other sources of compensation, will total more than 100 percent of normal pay, unless this is specified and explained in the proposal. Most federal agencies simply will not allow this and demand documentation of other sources of income for key project staff. Increasingly, private foundations and corporations are also asking for written verification on this issue. Although this is a budget item, it is mentioned here because the problem usually starts when one is planning the personnel narrative in the proposal.

A question frequently asked by novice proposal writers is: *How do I reconcile requirements for affirmative action procedures with requests from funding sources to include resumes for intended project staff?* This question is a good one because it presumes that most organizations must follow some type of open competition for available posts. This solicitation may not have taken place by the time the proposal must be submitted.

There are at least two ways this problem has been handled by others. The following examples are provided with the caveat that the advice of your local affirmative action officer should always be sought when planning projects involving the hiring of new staff.

● The project director or principal investigator can be named from among those in the organization who are expected to have some responsibility for the funded project anyway. Organizations frequently overlook the fact that a senior member of the faculty or staff is expected to provide informal supervision for most projects even though this person's salary is not charged to the project budget. By formally recognizing this already-presumed responsibility in the application and including a percentage of the person's time in the salary requests, the organization can avoid the problem of having to submit a proposal that includes none of the names or backgrounds of key personnel. To help share administrative duties, you may also choose to include a second leadership position (such as a co-director, assistant director, or senior research or development associate) to be hired once the funds are received.

● An existing staff member can be designated as a temporary or acting project director. The individual is presented as the one responsible for the project until staff who meet the qualifications listed in the application are found. In some cases, the continuation of the project past this initial phase may be contingent on the funding source approving the selection of the regular project director. The acting staff member may, at a later point, be moved to another position within the project or may be designated as the person in the organization to whom the regular project director will report. In any case, the resume and experience of this existing staff member can be included in the proposal to demonstrate personnel capability.

If an individual's hiring is contingent upon the approval of the proposal, this should clearly be specified in the proposal. The proposal should also provide some evidence that this individual is willing to accept the position if the funds are received.

Given the job market today, many experienced persons are willing to accept this arrangement if the project has a high probability of receiving approval. The individual may also be employed as a consultant during the proposal's preparation to make certain that he or she can live with its contents once an award is made.

These same approaches may be adapted to the filling of project positions other than that of the director.

Whenever possible, however, the project planner should always attempt to identify as many of the project staff as possible prior to submitting the proposal. Not only will the funding source consider it a plus that the project will not be delayed by personnel searches, but the availability of existing capability in the organization and the demonstration of the organization's prior experience within the project field are all important selling points in an application.

A second question frequently asked by beginners is: *How can you increase a project's competitiveness when you know that your age, status in the organization or lack of prior writings and project management may place you at a disadvantage?*

Again, there are several ways that this has been handled by others; but these ideas should be checked with key officials in the organization and scrutinized for their legality or applicability.

● The writer can choose to submit the proposal to a funding source that limits its awards to junior faculty members or beginning professionals. Some federal agencies, foundations and corporations have "small grants" or "young investigators" programs explicitly designed for those who are not yet ready to apply for funds in direct competition with senior individuals.

● You can choose to send the proposal to funding sources that are more interested in the quality of the idea and the application than they are in the prior reputation of project personnel. All funding sources want some assurance that the project personnel are capable of doing what is proposed. But some are more likely than others to base their judgments on the application and their personal impressions of the

quality of the director than to rely primarily on the extensiveness of prior activities.

● One can ask a more experienced colleague to serve as project director or principal investigator, with the initiator of the idea taking a less senior position. This is a time-honored approach used particularly in research applications originated by junior faculty members. And it is an accepted practice, as long as the person designated as project director has agreed to participate, is willing to assume the administrative and legal responsibilities, will actually play the role described in the application and is not overburdened with other assignments. A variation on this approach is to have a more senior person serve as co-director or co-investigator.

● One can have a more experienced person serve as an active consultant. Again, as long as the person truly intends to play this role, most funding sources are willing to accept this practice.

● Eaves (1972) suggests that beginning investigators include a brief biographical sketch of those who currently are serving or who previously served on the person's doctoral committee or supervised subsequent postdoctoral research. This can be particularly useful in applications to funding sources that use the peer review process. Such reviewers can be assisted in judging the likely capability of the applicant by seeing the quality of the applicant's mentors. This same approach can be useful to young applicants in other fields who may previously have worked under someone well known in the profession.

FACILITIES AND EQUIPMENT

You should provide an adequate description of the facilities and major equipment needed for the project and identify what the organization already has and what it is requesting funds to purchase, rent or renovate. Wherever possible, the project planner should minimize procedures that require extensive acquisition and should try to build on existing capabilities. Otherwise, the funding source may be negatively impressed by the amount of time that would be lost while arranging for the necessary facilities and equipment. Or it might decide that the project's real agenda was to acquire buildings and hardware needed by the organization.

In addition to describing the above, you should provide a justification for the facilities and equipment by showing how they will be utilized in the project. This is particularly important if these items represent a significant element in the budget.

Other guidelines include:

Whenever possible, you should emphasize any unusual or outstanding facilities or equipment in the organization. This may include: Particularly well-stocked or planned laboratories, exceptionally extensive or modern computer facilities, a large library or unusual materials collections, sophisticated or hard-to-secure equipment, ready access to other organizations with unusual capabilities, outstanding materials production capabilities, a complete range of advisory or consultative services (such as a survey research center or something of this kind), sites for research owned by the applicant and so forth.

If facilities or equipment from other organizations are essential elements of the proposal, you should provide documentation that these will be made available.

If any unusual or unproven facilities and equipment are to be used in the project, provide sufficient information to justify why they are being tried. Information should also be given on how they will be developed and/or evaluated and what provisions will be made if alternatives turn out to be necessary.

Any extensive renovation of facilities, particularly for office space, should be justified by providing a comparison to the cost of renting such space from a commercial source. Funding agencies are well aware that grants have been used on occasion to finance improvements that were not relevant to project activities. Some funding sources may also insist that such renovation be paid for from the project's indirect costs. Others may require that the indirect cost rate be reduced if a direct cost is being requested so that the changes can be made and paid for at the outset of the award.

This section of the application should be tailored to the specific requirements and needs of the project rather than simply lifted from previous proposals or taken from existing agency documents. The narrative should be made as readable as possible, with the reviewer directed quickly to the most important facts.

The writer should carefully check the funding source's policies on purchase vs. rental of equipment and also its approach to ownership of purchased equipment and materials after the project ends. The writer then should restate his or her interpretation of these in the proposal so that future conflicts can be avoided.

CHAPTER REFERENCES

Eaves, G.N., *Review of Research Grant Applications at the National Institutes of Health* (Bethesda, MD: Office of Grants Inquiries, National Institutes of Health, [1972], [first printing]).

Oetting, E.R., "Ten Fatal Mistakes in Grant Writing," *Professional Psychology, Research and Practice,* vol. 17, no. 6 (1986), 570-3.

THE BUDGET

This chapter discusses the importance of the budget in a proposal, provides suggestions on budget preparation, describes differences in budgets for public and private funding sources, and gives examples of a completed budget and required budget forms.

ROLE OF THE BUDGET

Budgeting is simply the process of translating the project plan into fiscal terms. Because it is one of the last things to be prepared, the weary writer may be tempted to slap it together and hope that any obvious mistakes can be corrected during negotiations or taken care of through supplemental requests after the program is started. *Not so!*

● The preparation of the budget is an important final check in clarifying the practicality of the proposed project.

● Its adequacy will be used by the funding source as an important consideration in judging whether you have the necessary experience and managerial capability to complete the project successfully.

● With few exceptions, most funding sources are distinctly hostile to organizations that later request substantive program modifications or ask for additional funds because original estimates were unrealistic.

● Unless you carefully develop the budget and understand the relationship between each item and the proposed plan of action, you will be unprepared to successfully answer questions or engage in final fiscal negotiations. Do not be misled because, on the proposal form, many foundations and corporations ask only for the total amount of the project budget. All will probe further prior to approving any significant award. Your ignorance, if you are unprepared, may lose you the grant. At worst, it could result in your being committed professionally and legally to a project whose resources are totally inadequate.

The complexity of the project, the procedures of your organization, and the instructions of the funding source will all determine the ease with which a budget is prepared. In any case, you will find that budgeting is essentially a three-step process:

● Determine the ground rules which will govern preparation and review of the budget.

● Identify the total costs of the project and estimate the utilization of these dollars during various phases of the project.

● Translate this information into appropriate budget categories and record this on required forms or in a suitable format.

Occasionally, you may find it necessary to take a fourth step: the redesign of project objectives and procedures in order to propose more realistic goals or use less costly means. If you find total project costs obviously exceeding amounts to be expected from funding sources, this fourth step should *always* be initiated. Only the foolhardy or irresponsible go forward with an application knowing that the budget request is simply inadequate to conduct the proposed scope of work.

Many authors claim that only inexperienced proposal writers have difficulty in preparing project budgets. It is true that the process becomes easier as one becomes familiar with fiscal terms, learns what kind of information is needed and begins to develop "rules of thumb" about probable costs of certain kinds of activities. But past experience can only provide general guidelines. The resource needs of each project are as unique as the proposed outcomes and planned methodology. And as much care should be given to the budget as to the development of the rest of the application.

To aid the reader, the following discussion is organized around the three steps enumerated above.

STEP ONE: Determine the Ground Rules

Early in the budgeting process, you should find what kind of help is available within your organization. Many institutions and agencies have personnel who specialize in the fiscal aspects of externally funded projects. These persons will probably know all of the necessary budgeting regulations, be familiar with the forms of most funding sources and be able to assist in estimating project costs.

Organizations may have developed budget worksheets which can help structure the identification of costs. Some examples of these are provided later. And your agency may also have developed a budgeting manual that explains fiscal terms, shows how to estimate costs and provides advice on other aspects of budget preparation and display.

Whether helped by someone else or not, try to identify all applicable regulations of both your organization and the agency to which the proposal will be submitted. Examples of the kind of questions which might be asked follow:

● What are considered allowable *direct costs*? This means determining which items of cost are specific to the project and should be overtly charged to its budget. In most projects, the largest single direct cost will be the salaries and wages of necessary staff.

● Are *indirect costs* allowed? And, if so, how should these be computed and what do they cover? Most governmental funding sources recognize that there are certain services, materials, facilities and personnel that are essential to a project but, because they are provided generally within institution, are difficult to cost out separately for each application. Examples of such items include the applicant's business services, library, central administration, and depreciation of buildings. To provide reimbursement for the project's access to such organizational resources, most governmental agencies allocate a lump sum which is usually computed by using a fixed percentage of total project salaries and wages or a percent of total budget. Normally, this percentage is negotiated annually between the applicant organization and the federal agency and remains the same for all projects submitted to that source.

● It is important to know that most private foundations and corporations will not allow *indirect costs*.

Many will also not permit a project budget to include as *direct costs* those items which the private donor assumes to be the normal responsibility of the applicant organization (such as the availability of a library or accounting service). It is therefore essential to secure a copy of the donor's guidelines prior to preparation of a budget and to call if any points need clarification.

● Will the funding source entertain a request for all of the project's costs or will part of the funds need to come from another source? Many foundations and corporations have fixed rules about only providing a certain percentage of a project budget and they expect that other private donors will be asked for the remainder. Government agencies, on the other hand, often ask for *matching funds* which they assume will be provided by the applicant organization itself.

● If *matching funds* are required, must these be provided in cash, or can they be "in kind" (i.e., assistance to the project that otherwise would be covered through direct or indirect costs)?

● If the project involves a contract, of what type will this be? Examples of types of contracts include *fixed-price, cost-reimbursement, cost-plus-fixed-fee* and *cost-sharing*. Each has its own unique set of budgeting requirements and the writer should get these sorted out early.

● What changes, if any, will be permitted in the budget once it is approved? Frequently, funding sources will allow the transfer of up to 10 per cent of one budget category (such as supplies and materials) to another (such as travel) without prior approval.

● Will the funding source require that the project budget be displayed by specific phases of time or will a total budget covering the entire period of the project be accepted? This question has to be answered early so that, if necessary, you can build estimates by time periods as well as by required categories.

Another question which must be answered early on is how to adjust the budget for unplanned developments. One can either add a little flexibility to the "scope of work" and then assume that the resulting budget will be sufficient to cover most contingencies *or* add a percentage to the estimates in major budget categories where some leeway is desired (i.e. use of consultants, travel, materials and supplies and so forth).

A related matter is the question of whether or not to add a specific amount to the budget to cover expected cuts by the funding source during negotiations. Since funding sources are much less likely nowadays to make arbitrary cuts, the author's advice is to keep the budget as realistic as possible and prepare a good defense for any reductions that might be suggested.

Beginning proposal writers also frequently ask how to estimate whether the total budget amount is "realistic," given the resources available to the funding source. This is where the information-gathering discussed in Chapter 4 is particularly useful. If that step has been done well, you will know the total dollars available to the funding source, and the approximate minimum/maximum range of prior awards in this program field. You can then tell if your total request is in the ball park.

In working with proposals submitted in response to an RFP, the writer can get an estimate of the acceptable budget range by computing the costs of the estimated staff time suggested by the funding source. In one recent solicitation from the National Science Foundation, for example, the RFP specified that the project would take an estimated "one person year of effort." NSF used a general "rule of thumb" that this would cost about $60,000. This figure thus became the average budget target for responding proposals. If none of these clues is available, you should ask for feedback from the funding source on an acceptable dollar amount during the preliminary inquiries submitted prior to proposal development.

It is also important to find out who in the funding source will be reading the budget and whether it will accompany the narrative or be considered as a separate document. Many federal agencies have contracting officers who read only the budget. Unless they initiate a special request, these persons may never see the rest of the application. This means that you may choose to submit more detail in the budget showing how various totals were arrived at (such as indicating a per-person amount for estimating office supplies and so forth). You may also want to include a column on each budget page indicating the page numbers of the narrative where the justification for each item is found.

Finally, you will want to determine the type of budget forms that must accompany the proposal. Examples of some of these are provided in the chapter attachments. If the funding source requires no specific budget format, these forms can be used as models.

As noted earlier, there is a considerable difference between the amount of budgetary detail required in proposals to private sources and to governmental agencies. However, it is important to prepare a carefully planned budget for all projects, even if you do not submit this in writing to the potential funding source. Not only can you expect to use the information during subsequent discussions, but you will need the budget for successful project management.

STEP TWO: Identify Total Costs of Program

Once familiar with the necessary regulations and expected information, work through the narrative of the proposal to identify activities and appraise the relative costs of each. The writer who uses a proposal design chart similar to that found in Chapter 7 will find this step greatly simplified.

Worksheets are a great aid in building the project budget. They:

● Provide a way to structure the budget planning so that no type of probable expense is overlooked.

● Make a record of how each item was computed so that you are prepared to discuss the possible impact of cuts proposed during the negotiations.

● Aid the writer in determining whether each request is sufficiently justified in the proposal narrative.

● Provide an expenditure plan for use in actual project operation. This is particularly valuable if the proposal writer or budget developer will not be included in project management once the funds are received.

Every experienced grants writer seems to have his or her own favorite type of worksheet. Some examples of those used in the past are provided in Tables 1, 2 and 3.

TABLE 1 | **THE BUDGET**

EXAMPLE OF BUDGET JUSTIFICATION WORKSHEET (BY COST CENTER)*

Cost Center /Item	Total	Requested from funding source	Local	Reference to Narrative	Justification or Explanation
Administration					
Advisory Board					
Salary	$3,000	-0-	$3,000	page 21,22	5 members x $50 each for 12 meetings
Supplies	100	$100	-0-	page 22	$20 each
Telephone (rental)	-0-	-0-	-0-	page 23	
(long-distance)	600	600	-0-		$10 each for 12 months
Travel (in-state)	1,800	1,800	-0-	page 23	$30/day x 5 members x 12 meetings
(out-of-state)	1,200	1,200	-0-	page 24	$600 for 2 members to attend national meeting
	6,700	3,700	3,000		
Project Director					
Salary	$24,000	$25,000	-0-	page 15,17,20	$2,000 x 12 months
Benefits	2,400	2,400	-0-	page 20	Institutional rate is 10% of salary
Supplies	480	480	-0-	page 17, 25	Agency requires $40 per person per month
Postage	240	240	-0-	page 17	Agency requires $20 per person per month
Telephone (rental)	240	240	-0-	page 17	1 instrument x $20 x 12 months
(long-distance)	1,200	1,200	-0-	page 15, 25, 30	$100/month x 12
	28,560	28,560	-0-		

*This just shows examples for two cost centers. The entire budget would require many pages. Advantages of this model are that it groups all planned expenditures for each cost center (i.e. administration) together and makes certain no needs are overlooked. However, it does not account for use of money over time and it does not organize expenditures by the categories normally required on most proposal budget forms.

TABLE 1

TABLE 2   **THE BUDGET**

EXAMPLE OF BUDGET JUSTIFICATION WORKSHEET (BY ACTIVITY)*

Page	Activity	Dates	Description	Amount	Explanation
13-17	Start-up	1/1 - 2/15	Salaries and Wages	$5,000	Director - $3,000 (45 days)
					Asst. - $2,000 (45 days)
			Benefits	1,000	Figured 20%
			Supplies/Materials	300	$150 each
			Travel/Transportation	600	$200 in-state/$400 other
			Postage/Shipping	100	$50 each
			Rent/Comm./Utilities	200	$100 each
			Other services	500	Consultants (5 x $100)
20-22	Literature Search	2/15 - 4/1	Salaries and Wages	3,000	2 Res. Assoc. x $1,500
			Benefits	600	Figured 20%
			Supplies/Materials	1,000	Acquire library
			Travel/Transportation	-0-	
			Postage/Shipping	100	$50 each
			Rent/Comm./Utilities	200	$100 each
			Other services	600	Computer searches (6)

*This example just shows cost estimates for two activities. Again, many sheets would be needed for the complete proposal. This model has the advantage of tying specific costs to specific activities and it does lend itself to estimating expenditures over time. However, it also has the disadvantage of not organizing the expenditures in the way normally requested in most proposal budget forms. For example, all salaries and wages for all activities would need to be totaled in order to build the type of information usually requested in the final proposal.

TABLE 3   **THE BUDGET**

EXAMPLE OF BUDGET JUSTIFICATION WORKSHEET (BY TIME PERIOD AND CATEGORY)*

Budget by Time Period

Description	Fiscal year					Total Budget
	Start Date					
	End Date					
Personnel Costs						
Salaries						
Personnel Benefits						
Consultant Claims						
Other Personnel						
Travel & Transportation						
Staff Travel						
Consultants Travel						
Other Travel						
Postage & Shipping						
Rent, Comm. & Utilities						
Facility Rental						
Equipment Rental						
Telephone & Telegraph						
Utilities						
Printing & Duplication						
Printing						
Duplication						
Other Services						
Data Processing						
Subcontracts						
Conference Expenses						
Other Services						
Supplies & Materials						
Office Supplies						
Printed Materials						
Other Supplies						
Total Direct Costs						
Equipment Purchases						
Indirect Cost @ %						
Total Costs						
Fee @ %						
Total Costs and Fee						

*This model has the advantage of collecting costs by the categories frequently found in required budget forms. It also allows their estimation by major time period (another kind of information usually requested by federal agencies). But it does not have the advantage of showing how the sums included in each category were computed, nor is it tied to costs of specific activities. It also does not include a reference to the page in the narrative where justification may be found. The form could be made more useful if it were completed separately for major cost centers (i.e., administration, training, materials development, evaluation and so forth) and if additional columns were added to capture the other information discussed above.

A brief description of normal budget categories follows.

PERSONNEL

Salaries (referring to income paid at a monthly or yearly rate) and *wages* (referring to remuneration figured by the hour) should be computed for all personnel associated with the project. The budget display should also indicate the amount of time each individual will allocate to the project (this can be shown as a percentage of total salary or in terms of number of staff days) and whether the amount is to be paid for by the funding source, by the local applicant, or by other donors to whom you are applying.

Salary/wage rates should be comparable to those regularly used by the organization. Grant funds should not be used to increase reimbursement rates above those the individual would normally receive. However, provision should be made to cover anticipated promotional increases.

In addition to including the salaries and wages of all regular project staff, the personnel category may also include funds for consultants and/or advisory board members. Consultants are usually hired as private contractors at a daily rate (which may be set by the funding source rather than the applicant). The daily rate should be mentioned somewhere in the narrative or referenced in the budget document itself.

EMPLOYEE BENEFITS

Employee benefits differ with each organization. Included in this category might be retirement, social security, fringe benefits, unemployment taxes and other similar payroll tax fees. Usually these are computed by applying a certain fixed percentage against the salaries and wages of project staff. The applicant's business office can provide advice on the percentage to use in this computation and the types of individual to exempt from its application. You should also find out whether funds must be included to cover the fringe benefits of consultants and advisors. Normally this is *not* done, but policies vary.

TRAVEL AND PER DIEM

This category usually covers all costs associated with the travel and transportation of individuals connected with the project. Some funding sources require that amounts be estimated separately for project staff, consultants and advisory boards. Others also require separate estimates of in-state costs and those associated with regional, national or international travel. The *per diem* expenses (money for food and lodging, parking and other such items on a daily basis) should be included as well as funds for actual air or ground transportation. It is quite permissible to include costs for travel to a national professional meeting in most grants—especially if you plan to report on the progress or results of the project.

Tables 4 and 5 give some examples of worksheets that are useful in estimating costs.

SUPPLIES, MATERIALS AND EQUIPMENT

Some funding sources require supplies and materials to be displayed separately, with "equipment" in a different category. Usually, supplies and materials include all office supplies, costs connected with duplicating and reproduction and funds to acquire documents and other project materials. Equipment may include office desks and chairs as well as laboratory and research equipment.

COMMUNICATIONS

This item usually refers to telephone charges. However, costs for telegrams, satellite time rental and other aspects of communication may also be included. You will want to determine if the budget should only show long-distance costs or should also include monies for the monthly rental of telephone equipment. If local and in-state telephone services are provided to the project without charge, the estimated cost of these can be computed and shown as matching funds.

SERVICES

This rather nebulous category will vary considerably from organization to organization and from one funding source to another. The items to be included should always be determined in advance. Examples of costs frequently recorded here include: data processing, computerized materials-searches, statistical services, page costs for articles in journals, editing and artistic services, printing and publishing services and, sometimes, all consultants or subcontractors.

FACILITIES

Office space and other facilities necessary for the project may either be charged directly to the project

TABLE 4 AND TABLE 5   **THE BUDGET**

CONSULTANT FEES AND TRAVEL

Name, Residence if known	Service to Be Performed	Consultant Fee			Per Diem			Travel	
		Days	Rate	Total	Days	Rate	Total	From - To	Total

STAFF TRAVEL

Destination	Purpose of Trips	Number of Trips	Transportation	Per Diem		
				Days	Rate	Total

It is usually a good idea to check with a travel agency and find out whether carrier costs are expected to increase substantially during the project period. Some individuals also include an inflationary factor to guard against unanticipated increases. Remember, many funding sources require that all travel planned outside of the United States be cleared in advance with the project monitor.

or provided by the applicant organization as a part of indirect costs. If the latter approach is used and any renovation is planned, a problem may arise during the project's operation. Indirect costs are usually released to the applicant by the funding source at the same rate as salaries and wages are paid out. For a twelve-month project, for example, only one-twelfth of the indirect costs are paid each month. If your organization insists on having "cash in hand" before renovation proceeds, it may be several months before sufficient monies are accumulated via receipt of indirect costs. You may thus want to consider inserting a direct cost for renovation or construction and reduce the indirect cost rate accordingly.

Other policies governing facilities should also be checked. If space is to be rented, some federal agencies pay a flat amount regardless of the availability of local space at this rate.

Also include any costs connected with the use of facilities for field-based research. If these are to be provided free of charge by the local organization or collaborating agencies, the costs of such services can also be estimated and included as a "match."

INDIRECT COSTS, OVERHEAD OR FEES

As noted earlier, most funding sources recognize that there are a variety of services provided by the applicant that are difficult to cost on a project-by-project basis. The availability of a modern laboratory, an outstanding library and effective organizational leadership are important to the success of any funded project. Yet because these facilities and personnel exist to serve all of the organization, it is almost impossible to determine their specific use or benefit to a single program.

To reimburse organizations for these generally available items, federal sources have adopted the policy of paying an indirect cost—a flat amount determined as a percentage of all or part of the project budget. Regulations governing these policies are periodically changed. So be certain that your business officials have the latest version.

Usually this percentage is negotiated by the applicant's business or research administrators annually and is simply applied to all proposals. In some cases, however, the funding source may require a different indirect cost rate, may pay no indirect costs at all, or may require a reduction in this rate as an aspect of cost-sharing.

You should always consult with your local business officials in determining the amount to include and its implication for other aspects of the budget. In addition to indirect costs (also called "overhead"), some organizations request a "fee" in their budgets. This amount is usually included to cover research and development activities which the organization conducts independently of any sponsored projects. Funding sources differ on whether they will honor this request.

Finally, one should determine how to handle indirect costs or fees for subcontractors that will be involved in the project. Many funding sources will not cover requests for a second organization's overhead and will insist that this be deducted from the amount due the primary applicant.

STEP THREE: Preparing the Final Budget Document

After completing all worksheets or writing down estimates of resources needed for various categories of project operation, insert this information on the forms required by the funding source or prepare a final budget in a format appropriate to the prospective donor.

Two examples of commonly-used federal budgeting forms are provided in Attachments 1 and 2. Attachment 3 shows a sample of a completed budget developed by the National Endowment for the Humanities to aid novice proposal writers. Attachment 4 is an example of a budget submitted to a corporate foundation. Note that it includes detail on sources of revenue anticipated by the organization, as well as expenses, for the period for which funding is requested. This is a frequent expectation of private donors as is shown in Attachment 5, examples of budget forms from the guidelines of several foundations and corporations.

SUMMARY

Several points have been made throughout this chapter which are worth repeating.

● The budget for a proposal can be developed only after the proposed program has been carefully planned and all activities detailed.

● The budget must be developed with the same care and deliberation as other parts of the proposal. Individuals experienced with budgeting can provide help, but decisions on time and cost can only be made by someone who thoroughly understands the intended operation of the project.

● The proposal writer must be aware of all pertinent regulations, both those of the applicant organization and those of the funding source.

● A record of the method used in computing all budget items (or copies of worksheets used to develop the budget) should be kept to aid in budget negotiation and later project operation.

● All expenses included in the budget should be well documented in the application, either in the narrative or through the use of appendixes. This is true even for proposals to private sources where detailed budget information may only be needed during subsequent negotiations.

● If the total budget obviously exceeds the amount of money that can be expected from the funding source, you should replan the project until it is more realistic. There is no fairy godmother for proposal writers.

EXAMPLE OF A COMMONLY USED FEDERAL BUDGET FORM

OMB NO. 29-R0218

PART III - BUDGET INFORMATION

SECTION A - BUDGET SUMMARY

GRANT PROGRAM, FUNCTION OR ACTIVITY (a)	FEDERAL CATALOG NO. (b)	ESTIMATED UNOBLIGATED FUNDS		NEW OR REVISED BUDGET		
		FEDERAL (c)	NON-FEDERAL (d)	FEDERAL (e)	NON-FEDERAL (f)	TOTAL (g)
1.		$	$	$	$	$
2.						
3.						
4.						
5. TOTALS		$	$	$	$	$

SECTION B - BUDGET CATEGORIES

6. OBJECT CLASS CATEGORIES	GRANT PROGRAM, FUNCTION OR ACTIVITY				TOTAL
	(1)	(2)	(3)	(4)	(5)
a. PERSONNEL	$	$	$	$	$
b. FRINGE BENEFITS					
c. TRAVEL					
d. EQUIPMENT					
e. SUPPLIES					
f. CONTRACTUAL					
g. CONSTRUCTION					
h. OTHER					
i. TOTAL DIRECT CHARGES					
j. INDIRECT CHARGES					
k. TOTALS	$	$	$	$	$
7. PROGRAM INCOME	$	$	$	$	$

HEW-608T

273

SECTION C - NON-FEDERAL RESOURCES

(a) GRANT PROGRAM	(b) APPLICANT	(c) STATE	(d) OTHER SOURCES	(e) TOTALS
8.	$	$	$	$
9.				
10.				
11.				
12. TOTALS	$	$	$	$

SECTION D - FORECASTED CASH NEEDS

	TOTAL FOR 1ST YEAR	1ST QUARTER	2ND QUARTER	3RD QUARTER	4TH QUARTER
13. FEDERAL	$	$	$	$	$
14. NON-FEDERAL					
15. TOTALS	$	$	$	$	$

SECTION E - BUDGET ESTIMATES OF FEDERAL FUNDS NEEDED FOR BALANCE OF THE PROJECT

(a) GRANT PROGRAM	FUTURE FUNDING PERIODS (years)			
	(b) FIRST	(c) SECOND	(d) THIRD	(e) FOURTH
16.	$	$	$	$
17.				
18.				
19.				
20. TOTALS	$	$	$	$

SECTION F - OTHER BUDGET INFORMATION (attach additional sheets if necessary)

21. DIRECT CHARGES:

22. INDIRECT CHARGES:

23. REMARKS:

PART IV - PROGRAM NARRATIVE (attach per instructions)

HEW-608T

274

166

SAMPLE OF A BUDGET FORM, WITH INSTRUCTIONS,
FROM THE NATIONAL INSTITUTES OF HEALTH

Detailed Budget For First 12-Month Budget Period. List only the direct costs requested in this application. Do not include any items that are treated by the applicant organization as indirect costs according to a Federal rate negotiation agreement except for those indirect costs included in consortium/contractual costs. For a SUPPLEMENTAL application, show only those items for which additional funds are requested, prorating the personnel costs and other appropriate parts of the detailed budget if the first budget period of the application is less than 12 months.

Personnel. Whether or not salaries are requested, list the names and roles of all applicant organization personnel to be involved in the project during the 12-month budget period. Starting with the P.I., list all key personnel first and then support personnel. Key personnel are those individuals who participate in the scientific development/execution of the projects. This will generally include individuals with professional degrees, i.e., Ph.D., M.D., D.D.S., D.O., D.V.M., B.S.N., or B.S.E., but in some projects this may also include individuals with other degrees at the masters and baccalaureate levels. Support personnel are those individuals who provide administrative or technical assistance to the project, i.e., dishwashers, animal caretakers, histopathology technicians, electron microscopy technicians, and in some instances research technicians or associates.

Column 1 indicates whether the type of appointment at the applicant organization is full-time or part-time for each individual. A full-time 12-month appointment is coded 1.0. If an individual has outside commitments or concurrent appointments with other organizations, enter only that portion of 1.0 which is allocable to *this* applicant organization. If the 12-month year is divided into academic and summer periods, identify and enter on separate lines the types of appointment for each period.

For example:

Half-time appointment for 12 months (0.5 × 12/12) = 0.5
Full-time appointment for 6 months (1.0 × 6/12) = 0.5
Half-time appointment for 9 months (academic year) (0.5 × 9/12) = 0.38
Full-time appointment for 3 months (summer) (1.0 × 3/12) = 0.25

Column 2 indicates the percentage of each appointment at the applicant organization to be devoted to *this* project. Enter on the appropriate separate lines the percentages for the academic and summer periods. If an individual engages in other institutional responsibilities, such as teaching, the *total* percentage devoted to *all* research activities by the individual must be less than 100%.

Column 3 is the effort on the project. This is calculated for each line by multiplying Column 1 by Column 2 and expressing the result as a decimal.

Enter the dollar amounts for each position for which funds are requested. The maximum salary that may be requested is calculated by multiplying the individual's base salary, defined below, by the percentage of the appointment to be devoted to the project (Column 2). If a lesser amount is requested for any position, explain on page 5 (for example, endowed position, institutional sources, other support). Enter on the appropriate separate lines the salaries requested for the academic and summer periods. The monthly base for summer salaries is calculated by dividing the base salary for the academic period appointment by the number of months of that appointment.

Base salary is defined as the compensation that the applicant organization pays for the individual's appointment, whether that individual's time is spent on research, teaching, patient care, or other activities. Base salary excludes any income that an individual may be permitted to earn outside of duties to the applicant organization. Base salary may not be increased as a result of replacing institutional salary funds with grant funds.

Fringe benefits may be requested provided such costs are treated consistently by the applicant organization as a direct cost to all sponsors.

Calculate the totals for each position and enter the subtotals in each column where indicated.

The applicant organization has the option of having specific salary and fringe benefit amounts for individuals omitted from the copies of the application that are made available to non-Federal reviewers. If the applicant organization elects to exercise this option, use asterisks on the original and copies of the application to indicate those individuals for whom salaries and fringe benefits are being requested; the subtotals must still be shown. In addition, submit one copy of page 4 of the application, completed in full with the asterisks replaced by the salaries and fringe benefits requested. This budget page will be reserved for PHS staff use only.

Consultant Costs. Whether or not costs are involved, provide the names and organizational affiliations of any consultants, other than those involved in consortium/contractual arrangements, who have agreed to serve in that capacity. Include consultant physicians in connection with patient care. Briefly describe and justify on page 5 the services to be performed, including the number of days of consultation, the expected rate of compensation, travel, *per diem*, and other related costs.

Equipment. List separately each item of equipment with a unit acquisition cost of $500 or more. If funds are requested to purchase items of equipment that appear to duplicate or to be equivalent to items listed on the Resources and Environment page or items used in preliminary studies, justify the reasons for the duplication on page 5.

Supplies. Itemize supplies in separate categories such as glassware, chemicals, radioisotopes, etc. Categories in amounts less than $1,000 do not have to be itemized. However, if animals are involved, state how many are to be used, their unit purchase cost, and their unit care cost.

Travel. State the purpose of any travel, giving the number of trips involved, the destinations, and the number of individuals for whom funds are requested, bearing in mind that PHS policy requires that less than first class air travel be used. Justify foreign travel in detail on page 5, describing its importance to the accomplishment of the project.

Patient Care Costs. If inpatient and outpatient charges incident to the research are requested, on page 5 provide the names of the hospitals or clinics to be used and the amounts requested for each. State whether each hospital or clinic has a currently effective DHHS-negotiated patient care rate agreement, and if not, what basis is used for calculating charges. If there is "limited" patient care activity that does not require the establishment of a DHHS-negotiated rate, an institutional patient care rate may be provisionally approved by the PHS awarding component. Indicate in detail the basis for estimating costs in this category, including the number of patient days, estimated cost per day, and cost per test or treatment. Patient care costs do **not** include travel, lodging, and subsistence *or* donor/volunteer fees; request these costs in the "Other Expenses" category. Request consultant physician fees in the "Consultant Costs" category. Patient care costs will be provided to foreign organizations only in exceptional circumstances.

Alterations and Renovations. The costs of construction *per se* are not permissible charges. If the costs of essential alterations of facilities, including repairs, painting, removal, or installation of partitions, shielding, or air conditioning, are requested, itemize them by category and justify them fully on page 5. When applicable, indicate the square footage involved, giving the basis for the costs, such as an architect's or contractor's detailed estimate. When possible, submit a line drawing of the alterations being proposed. Cost for alterations and renovations are not allowed on grants made to foreign applicant organizations.

Consortium/Contractual Costs. Consortium arrangements may involve costs such as personnel, supplies, and any other allowable expenses, including indirect costs, for the relatively independent conduct of a portion of the work described in the Research Plan. Contractual arrangements for major support services, such as the laboratory testing of biological materials, clinical services, etc., are occasionally also of sufficient scope to warrant a similar categorical breakdown of costs. For either of the above arrangements, enter the total direct costs and indirect costs, if any, separately for each participating organization. Use photocopies of pages 4 and 5 to itemize and justify separate detailed budgets for the first 12-month budget period and for the entire proposed project period for each participating organization. Itemize any indirect costs and provide the basis for the rate in the "Other Expenses" category of these supplementary budget pages. Insert the supplementary budget pages after pages 4 and 5 and number them sequentially.

Other Expenses. Itemize by category and unit cost such other expenses as publication costs, page charges, books, computer charges, rentals and leases, equipment maintenance, minor fee-for-service contracts, etc. Reimbursement is allowable for tuition remission in lieu of all or part of salary for student work on the project. State on page 5 the percentage of tuition requested in proportion to the time devoted to the project. Reimbursement is allowable for donor/volunteer fees and for travel, lodging, and subsistence costs incurred by human subjects participating in the project, including travel of an escort, if required. This reimbursement is applicable to all classes of human subjects, including inpatients, outpatients, donors, and normal volunteers, regardless of employment status. Detail such costs on page 5.

PRINCIPAL INVESTIGATOR/PROGRAM DIRECTOR: _____

DETAILED BUDGET FOR FIRST 12-MONTH BUDGET PERIOD
DIRECT COSTS ONLY

FROM | THROUGH

PERSONNEL (Applicant organization only)		1 TYPE APPT.	2 % OF APPT.	3 EFFORT ON PROJ.	DOLLAR AMOUNT REQUESTED (Omit cents)		
NAME	ROLE IN PROJECT				SALARY	FRINGE BENEFITS	TOTALS
	Principal Investigator						
	SUBTOTALS ⟶						

CONSULTANT COSTS

EQUIPMENT (Itemize)

SUPPLIES (Itemize by category)

TRAVEL	DOMESTIC
	FOREIGN
PATIENT CARE COSTS	INPATIENT
	OUTPATIENT

ALTERATIONS AND RENOVATIONS (Itemize by category)

CONSORTIUM/CONTRACTUAL COSTS

OTHER EXPENSES (Itemize by category)

TOTAL DIRECT COSTS FOR FIRST 12-MONTH BUDGET PERIOD (Item 7a) ⟶ $

PHS 398 (Rev. 9/86)   Page 4*

*Number pages consecutively at the bottom throughout the application. Do *not* use suffixes such as 5a, 5b.

REMOVE AND USE FOR DRAFT COPY

170

BUDGET FOR ENTIRE PROPOSED PROJECT PERIOD
DIRECT COSTS ONLY

BUDGET CATEGORY TOTALS		1st BUDGET PERIOD (from page 4)	ADDITIONAL YEARS OF SUPPORT REQUESTED			
			2nd	3rd	4th	5th
PERSONNEL (Salary and fringe benefits) (Applicant organization only)						
CONSULTANT COSTS						
EQUIPMENT						
SUPPLIES						
TRAVEL	DOMESTIC					
	FOREIGN					
PATIENT CARE COSTS	INPATIENT					
	OUTPATIENT					
ALTERATIONS AND RENOVATIONS						
CONSORTIUM/ CONTRACTUAL COSTS						
OTHER EXPENSES						
TOTAL DIRECT COSTS						

TOTAL DIRECT COSTS FOR ENTIRE PROPOSED PROJECT PERIOD (Item 8a)⟶ | $

JUSTIFICATION (Use continuation pages if necessary): Describe the specific functions of the personnel, consultants, and collaborators. For all years, explain and justify any unusual items such as major equipment, foreign travel, alterations and renovations, patient care costs, and tuition remission. For additional years of support requested, justify any significant increases in any category over the first 12-month budget period. Identify such significant increases with asterisks against the appropriate amounts. If a recurring annual increase in personnel or other costs is anticipated, give the percentage. In addition, for COMPETING CONTINUATION applications, justify any significant increases in any category over the current level of support.

PHS 398 (Rev. 9/86)   Page 5*
*Number pages consecutively at the bottom throughout the application. Do *not* use suffixes such as 5a, 5b.

171

REMOVE AND USE FOR DRAFT COPY

SAMPLE OF A COMPLETED BUDGET FROM THE NATIONAL ENDOWMENT FOR THE HUMANITIES

Sample Planning Grant Budget

	NEH	College	Total
A. Salaries			
1. Professor Charisma			
1/2 released time for academic year; salary $18,000	4,500	4,500	9,000
2. Professor Pensive			
1/2 released time fall semester; salary $16,000	4,000		4,000
3. Professor Somnambule			
1/4 released time spring semester; salary $20,000		2,500	2,500
4. Professor Pompous			
1/4 released time spring semester; salary $20,000	2,500		2,500
5. Secretary			
1/2 time; salary $8,000	2,000	2,000	4,000
Subtotal:	13,000	9,000	22,000
B. Staff Travel			
1. Professor Charisma: 1 trip by surface to American College to observe similar program. 250 mi. each way x 12 cents per mile = $60. Per diem $25 for 3 days = $75	135		135
2. Professors Pensive and Pompous:			
1 trip to National University for (state purpose). Plane fare est. $300 for each = $600. Per diem $25 for two days each = $100	700		700
Subtotal:	835		835
C. Supplies			
1. Instructional materials (slides, tapes)	600	200	800
2. Office supplies (paper, ribbon, etc.)	500	100	600
Subtotal	1,100	300	1,400

CONTINUED

	NEH	College	Total
D. Equipment Purchase			
(All equipment purchases must be itemized and fully justified. NEH authorization is required.)			
E. Other			
1. Fringe benefits (if not included in indirect costs): 10% of salaries and wages	1,600	600	2,200
2. Consultants honoraria: 5 for 5 days @ $150 per day	2,500	1,250	3,750
3. Consultants travel: Est. travel $200 each = $1,000. 5 days per diem each @ $25 = $625	1,168	457	1,625
4. Communications (telephone, mail, etc.) @ $200 per month for 12 months	1,468	932	2,400
5. Equipment rental: 2 tape recorders @ $200-$400; 1 8mm projector @ $150	550		550
6. Library acquisitions (attach breakdown)	1,200	800	2,000
7. Evaluation	200	650	850
8. Dissemination	400	450	850
Subtotal:	9,086	5,139	14,225
F. Indirect Costs			
60% of salaries and wages in accordance with negotiated agreement with HEW dated 5/13/74	5,979	7,221	
Total:	30,000	21,660	
	(58%)	(42%)	

Sample Program Budget Summary

	NEH	College	Total
First year	72,411 (69.0%)	32,444 (31.0%)	104,855
Second year	58,326 (58.3%)	41,745 (41.7%)	100,071
Third year	38,455 (41.8%)	53,631 (58.2%)	92,086
TOTAL	169,192 (57.0%)	127,820 (43.0%)	297,012

SAMPLE OF A BUDGET SUBMITTED TO A CORPORATE FOUNDATION ACCOMPANYING A REQUEST FOR GENERAL SUPPORT OF THE ORGANIZATION DURING 1986-87

1985-86 Fiscal Year
9-1-85 to 8-31-86
Operating Budget

REVENUES	1985-86 Budget	Actual Year End	Proposed 1986-87 Budget
Gifts-Corporate	$31,000	$34,100	$33,600
Gifts-Individual	2,000	1,350	1,000
Seminars	500	——	——
Publications	100	149	——
Interest Income	1,500	2,195	1,750
Miscellaneous	300	——	——
Total	$35,400	$37,794	$36,350
EXPENSES			
Salaries	23,117	$22,650	$22,550
Employee Benefits	4,636	3,642	4,000
Payroll Taxes	2,485	2,239	2,500
Printing & Off. supplies	1,815	1,275	1,800
Postage & Deliveries	1,000	523	600
Telephone	700	456	600
Local Expenses	450	358	500
Fees & Licenses	100	120	150
Miscellaneous	467	326	400
Depreciation & Maintenance	330	326	350
Travel	300	469	500
Rent	---	——	1,400
Contingency	---	——	1,000
Total	$35,400	$32,384	$36,350
Revenue over (under) expenses	-0-	$5,410	

THREE EXAMPLES OF BUDGET INFORMATION REQUIRED IN PROPOSAL GUIDELINES FROM PRIVATE FOUNDATIONS AND CORPORATE GIVING PROGRAMS

SAMPLE 1: EXCERPT FROM CORPORATE CONTRIBUTION APPLICATION OF BOISE CASCADE CORPORATION

FINANCES

What is the fiscal year of the organization? _____ _____ to _____ _____
                                              Month   Day   Month   Day

Total Support/Revenue last fiscal year: $ _____
(Source of funding — % Federal, % private grants, etc.)

Total expenditures last fiscal year: $ _____

Total approved budget for current
fiscal year: $ _____

Total project budget: $ _____

Amount requested: $ _____

What methods of fund raising are used or planned (e.g., direct mail solicitation, membership solicitation, corporation or foundation solicitation etc.)?

_____

Are outside fund raisers employed?   Yes _____   No _____

If yes, please list names and addresses: _____

_____

_____

On commission? Yes _____   No _____   On fee basis? Yes _____   No _____   Other:

How often are accounts audited? _____

What percentage of funds raised during your last fiscal year was used for fund raising? _____%

What percentage of funds raised during your last fiscal year was used for administrative costs? _____%

What is the current salary range of the executive staff (including deferred compensation, if any?) $ _____ to $_____

How many full-time paid staff members do you employ? _____

How many part-time? _____

What was the total compensation for staff salaries (full- and part-time), including deferred compensation, for the last year? _____

List other business contributors to this project.

_____

_____

_____

4. AGENCY DIRECTOR: Name: _____

                    Address: _____

                    City _____ State _____ Zip _____

                    Telephone No. _____

5. A. Grant Amount Requested: $ _____

   B. Total Project Cost: $ _____

6. SUMMARY OF BUDGET RELATING TO GRANT REQUEST:

                              a. Personnel Compensation $ _____
                              b. Consultants   _____
                              c. Travel   _____
                              d. Equipment   _____
                              e. Supplies & Operating Expense _____
                              f. Other: _____
                                                             _____
                                                             _____
                                                             _____

                                    Total: $ _____

7. IDENTIFY OTHER SOURCES OF FUNDING, EITHER CURRENT OR APPLIED FOR.

8. PROPOSED PROJECT PERIOD:

                    From: _____ to: _____

6. Total proposal budget $ _____   Amount requested from OCF $ _____

    Indicate with check mark whether request is for:

    Special Program _____   One Time Capital Expenditure _____   Operating Support _____

7. List other sources of support being approached:

    Source   **Amount Requested**   **Current Status**

ORGANIZATION INFORMATION

10. Brief description of your organization and its primary objectives:

11. Date established _____ ; number of paid employees _____ ; number of volunteers _____ .

12. Current annual budget $ _____ ; amount budgeted for administration $ _____ (staff and support costs).

13. Total financial support received **last** fiscal year $ _____ .

    Sources of this support:

    Memberships & Individual Contributions: $ _____   Ticket Sales & Fees: $ _____

    Fund Raising Benefits: $ _____   United Way: $ _____

    *Corporations: $ _____   *Government Programs: $ _____   *Foundations: $ _____
    *Identify and indicate dollar amount of support from each during last fiscal year.

Source	**Amount**	**Source**	**Amount**

14. Amount raised through fund raising activities last year (include membership drives, benefits, etc.)
$ _____ ; identify the costs you incurred in raising those funds (include salaries, brochures, mailings, professional services, grant writing) $ _____ .

15. List previous grant applications to the Oregon Community Foundation during the last 5 years:

DATE OF APPLICATION	PURPOSE Program / Capital / Operating	AMOUNT REQUESTED	AMOUNT APPROVED

16. Attach **single** copies of the following to **original only:**

_____	Current Financial Statement	_____	List of Officers and Board Members
_____	Detailed Agency Budget	_____	Resume(s) of **key** staff person(s)
_____	Detailed Project Budget	_____	Copy of IRS 501(C)(3) Tax Exemption
_____	Descriptive brochure(s) if available and related to funding request		

_____ TEN copies of application form without above attached.

178

REVIEW, SUBMISSION, NOTIFICATION AND RENEWAL

This chapter discusses the final steps in the proposal development process and discusses what typically occurs after the proposal is submitted. It also describes reasons why proposals are not funded and suggests issues to consider when trying to renew or refund a project.

REVIEW OF THE FINAL PROPOSAL DOCUMENT

At this point you have completed the proposal and had it typed in the required format. If not done previously, you should now ask someone (preferably a critically-minded colleague) to read the final application and:

❏ Check for typographical errors.

❏ Determine the soundness of content.

❏ See that all information requested by the funding source has been provided.

❏ Make certain that the document is well written and easily understood..

Depending on the severity of the criticism, the proposal may need to be redrafted before it is sent forward for the necessary pre-submission review and clearance.

In developing the time schedule for the proposal development process mentioned in Chapter 5, you will already have determined what reviews and clearances are needed by your organization and by any local, state or regional bodies. Hopefully, you have also discussed the project idea and approach with these groups so that this final review can be handled expeditiously. Even if this has been done, it is a good idea to leave some extra time in case last minute complications develop.

If the proposal is being sent forward from a large bureaucracy or if many different levels of local and

state review are required, it may be necessary to personally carry the application through the clearance process. Another useful technique is to incorporate the anticipated review steps into a schedule so that each can be monitored and checked off as it is completed. Such a schedule, completed, might look like this:

	Jan. 1-20	Jan. 21-31	Feb. 1-14	Feb. 15
Applicant Agency				
Department chair	✔			
Internal review committees*	✔			
Business office	✔			
Administrator	✔			
Governing board	✔			
Cooperating Agencies				
Business office	✔			
Administrator	✔			
Governing boards	✔			
Local council of government		✔		
State review agency		✔		
State A-95 process agency		✔		
Federal regional office			✔	
Sent to funding source				✔

*Example includes peer review committee on protection of human subjects.

**Some private foundations also have local or regional contributions committees that initially screen proposals from their areas.

To minimize delay, one should have several extra copies of the proposal prepared so that review can take place at different levels simultaneously.

Some other details that need attention include:

❏ Gathering the necessary signatures on the required number of title pages.

❏ Making certain that any internal forms required by your organization or by other groups involved in the pre-submission review are completed and processed.

❏ Determining if a separate form (in addition to the proposal) must be submitted to the state's A-95 review process and, if so, seeing that this is forwarded.

❏ Arranging for preparation of the necessary letter of transmittal.

❏ Securing any desired letters of support to be included with the proposal or sent to the funding source separately. Remember, private foundations and corporations will be particularly interested in evidence of community support for your project.

While somewhat mundane, each of these steps is important and must be completed. Ignorance of the internal review requirements has caused more than one writer to miss a submission deadline.

SUBMISSION TO THE FUNDING SOURCE

Most funding sources offer clear guidance on how many copies of the proposal document to submit. Governmental agencies may ask for as many as thirty copies, of which six or seven must carry original ink signatures from your agency's administrators.

Private foundations and corporations, on the other hand, normally expect no more than one or two copies. Be certain to know their requirements. Foundations (even those whose assets may come from a firm that sells paper) have a negative impression of applicants who send stacks of proposal copies, particularly if it appears that the document was originally prepared for submission to a federal agency. A foundation manager may justifiably wonder why funds should be given to an organiza-

tion that did not care to check on a simple issue such as determining how many copies of the application to send.

Unless otherwise directed, a letter of transmittal should accompany the proposal(s). For federal sources, the letter typically says that the application is being officially submitted on behalf of your organization for the particular program to which you are applying. The letter can also call attention to a unique or important aspect of the application and can indicate the level of priority the applicant organization gives to receiving support for the project. However, since such letters are **expected** to say these things (and are thus generally ignored), you should never expect the letter of transmittal to a governmental agency to carry a significant message that is not contained, in some way, within the proposal itself.

For private donors, the content and signer of a letter of transmittal is much more important. Since these sources have probably instructed you to limit the proposal itself to only a few pages, you can use the letter of transmittal for important messages that may not be repeated in the application. These messages may include:

● Why you believe your project to be of particular importance to this specific foundation or corporation.

● Why the funding of this project is critical to your organization.

● A status report on your solicitation of funds for this project from other sources (remember, few foundations or corporations pay the entire cost of a project and thus expect that you will be seeking a portion of the necessary resources from someone else).

The question of who should sign a transmittal letter for a funding request to private sources should also be considered with care. Options may include the chair of the organization's board of directors; the president or director of your agency; an important civic or business leader who is interested in the project; the head of another foundation that has already made a commitment to the project; or someone who is personally significant to the foundation or its trustees. Using a "big gun" to transmit your proposal will not, by itself, get you a grant. But, it may insure that a more careful and thoughtful review is made of your application. It is also a means of demonstrating that your project is considered to be a priority to someone other than your agency.

Finally, in the case of corporate donors, a transmittal letter for submission of the proposal to the firm's headquarters might be requested from the most senior manager of that business's facility in your community. Few corporate foundations or corporate giving programs will make a grant to a locale in which they have operations without at least consulting with that key manager. You are already one step ahead of the process if you can sell the project idea to that business person and ask him or her to send the proposal to their headquarters with a recommendation of support.

Some funding sources establish very tight application deadlines. These may be one of two types: *a postmark deadline*, which indicates that the proposal was put in the mail prior to a specific time or date, or a *receipt deadline*, which requires that a proposal be in the hands of the funding source by a specific time and date. Be certain to clarify what type of deadline you are working against.

Proposals can usually be sent to a private foundation or corporation at any time. However, since most private sources operate on a calendar year, the most experienced fundraisers either:

● Submit the proposal during the fall months preceding the year for which they are requesting funds. This is the period when most private donors are preparing their next year's budget and it may be possible for you to be included as a "line-item" in their budget plans if you have reached them early enough;

or, if you have been unable to do the above,

● Submit the proposal during January or February of the year when you expect to start the project. Private donors are likely to have the greatest amount of discretionary monies at the start of their fiscal year. It is not uncommon for some private donors to have fully expended their annual budget by mid-year. If you wait until late in the year to send your request, it probably cannot be acted upon until the donor's next budget year.

One of the last minute traumas which the unwary writer may experience is the decision about how to physically transmit the proposal to the funding source. Some argue that proposals should always be sent with a delivery receipt requested. Others say that when dealing with federal agencies, this special mailing process actually takes longer than the use of normal first-class mail. Still others follow a process of hand-carrying all significant applications, feeling that the costs are justified in knowing that the proposal reached its correct destination on time.

The author's preference is to simply use first-class mail with both private and governmental sources. If the writer simply cannot tolerate the uncertainty of this approach, then a "receipt requested" mailing is next best, realizing that some extra time should be planned for the proposal to make its way to the individual or specific federal programmatic unit to whom you have sent the material.

RECEIPT BY FUNDING SOURCE

The majority of federal agencies require that a self-addressed postcard be submitted with the proposal. The return of this postcard, indicating that the proposal has been received, should be expected no later than thirty days after the application is mailed. If nothing has been heard by then, a phone call to the funding source is warranted.

Procedures by private foundations, corporations, state agencies and other types of funding sources differ. You should ask about the notification process during the initial information-gathering on the funding source discussed in Chapter 4. If you have not bothered to do this, wait a minimum of thirty days before calling any private donor to determine if your application has been received. When you call, be sure to indicate that you are *only checking on whether the material was received, not expecting a decision on the request itself.*

Federal agencies usually assign a processing number to proposals as they are received and, in most cases, this number is indicated on the self-addressed postcard when it is sent back to the applicant. This number should be referred to in any subsequent correspondence or negotiation with the agency.

Almost all funding sources (governmental and private) maintain some type of register in which they "log in" the proposal as it is received. Usually these records are organized alphabetically by state or by the name of the applicant organization. Such registers also record the name of the individual and/or program staff to whom the proposal is sent for review and disposition.

For smaller foundations or those foundations and corporations that receive a large number of requests, it is not unusual for it to take as long as sixty days before a proposal is actually "logged-in." So, always be courteous if you call to determine receipt of your application and, if they cannot immediately find it, ask when or if it would be appropriate to call back. Calling back repeatedly and thus being perceived as a nuisance does not help your cause. Such behavior is one of the reasons why "philanthropoids" (donors) sometimes jokingly refer to applicants as "philanthropests."

REVIEW BY THE FUNDING SOURCE

There are so many different policies and procedures used by funding sources to review proposals that a whole body of literature has developed on this process. Jones (1982), Troy (1980), Klepper and Mackler (1986) and Mahoney (1976) give particularly useful descriptions of processes and criteria used by private foundations or corporations. On the governmental side, Niederhuber (1985) provides an excellent overview of the review process at the National Institutes of Health, and Lippincott (1981) does the same for the National Endowment for the Humanities. Other helpful descriptions of review procedures and the basis for public or private decisionmaking on proposals can be obtained by consulting your library.

Even given this variation, there are some common elements.

1) *Most proposals are given an initial screening by someone to see if the proposal meets the purpose of the program and/or funding source to which it was submitted.* Townsend (1974), in studying a hundred governmental and private funding sources, found that the mismatch between purposes of proposals and funding sources was one of the most common reasons why applications were rejected. Hall (1982), in preparing for a speech, made an informal survey of the thirty largest corporate donors in the United States and was told that, on the average, as many as 60 percent of all funding requests were being immediately rejected because they were inappropriate to

the corporation's philanthropic guidelines. This is a cogent argument for the writer doing the necessary pre-investigation outlined in Chapter 4.

Funding sources differ on whether they will immediately notify an applicant that the proposal is not appropriate. Some wait until all applications for a particular program have been judged or a round of grantmaking completed before sending any kind of notification on the request's disposition. Others send the bad news as soon as possible.

2) *Proposals that are worthy of further consideration are subjected to additional reviews of one or more type.* Some of the most common include:

● An internal review by the programmatic staff of the funding agency to see if all the required information has been furnished and to determine the staff's opinion on the merits of the application.

● A written and/or oral review by a group of outside experts, an advisory body or the donor's representative in the community in which the applicant organization is based. Most governmental sources now furnish the names and affiliations of those who serve on their review panels. Few corporations or foundations do so.

● An on-site visit or telephone interview by staff of the funding source or their representatives. This is more frequent in those cases where significant sums of money are at stake or where support for several years has been requested.

● A fiscal and/or legal review to determine the adequacy of the proposed budget and to see that all regulations of or restrictions on the funding source have been observed.

● An administrative review of the entire proposal or its abstract by top officials in the agency, members of a foundation's board or a firm's contribution committee to see if they concur with staff and/or external reviewer recommendations.

3) *Specific criteria against which to judge the merits of the proposal are utilized.* Examples of criteria used by private foundations and corporations are provided in Attachment 1; those for a state-funded program, in Attachment 2; and criteria from federal agencies, in Attachment 3. It is important to know that the evaluation criteria for federally-funded programs are always included in the *Federal Register*

when the regulations governing that program are issued. In addition, most foundations and corporations list at least some of their criteria in their written application guidelines. Securing these, in advance of writing the proposal, should always be part of the research mentioned in Chapter 4. Although mentioned previously, it cannot be overemphasized how important it is to *write the proposal to the evaluative criteria* of the particular source of funding to which you are applying.

4) ***The majority of funding sources maintain some type of record of the reasons why a proposal was approved or disapproved.*** In the case of federal agencies, the reviewers' comments are a matter of public record and must be furnished under provisions of the Freedom of Information Act. Private foundations and corporations are not obligated to furnish this type of information, nor to provide a specific reason for rejecting a request. Most, however, give at least a general reason in their turndown letter or may be willing to visit with you on the telephone about ways is which the application could have been strengthened.

5) ***Funding sources typically assign evaluated proposals to one of the following categories:***

● *Approval* (proposal worthy of support as proposed.

● *Provisional approval* (proposal worthy of support with negotiated modifications).

● *Disapproval* (proposal not worthy of support).

● *Deferral* (proposal unable to be evaluated without additional information—or its consideration postponed without prejudice to the next round of review).

6) ***Funding sources engage in some type of process to assign a final weighting to all proposals that have been recommended for "approval" or "provisional approval."*** This process leads to the ranking of the applications in the order in which they should be funded. Sometimes this process is purely subjective and sometimes it is, at least theoretically, made more objective by the accumulation of rating scores. This process may be conducted solely by the funding source's staff or it may also involve outside reviewers and/or an advisory council. Whatever the case, a final decision is then made by the foundation's trustees or designated officer, the corporate contribu-

tions committee or the appropriate senior officials in state or federal agencies.

NOTIFICATION AND NEGOTIATION

On completion of the funding agency's review, you will receive a notice that the proposal has been approved or rejected. With federal agencies, this information may first be received in a telegram from members of your congressional delegation. Usually, federal agencies advise Members of Congress of the approval of a project in their area at least twenty-four hours in advance of this notice being sent to the applicant. This allows the politicians the opportunity to be the first to give you the "good news."

However, you should never start spending money just because you hear that your application is successful. Until an official confirmation of expenditure authority is received from the federal agency, any premature expenses may be disallowed.

With private foundations, you may or may not receive a check along with the notice of the grant's approval. Frequently, private donors will send a letter *pledging* a certain sum towards the project or organization, but indicating that the actual check will be furnished at some later date or after the applicant has met certain *contingencies* (such as raising the remainder of the money needed for the project).

In the case of both private and public funding sources, you may also be asked to enter into further negotiations—either on the project's content, its budget or both. Private foundations and corporations may ask you to negotiate a detailed memorandum of understanding governing administration of the grant.

The reasons for negotiations and the way they are conducted vary so much that it is hard to generalize about them. But the following ideas may be helpful.

● One experienced colleague says that the key to successful negotiations is to enter the process *knowing that the project is important*, that it is well-planned and that the proposed staff has the capability to be successful. He claims that a positive attitude on the part of everyone representing the applicant's organization will carry more weight than any behind-the-scenes political machinations or defensive arguing.

● Another colleague stresses the importance of *assembling the proper negotiating team*. In dealing with governmental agencies, this may be the project director or principal investigator and the appropriate administrator or business officer of the applicant's agency. The former is the only one who can judge the impact of suggested modifications on the project design; the latter may be the only one who can legally agree to any changes in the proposed budget. In dealing with private funding sources, a good team might be the agency director and the chair of the organization's board.

● If at all possible, you should try to *determine in advance which items or issues will be subject to negotiation*. Be careful in using this approach with private foundations or corporations, because the last impression you want to give is that you are proposing to enter discussions combatively. However, you can sometimes get leads through an advanced phone call asking whether there is any additional information you need to bring to the meeting. Governmental sources may be willing to give you a written list of items to be negotiated. Not only will this list help you prepare an effective explanation or justification, but it will force the funding source to be specific during the subsequent discussions.

● You should *resist any efforts to make you concur in major modifications on the spur of the moment*. Novice negotiators, in their eagerness to get the project approved and operational, sometimes forget that they have spent weeks, months or even years planning the content of a proposal. To immediately respond to requested changes may suggest either a lack of commitment to the project or significant "slush" in the budget. It is not at all unreasonable to ask for a period of time to discuss and weigh revisions or even to request an opportunity to prepare a new plan of action or budget that may later be considered in a second negotiation meeting.

● Cuts in the budget should not be made *unless the "scope of work" is also reduced*. To do otherwise indicates that the budget was unreasonably padded in the first place. If a substantial scaling-down of the project is expected, ask for an opportunity to prepare a written revision rather than leaving the negotiation session with only aural recollections of what was eliminated or retained. In the case of negotiations with a private foundation or corporation, you might also request additional time to raise money from other sources rather than make a significant reduction in the proposed program. They may even have ideas about who else you could approach or be willing to assist with the fundraising if they are significantly committed to the project, but do not have sufficient resources to provide all that you have requested.

● Don't engage in substantive negotiations with programmatic staffs of governmental agencies *unless the contracting officer in the funding source is present* at the meeting. Too many people see the contracting officer as a "bad guy" in the negotiations, but this is often not the case. This person is the one who knows all of the applicable regulations; is the most experienced in forecasting fiscal needs; is frequently your best friend in dealing with improper, unwarranted or irresponsible requests from program officials.

● Resist any impulses to *haul out the "big guns" prior to negotiations*. Asking a congressional office to intervene in the negotiation process is seldom helpful and always harmful. So, too, is asking important individuals to contact a foundation's trustees or corporate officers prior to talking with the foundation or corporate contributions staff. You may be able to successfully browbeat or intimidate such staff to get one grant, but the practice will haunt your organization for a long time. The world of those who professionally staff foundations and corporate contributions programs is a small one, and word quickly gets around about any organization that has not "played by the rules."

● Finally, take good notes on agreements made during the negotiation process and get the signals straight on who is to reduce these agreements to writing.

REASONS FOR DISAPPROVAL

There are a number of books and articles available discussing the most common reasons why proposals are rejected. Tringo (1982) found in his studies that the most frequent sins were "faults in writing or organizing the proposal, rather than poor content." Meador (1985) reported that at least one-third of proposals were not funded because they proposed to "reinvent the wheel."

Townsend (1974) is still one of the classics in terms of a study of the reasons for approval or rejection by both governmental bodies and private funding sources. His design was to ask 100 foundation and government agency directors to use a six point rating scale in judging the degree to which twenty criteria influenced decisions on funding.

Factors included in the "very important" category were:

● *Purpose* - the degree of match between interest and priorities of the funding source and those of the applicant.

● *Community need* - The extent to which the project addressed a significant need and the adequacy with which this was rationally displayed in the application.

● *Accountability* - whether the applicant could be expected to implement the project successfully, provide meaningful results and spend the money legally.

● *Competence* - the level of previous experience and preparation of project personnel and the degree to which the applicant's organization had a good track record.

● *Feasibility* - whether the applicant either had or was requesting sufficient staff, money and materials to "do the job."

Five other criteria were rated in the next category of importance. These included:

● *Project logic* - whether "method 'A' can reasonably be expected to achieve result 'B'" was the way one respondent stated this criterion.

● *Probable impact* - the extent to which the project's idea, methodology and results could be expected ultimately to affect other human lives.

● *Language* - the degree to which the proposal was well written, easy to understand, concise, appropriately phrased and used explicit language.

● *Money needed* - whether the funding source had sufficient funds to support the project and whether the level of a project's request seemed reasonable.

● *Community support* - whether the environment in which the project would be carried out was conducive to success and whether there was evidence that the people to be served or benefited by the project really were behind it.

One of Townsend's more interesting findings was the extent to which these variables interacted during the funding source's decision-making process. Many of the respondents noted that the absence of only one or two of the criteria would probably not automatically doom an application. But they explained that there was a "law of cumulative effect" in which the reviewer began to build an impression that several things were wrong with the proposal—and at this point usually decided that the project was not worth trying to salvage.

This finding tends to point up the importance of your doing a good job on all of the components of a proposal. It also suggests that you cannot rely on just one factor (such as an idea that addresses a terribly important need) to overcome obvious defects in several other aspects of the project's design.

RESUBMISSION AND REFUNDING

It is important to recognize that few individuals are fortunate enough to receive a significant grant in this highly competitive field on their very first try. The odds can be improved by the quality of the pre-proposal research and the care with which the application is developed. However, all funding sources (both public and private) receive far more eligible and excellent requests than they can normally support at any given time.

Tringo (1982) makes an excellent point when he notes "because writing an original proposal is such a large investment and offers such a valuable learning experience, probably the single most important thing a grant applicant can do is profit from an unsuccessful application."

By securing copies of the review comments (from public agencies) or discussing in person by phone the reasons for disapproval (with corporations or foundations), you can make the critical judgment of whether the idea is still worthy of pursuing for support or whether you might as well move on to another project. If the former, prepare a new proposal. Much of the work may already be done and it will be a matter of fine tuning those issues that caused problems during the initial submission.

A similar challenge faces the principal investigator or project director whose proposal was successful, particularly if support was secured for only one year at a time. *Always be certain to determine, in advance, if the funding source (whether public or private) will entertain a request for multiple-year support.* If they do, ask for it. You can always scale the request down to a one-year commitment, if necessary, during negotiations.

More commonly, however, you are faced with needing to submit an application for renewal before the first year of the funded project is even half over. Usually, this is done in accordance with well-established procedures of the funding source and in most cases will involve both a progress report on the project and a presentation of the next year's operation. The refunding document is seldom as lengthy as the original application, but still requires careful thought. It also takes time, so it is important that you plan for this. Additionally, you will want to have planned the project's evaluation to produce data early which will be useful in this second application.

In some cases, however, the funding source has committed itself to only a one-year grant and has indicated that some other source of support must be secured for further project operation. Too, the current project may be nearing its end, but have produced a whole set of new needs or ideas that should be explored in a follow-up proposal.

In these cases, the project director and/or proposal writer is faced with going through the entire process again of determining appropriate funding sources, writing abstracts and letters of inquiry and submitting another application.

This can be very discouraging if it hasn't been anticipated in advance. One colleague noted that he typically develops a long-range plan for possible funding sources of an idea that is worthy of study or development for several years. He then sorts these potential sources into categories such as: most likely to support the planning phase; most likely to support early research; most likely to be interested in application and utilization of the research in development or demonstration; and finally, the funding source that might be willing to finance necessary dissemination and training or installation. Such an approach allows the individual to plan time necessary for writing a proposal for each subsequent source of support. It

also helps structure continuing communication with private foundations and governmental bodies so that the necessary groundwork can be laid in advance of the applications.

All of this may be rather overwhelming to the person who has just completed a first proposal and has vowed never to do another one (at least not immediately). But writing proposals is akin to the well-known potato chip ad: it is difficult to stop at one. The mark of a good project is the extent to which it does prompt exciting new ideas that are worthy of external support. If, during the preparation of a debut proposal, you have realized that proposal preparation is really a process that, with some variation, is similar from application to application, *the second and third proposals really will be easier to digest.*

CHAPTER REFERENCES

Hall, M.S., "Securing Funds from Corporations and Private Foundations," speech to the Annual Conference of the Pacific Northwest Grantmakers Forum, September 10, 1982.

Jones, F.W., "Policies and Procedures for a Corporate Philanthropy Program," in *Corporate Philanthropy* (Washington, D.C.: Council on Foundation 1982), 55-57.

Klepper, A., and S. Mackler, *Screening Requests for Corporate Contributions* (New York: The Conference Board, 1986).

Lippincott, J., "Grantmaking at the National Endowment for the Humanities," *Grants Magazine*, vol. 4, no. 2 (1981), 125-33.

Mahoney, M.F., "Evaluation Can Help Make the Manager's Life Easier," *Foundation News*, vol. 17, no. 6 (November/December 1976), 29-34.

Meador, R., *Guidelines for Preparing Proposals* (Chelsea, MI: Lewis Publishers, 1985).

Niederhuber, J.E., "Writing a Successful Grant Application," *Journal of Surgical Research*, vol. 39, no. 4 (October 1985), 277-84.

Townsend, T.H., "Criteria Grantors Use in Assessing Proposals," *Foundation News*, vol. 15, no. 2 (March/April 1974), 33-38.

Tringo, J., "Learning from Failure: Resubmitting Your Rejected Proposal," *Grants Magazine*, vol. 5, no. 1 (March 1982), 18-22.

Troy, K., *Managing Corporate Contributions* (New York: The Conference Board, 1980).

THREE EXAMPLES OF SELECTION CRITERIA FROM FOUNDATIONS AND CORPORATIONS

SAMPLE 1: SELECTION CRITERIA PREPARED BY BORDEN FOUNDATION FOR USE BY THEIR FIRM'S LOCAL MANAGERS IN REVIEWING AND RECOMMENDING COMMUNITY REQUESTS

Determining the Value of a Local Request

1. Is the contribution tax-deductible?

2. Will the contribution benefit the company?

3. Does the soliciting organization's record and reputation indicate effectiveness, results, efficient management, sound budgeting and planning?

4. How does the soliciting organization aid a social service?

5. Will it advance our community and public relations within the community? Would a grant to the soliciting organization create a non-defensible position for other similar requests?

6. Is there a duplication of efforts by other similar organizations to which the company has contributed?

7. Is the project best served by private funding or could it be financed by public funds?

8. What will be the reaction of the general public if we do not give?

9. Will a positive response to the appeal solve a community problem, or at least have a strong influence toward the solution?

10. What is the reaction of other companies and the community in general to the appeal?

11. Can a contribution be justified in view of the company's current commitments and business position?

The following questions will help you determine the size of a contribution to be considered:

12. If the organization is not a new one, what has been the principal source of support in the past?

13. What is the total amount being asked for in the campaign?

14. What other organizations have been or will be approached for funding of this project and what amount of support will be requested from each?

15. What is the relationship of the size of the corporation's local operation to the size of the community?

16. What is the relationship of the number of employees to the total number of people employed in the community?

17. Is it a one-time or ongoing appeal?

18. Does the company's present business position justify the requested amount?

SAMPLE 2: REVIEW CRITERIA FROM THE GUIDELINES OF THE M.J. MURDOCK FOUNDATION

QUESTIONS TO ASK ABOUT A PROPOSAL

1. SIGNIFICANCE/WORTHINESS

a. How important to society is the problem?

b. Is the proposal consonant with the objectives of the Trust?

c. Does it get at root causes of the problem rather than deal with symptoms?

d. Are there elements of creativity and innovation, or will it merely continue or extend what is already well-known or established?

e. Are the goals well-defined and will achievement be measurable?

f. Will the proposed effort toward solution make a significant difference?

g. Will the solution benefit many or few? To what extent?

h. Will the solution produce impact or multiplier effect? Will it arouse to action?

i. Will the benefit be long-term or short-term?

j. Is the anticipated benefit commensurate with the cost?

k. Will successful completion lead to a generally useful model?

l. What is the potential for increased self-sufficiency?

m. How is the proposal rated by those qualified to judge?

2. PEOPLE

a. Are they qualified for and capable of accomplishing what is proposed? What is their track record or potential?

b. Is there a critical mass of persons for getting the job done?

c. How are they regarded by those best able to judge?

d. What is the availability of other needed persons with requisite skills?

3. ORGANIZATION

a. Does it have a clear and important mission?

b. What are its distinctive features or outstanding characteristics?

c. Is the leadership able, sincere, dedicated, energetic?

d. Is it well supported, administered and operated?

e. How is it regarded by those best able to judge?

CONTINUED

4. PLAN

a. Is the plan carefully thought out and organized?

b. Is it presented clearly?

c. Is it sensible and realistic?

d. Does it proceed directly to the heart of the matter?

e. If a departure from orthodoxy, is it well-reasoned?

f. Have ways around possible obstacles been foreseen?

g. Does it make use of resources effectively and efficiently?

h. What is the opinion of those best able to judge?

5. RESULTS-EVALUATION

a. How will accomplishments be evaluated qualitatively and/or quantitatively?

b. What use will be made of results?

c. Will results be disseminated? How?

d. What effects might be anticipated from the results?

6. FINANCING

a. Is the budget appropriate, cost-effective and commensurate with needs?

b. What in-house support is being offered?

c. What other support is available, has been and is being sought?

d. Are other sources of funds more appropriately or readily available?

e. Is the request for picking up support which has been lost or for filling a gap between other funding?

7. OTHER CONSIDERATIONS

a. Have other grants been made to this organization? If so, what were the results?

b. Must other proposals be denied if this one is approved? If so, how do they compare as to worthiness?

c. Is this such a special situation as to call for suspension of the usual Trust guidelines?

SAMPLE 3: REVIEW GUIDELINES FROM THE WEYERHAEUSER COMPANY FOUNDATION

SOME ISSUES TO CONSIDER IN JUDGING A GRANT REQUEST

THE PROBLEM

1. Is the group clear about the problem it is trying to resolve?

2. Is it a problem which the group can realistically do something about?

3. How important is the problem? Would you give your own money for this cause?

4. Are they proposing to help those who are most seriously affected by this problem?

5. What evidence is there that the community also feels this is a priority problem?

6. How immediate is the problem? What will happen if nothing is done now?

THE APPROACH

1. Is the group specific about what they propose to do? How they will do it? When they'll do it?

2. Why do they believe this approach will be successful? What evidence do they have on how this approach worked elsewhere?

3. Is their approach feasible? Creative? Cost-effective?

4. Is this really a special project that will result in new services and outcomes or is the group simply trying to find a new way to fund their ongoing programs?

5. Do they know who else in the community is providing similar services or dealing with similar populations? Is what they propose to do complementary or duplicative?

6. How will they or anyone else know whether the project is succeeding or failing before all of the money is spent? Do they have a specific plan for evaluation? What kind of interim reports will we receive?

7. Does this approach foster self-reliance?

8. Is it appropriate for the private sector to help pay for this project?

THE AGENCY

1. How is the organization governed? Who is on the board? What does it do? Are these roles confirmed in the minutes from the last two board meetings? How many of the board attended these last two meetings?

2. How is the organization managed? Is top management competent, proven and hardworking? What is the salary for the five highest paid staff? Are these sums similar to those paid in other such organizations?

3. Who will staff the special project? Are they competent? If they have previously been on staff, then presumably they've been performing important functions and who will do these while they work on the project?

CONTINUED

4. If volunteers are to be used, are their roles appropriate?

5. What experience does this organization have that will likely make it succeed with this project?

6. Is adequate space and equipment available for this project?

7. Has this agency received any large grants from other foundations or corporations in the past? If not, why? If so, what do these donors have to say about the organization?

FINANCE

1. What is the total budget this year for this agency? For what is it spent? Is the amount significantly different from last year and if so, why?

2. What are the major current sources of revenue for this agency? Are they sufficient to cover the budget? Are these sources stable? Does this organization appear to have a broad base of support? Does their own board contribute?

3. What is the total budget for this project? Over what period of time? How is it to be spent? Do these amounts seem reasonable to you?

4. How much do they want Weyerhaeuser to contribute? Specifically, how will they use our funds? Is the amount requested from us appropriate?

5. Who else has been asked to contribute? Have any of them said "no"? How much has definitely been pledged or paid and by whom? When do they expect to hear from other donors? How will any additional funds be obtained? Do these plans seem realistic? Should we insist that more of the project funds be obtained before we pledge or pay our grant?

6. Is the agency itself contributing anything to this project? If so, how much and for what?

7. If this project is successful, how will it be funded in the future? Are these plans realistic?

8. Will those being served by the project pay anything?

AN EXAMPLE OF PROJECT SELECTION CRITERIA FOR A STATE-FUNDED PROGRAM

EVALUATION CRITERIA FOR 1988-89 CHALLENGE GRANTS FOR ENDOWMENT DEVELOPMENT, MONTANA ARTS COUNCIL

Recommendations for funding will be based on evaluation of these considerations:

1. **Quality of the Project**

   A. Does the applicant and its staff and/or volunteers have the technical, artistic and administrative **abilities and experience** to complete and implement the project within the grant period?

   B. Is the project **creative, innovative, practical or beneficial**?

2. **Cultural Impact of the Project**

   A. Will the project contribute to or improve the cultural development of the service area community(s), county(s), region or state?

   B. Does the project address an **identified need** within the proposed service area?

   C. Will the project **establish** or **augment** an activity or service?

   D. Does the project have stated goals that are **within the resource capability** of the applicant and is there a reasonable likelihood that the **goals will be attained** within the grant period?

   E. Will the project have **benefit, availability and accessibility to the public**?

3. **Cost Factors of the Project**

   A. Is the project requesting special project, operational, capital expenditure or challenge grant support?

   B. Is the project **cost-effective**? How will the funds be spent? Is the cost reasonable?

   C. Is the relative level of **local support** demonstrated by cash match from local sources or donation of in-kind goods and services?

   D. Is there a **"mix" of revenue sources** for the project? If the application is being made by or on behalf of an organization which owns a cultural facility, what is the extent and type of local government support?

   E. What is the project's potential to **stimulate other sources of funding** or to become self-supporting?

   F. What is the probability that the project will be **accomplished within budget** and with available resources?

CONTINUED

CRITERIA FOR COMMITTEE RECOMMENDATIONS

Committee recommendations to the legislature of those projects which meet the evaluation criteria will also address these considerations:

1. **Geographical Diversity** - The variety of grants recommended should, when taken as a whole, assist the entire state.

2. **Cultural Diversity** - Recognizing the special needs of access to cultural and aesthetic projects and the unique perspective, skills, talents and contributions of the variety of Montanans, the grants recommended, as a whole, should reflect and affirm that diversity, and provide enrichment to the population at large. These projects should encourage the expansion of opportunities for all Montanans to create, participate in and appreciate the wide range of all cultural and aesthetic activities regardless of age, sex, race, ethnic origin, income, physical and mental ability, or place of residence.

3. **Project Diversity** - A variety of different interests and disciplines within the eligible projects should be served including:

   A. service to local communities or counties, multi-county regions and the state

   B. Special projects, operational support, capital expenditures, and challenge grants.

   C. Single sponsors and those representing coalitions of a number of organizations.

4. **Cost Diversity** - Consideration will be given to projects requesting all levels of funding.

EXAMPLES OF EVALUATIVE CRITERIA USED IN VARIOUS FEDERALLY-FUNDED PROGRAMS

SAMPLE 1: EVALUATIVE CRITERIA FOR FY 1987, APPLICATIONS FOR GRANTS UNDER HANDICAPPED CHILDREN'S EARLY EDUCATION PROGRAM DEMONSTRATION PROJECTS

PLAN OF OPERATION   Maximum 40 points

(a) The Secretary reviews each application for information that shows the quality of the plan of operation for the project.

(b) The Secretary looks for information that shows:

(1) High quality in the design of the project;

(2) An effective plan of management that insures proper and efficient administration of the project;

(3) A clear description of how the objectives of the project relate to the purpose of the program;

(4) The way the applicant plans to use its resources and personnel to achieve each objective;

(5) A clear description of how the applicant will provide equal access for eligible project participants who are members of groups that have been traditionally underrepresented, such as (i) members of racial or ethnic minority groups, (ii) women, (iii) handicapped persons and (iv) the elderly.

QUALITY OF KEY PERSONNEL   Maximum 20 points

(a) The Secretary reviews each application for information that shows the qualifications of the key personnel the applicant plans to use on the project.

(b) The Secretary looks for information that shows:

(1) The qualifications of the project director;

(2) The qualifications of each of the other key personnel to be used in the project;

(3) The time that each person referred to in paragraph (b)(1) and (2) of this section will commit to the project; and

(4) The extent to which the applicant, as part of its nondiscriminatory employment practices, encourages applications for employment from persons who are members of groups that have been traditionally underrepresented, such as (i) members of racial or ethnic minority groups; (ii) women; (iii) handicapped persons; and (iv) the elderly.

EVALUATION PLAN   Maximum 15 points

(a) The Secretary reviews each application for information that shows the quality of the evaluation plan for the project.

(b) The Secretary looks for information that shows methods of evaluation that are appropriate for the project and, to the extent possible, are objective and produce data that are quantifiable.

CONTINUED

ADEQUACY OF RESOURCES   Maximum 10 points

(a) The Secretary reviews each application for information that shows that the applicant plans to devote adequate resources to the project.

(b) The Secretary looks for information that shows:

    (1) The facilities that the applicant plans to use are appropriate, adequate; and

    (2) The equipment and supplies that the applicant plans to use are adequate.

BUDGET AND COST EFFECTIVENESS   Maximum 15 points

(a) The Secretary reviews each application for information that shows that the project has an adequate budget and is cost effective.

(b) The Secretary looks for information that shows:

    (1) The budget for the project is adequate to support the project activities; and

    (2) Costs are reasonable in relation to the objectives of the project.

SAMPLE 2: CRITERIA USED BY THE NATIONAL INSTITUTES OF HEALTH IN EVALUATING TRAINING PROPOSALS

1. The degree to which the proposed program delineates an *important need* in the field.

2. The indication of a *well-coordinated* program which has promise of meeting identified needs.

3. The extent to which the program will *expose* participants to new approaches, techniques, and new instructional materials.

4. The extent to which the participants actually will be *involved* in innovative and creative experiences.

5. The extent to which the program is focused on a discipline *or a group of related disciplines.*

6. The consistency and clarity of *statement on procedure* for selecting participants as related to purposes of the program.

7. The level of *professional competence and leadership* of the program director and of the professional staff which will assist him.

8. The indication that the professional staff will have *sufficient time* to prepare for and to conduct the program.

9. The extent to which the sponsoring institution will make *available adequate* classrooms, laboratories, library, and other needed facilities, and satisfactory instructional materials and equipment.

10. The degree to which the proposed program will result in the *improvement of instruction.*

11. *Completeness* in format, body of proposal, budget, etc.

SAMPLE3: SPECIFIC CRITERIA DEVELOPED TO JUDGE A REQUEST FOR PROPOSAL (RFP) BY THE NATIONAL INSTITUTE OF EDUCATION

PROPOSAL EVALUATION CRITERIA

NIE will consider the merits of each submission in accordance with the evaluation criteria and weightings set forth below. All offerors are required to provide sufficient information in their proposals to permit evaluation by reviewers on all factors covered by the following criteria.

A. **Problem Definition.** Significance of the proposed project, as measured by the following factors (30 points):

1. Potential of the project for improving educational practices and resolving educational problems at the local level.

2. Likelihood that the experience acquired through this project will expand the dissemination knowledge base.

3. Evidence of importance of selected problem area in terms of user needs and user commitment to the project.

B. **Equal Educational Opportunity**. Potential contribution of the project to the achievement of equal educational opportunity (20 points).

C. **Technical Quality of Proposal** as evidenced by the following factors (40 points):

1. Quality of technical work plan as measured by:

*Soundness of proposed project objectives and potential for being achieved.

*Appropriateness of proposed sequencing/phasing of activities and adequacy of time and resources allocated to each phase of program operation.

2. Appropriateness of proposed technical services as measured by:

*Quality of plans for achieving sustained local school involvement in project planning and implementation.

*Extent to which proposed services reflect intent to be responsive to user needs.

3. Appropriateness of evaluation activities as measured by:

*Quality of proposed major evaluation activities and tasks to be undertaken by program contractor to improve project management.

*Evidence of local clients' willingness to permit collection of data for evaluation purposes.

4. Soundness of the plan for involving a variety of agencies in the project activities as evidenced by the potential effectiveness of linkage proposed among involved agencies.

D. **Capability of the offeror** to carry out the proposed project as measured by the following factors (30 points):

1. Strength and experience of each of the key individual organizations participating in the project, and the appropriateness of this collective experience in terms of the educational problems addressed by the proposed project.

2. Capabilities, experience and time commitment of the proposed project director, evaluation director, project staff, and staff of sub-contracting organizations.

3. Adequacy of management structure to integrate the performance of activities at different sites by various sub-contractors.

PROPOSAL DEVELOPMENT CHECKLIST

SECTION 1: ASSESSING YOUR CAPABILITY

HAVE YOU:

❑ Analyzed your personal ability to compete for external funds? Considered your professional reputation, prior experience, appropriate preparation and ability to write an effective proposal?

❑ Identified whether you have alternatives to help increase your likelihood of success, i.e., securing a more experienced co-director, joining a consortium of applicants, submitting the proposal through another organization?

❑ Made certain that your organization has the necessary legal basis to be eligible for external funds?

❑ Identified the unique aspects of your organization that will appeal to funding sources?

❑ Determined the kind and amount of help that will be made available to you in developing the proposal?

❑ Considered the relative competitiveness of your organization vis-a-vis others who might be proposing the same idea? Or seeking the same funds?

❑ Determined the reputation of your organization with potential funding sources?

❑ Reviewed the adequacy of other colleagues who might be involved in the project as staff or administrators?

❑ Determined the kind and amount of external professional or political support available to you?

❑ Analyzed the adequacy of the environment in which the project would be implemented?

❑ Reviewed the potential fiscal impact of the project on your organization and determined if there is the necessary time and money to support proposal development as well as project implementation?

❑ Determined if your organization has the essential support systems to effectively compete for and administer external funds? If not, considered whether these could be provided by others?

SECTION 2: DEVELOPING THE IDEA

HAVE YOU:

❑ Developed a clear-cut statement of the problem or need that your idea is trying to address?

❑ Determined what has been the experience of others with similar project ideas?

❑ Gained an understanding of the previous literature and research addressing this same problem or idea?

❑ Assessed the priority of your idea given other problems and needs that your organization should address?

❑ Determined whether the idea is related to your organization's goals/mission?

❑ Discussed the idea with colleagues and administrators in your organization to see if they are willing to provide support for further planning and development of a proposal?

Continued

This handout taken from *Getting Funded: A Complete Guide to Proposal Writing* by Mary Hall, 1988. Available from Continuing Education Publications, P.O. Box 1491, Portland, OR 97207.

❏ Determined what makes your idea innovative? Necessary? Timely? Significant?

❏ Identified other factors which indicate why your idea should receive priority by your organization and others, particularly potential funding sources?

❏ Identified the population that will benefit most from implementation of your idea and documented the extent of their need?

❏ Gathered relevant statistical data both locally and nationally to help document the need and its importance?

❏ Considered alternative approaches and means of implementing your project and analyzed the cost-benefit and potential impact of each?

❏ Determined the feasibility of others replicating your project or using its results effectively?

❏ Discussed the idea with potential participants or secured the opinions of the population to be served?

❏ Met with local and state organizations to see if they are interested in participating in the project or are supportive of its goals?

❏ Identified the constraints or difficulties that should be anticipated in implementing the idea?

❏ Classified the idea by major characteristics? Considered the impact on the choice of funding source?

❏ Decided whether your idea will result in a solicited or unsolicited proposal? Determined what this will mean in planning the proposal's development? Considered how this will affect the proposal's contents or the choice of funding source?

❏ Written a short description of your idea and approach to assist in clearly communicating with others during preliminary planning?

SECTION 3: SELECTING THE FUNDING SOURCE

HAVE YOU:

❏ Considered the full gamut of types of funding sources that might be interested in your idea— private foundations, state agencies, federal agencies, private businesses and professional associations?

❏ Consulted appropriate information sources to develop a preliminary list of possible sources of support?

❏ Gathered the necessary information to identify those sources most worthy of immediate attention?

❏ Identified the person with whom to communicate for each source?

❏ Made an initial inquiry to verify which of these sources might be most interested in your idea?

❏ Asked these sources to provide any comments or suggestions on ways to improve your project idea?

❏ Contacted the most likely prospects to gather all information necessary to guide proposal preparation? Made certain this includes deadlines, writing instructions, forms, regulations, guidelines, priorities and any legal or fiscal requirements?

❏ Identified the criteria and process used for proposal review and selection?

❏ Talked to others familiar with the funding sources and reviewed previously approved proposals to gather informal information on things like language preference, proposal style and so forth?

❏ Identified whether the funding source is likely to approve the project as a grant or as a contract and considered the implications of this for proposal content, submission, review and project operation?

❏ Prepared and submitted a statement of capability or initiated a request to be placed on future bidder lists for contracts and requests for proposals?

❏ Asked funding sources to place you on their mailing lists to receive future program announcements and any other information on external funding opportunities?

❏ Assessed the preferences, interests and priorities of the funding sources against the capabilities of yourself and your organization and selected the source most appropriate to receive the proposal?

Continued

 This handout taken from *Getting Funded: A Complete Guide to Proposal Writing* by Mary Hall, 1988. Available from Continuing Education Publications, P.O. Box 1491, Portland, OR 97207.

SECTION 4: PLANNING THE PROPOSAL WRITING

HAVE YOU:

❏ Identified the components that should be in your proposal and outlined the kind of information that should be furnished in each section?

❏ Collected the information necessary for writing the proposal and organized it for ease of presentation?

❏ Prepared a timeline for proposal development and submission?

❏ Identified all individuals and groups that must review and approve the proposal prior to submission and studied each of their requirements and processes?

❏ Selected the individuals necessary to help write the proposal and made certain that they understand their assignments?

❏ Arranged for the necessary support systems for the proposal's development (such as typing, art work, editing and so forth)?

❏ Arranged for one or more colleagues to read the proposal after it is written to check for typographical errors, clarity, effectiveness of communication and compliance with informational requirements of the funding source?

SECTION 5: WRITING THE PROPOSAL - GENERAL CRITERIA

DOES THE PROPOSAL:

❏ Use language and editorial style appropriate to the discipline and the funding source?

❏ Establish the scholarship and competence of the applicant?

❏ Read easily? Is the language clear and concise?

❏ Use language that is intelligible to the non-specialist?

❏ Call attention to the most significant points through the use of underlining, differences in type, spacing, titles and appropriate summaries?

❏ Flow logically from section to section?

❏ Demonstrate a match between the various proposal components in degree of innovativeness? Appropriateness? Feasibility? Presentation (i.e., are the needs, objectives, procedures and evaluation linked)?

❏ Include enough detail?

❏ Obviously address the review criteria of the funding source?

❏ Identify constraints or problems associated with the idea or its implementation and indicate how these will be handled?

❏ Make appropriate use of diagrams, charts and other visual displays?

❏ Include appropriate and sufficient citations to prior work, research and related literature?

❏ Provide all of the information requested by the funding source in the required format?

SECTION 6: PREPARING THE TITLE, ABSTRACT, FORMS

DOES THE PROPOSAL:

❏ Have an appropriate and imaginative title? Is it descriptive? Suitable for indexing? Catchy?

❏ Include a title page with the necessary information? Signatures?

❏ Have a suitable binding?

❏ Include an abstract that provides an effective and informative summary of the project? Does the abstract place appropriate emphasis on various components in the proposal? Does it state the

Continued

This handout taken from *Getting Funded: A Complete Guide to Proposal Writing* by Mary Hall, 1988. Available from Continuing Education Publications, P.O. Box 1491, Portland, OR 97207.

201

outcomes of the project? Does it comply with the length or word requirements of the funding source?

❏ Include all of the necessary forms and assurance statements?

❏ Include appropriate attachments and appendixes?

SECTION 7: DEVELOPING THE PURPOSE

DOES THE PROPOSAL:

❏ Include a clear description of the project's purpose, objectives, hypotheses and/or research questions?

❏ Signal the reader clearly to the project's objectives? Has the writer avoided burying them in a morass of narrative?

❏ Demonstrate that the objectives are important, significant and timely?

❏ Include objectives which comprehensively describe the intended outcomes of the project?

❏ Include objectives that are well-written? Concise? Clear?

❏ Display the objectives appropriately? Signal the reader to the most important ones first? Show how

the objectives relate to project hypotheses or questions?

❏ State the objectives, hypotheses or questions in a way that they can later be evaluated or tested?

❏ Demonstrate why the project's outcomes are appropriate and important to the funding source?

❏ Include objectives of an appropriate type for the project (i.e. process, product, behavioral, research or performance objectives)?

❏ Indicate that the project's hypotheses rest on sufficient evidence and are conceptually sound?

❏ Justify that the project's outcomes are manageable and feasible?

❏ Provide an appropriate and compelling introduction to the rest of the application?

SECTION 8: WRITING THE STATEMENT OF NEED

DOES THE PROPOSAL:

❏ Demonstrate a precise understanding of the problem or need that the project is attempting to meet or remedy?

❏ Clearly convey the need for the project early in the narrative?

❏ Indicate the relationship of the project to a larger set of problems and explain why its particular focus has been chosen?

❏ Obviously relate to the purposes of the project?

❏ Establish the importance and significance of the problem/need—especially to a national audience?

❏ Signify the potential generalizability and contribution of the project?

❏ Provide effective coverage of related research and demonstrate how the project will build on these earlier studies?

❏ Include citations to ongoing studies as well as earlier research findings?

❏ Establish the theoretical or conceptual base for the project?

❏ Provide initial justification for the project's methodology?

❏ Justify why the problem should be of interest to the funding source?

❏ Include necessary statistical data?

❏ Demonstrate that the problem is feasible to solve?

Continued

This handout taken from *Getting Funded: A Complete Guide to Proposal Writing* by Mary Hall, 1988. Available from Continuing Education Publications, P.O. Box 1491, Portland, OR 97207.

SECTION 9: WRITING THE PROCEDURES

DOES THE PROPOSAL:

❏ Include procedures for every objective? Hypothesis? Research question?

❏ Justify why the approach and methodology is suitable to the stated objectives or purpose?

❏ Provide sufficient detail on the procedures so that their adequacy can be evaluated?

❏ Demonstrate that the procedures are feasible and likely to succeed?

❏ Explain why the procedures are suitable to the amount of time and resources requested?

❏ Provide a clear description and justification of the theoretical base of the methodology?

❏ Describe the procedures clearly so that the reviewer easily understands what will take place during the project period?

❏ Make appropriate use of tables, diagrams and other visual displays and summaries?

❏ Include information that addresses all of the questions asked by the funding source about the approach?

❏ Present the procedures in a format so that they follow logically from section to section?

❏ Demonstrate why the procedures are technically sound?

❏ Clearly describe the project's population and how it will be selected?

❏ Include a description of any accomplishments-to-date of the applicant that bear specifically on the project?

❏ Describe any data to be gathered, instruments to be used, timetable and procedures for collection, analysis, reporting and utilization?

❏ Signal the reader to a summary of the intended results, benefits or anticipated products of the project?

❏ Demonstrate that the procedures are imaginative?

❏ Describe how the project will make certain that its results are generalizable and usable? Addresses how any potentially contaminating factors will be identified and controlled?

❏ Include a discussion of how unanticipated events and problems will be addressed?

❏ Clearly discuss the intended role of the funding source in monitoring the implementation of the procedures? Indicate the type and amount of information to be provided to the funding source to assist with its monitoring?

SECTION 10: DESCRIBING THE EVALUATION

DOES THE PROPOSAL:

❏ Describe why evaluation is needed in the project?

❏ Clearly identify the type and purpose of the evaluation and the audiences to be served by its results?

❏ Demonstrate that an appropriate evaluation procedure is included?

❏ Provide a general organizational plan or model for the evaluation? Justify its technical and theoretical soundness?

❏ Demonstrate that the scope of the evaluation is appropriate to the project?

❏ Describe what information will be needed to complete the evaluation, the potential sources for this information and the instruments that will be used for its collection?

❏ Provide sufficient detail to demonstrate the technical soundness of all data collection instruments and procedures?

❏ Identify and justify procedures for analysis, reporting and utilization?

Continued

This handout taken from *Getting Funded: A Complete Guide to Proposal Writing* by Mary Hall, 1988. Available from Continuing Education Publications, P.O. Box 1491, Portland, OR 97207.

❏ Define standards that will be used in judging the results of the evaluation?

❏ Clearly summarize any reports to be provided to the funding source based on the evaluation and generally describe their content and timing?

❏ Identify any anticipated constraints on the evaluation?

❏ Discuss who will be responsible for the evaluation and the role of any consultants or external personnel?

SECTION 11: DEVELOPING DISSEMINATION AND PUBLICITY

DOES THE PROPOSAL:

❏ Indicate why dissemination activities are important to the project?

❏ Clearly identify the intended outcomes of the dissemination effort?

❏ Include a feasible and appropriate plan for dissemination?

❏ Succinctly describe any products to result from the dissemination effort?

❏ Demonstrate that the applicant is well-grounded in theory and research on the dissemination and utilization of knowledge?

❏ Provide sufficient detail on proposed dissemination procedures to justify the budget request?

❏ Describe any publicity planned for the project?

❏ Signal intent to give suitable recognition to the donor?

❏ Include dissemination strategies and procedures that are imaginative and suitable to the project?

❏ Specify clearly who will be responsible for dissemination and why they are capable?

❏ Speak to internal as well as external project dissemination?

❏ Provide techniques for evaluating the effectiveness of the dissemination/utilization efforts and products?

❏ Lay the groundwork for approaching the funding source at a later date with another proposal focusing exclusively on dissemination/utilization of the results expected from the current effort?

SECTION 12: DESCRIBING CAPABILITIES

DOES THE PROPOSAL:

❏ Describe the role, responsibilities or assignment of each member of the project staff?

❏ Identify the role and responsibility of consultants?

❏ Show how the project staff and major consultants complement and balance each other and provide the breadth of experience and skills necessary for the project?

❏ Provide the names and qualifications of all key project staff and give sufficient detail on their experience and training to justify their capabilities?

❏ Describe how any staff and/or consultants not yet identified will be recruited and the criteria for their selection?

❏ Indicate how state and federal laws governing affirmative action and non-discrimination in personnel selection will be implemented?

❏ Describe the organizational and management structure of the project?

❏ Define any intended role of advisory boards?

❏ Include evidence that consultants and external organizations essential to the project's success have agreed to participate?

❏ Demonstrate appropriate community support?

❏ Signal the readers easily to which staff will be responsible for what set of procedures and other project activities?

❏ Clearly identify the facilities and major equipment needed for the project?

Continued

This handout taken from *Getting Funded: A Complete Guide to Proposal Writing* by Mary Hall, 1988. Available from Continuing Education Publications, P.O. Box 1491, Portland, OR 97207.

❏ Show which facilities and equipment are available and which must be acquired after the project starts?

❏ Direct the reader's attention to any facilities, equipment or special capability of the organization

that enhances the likelihood of the project's success, and the applicant's uniqueness and competence?

❏ Show that the applicant is aware of all policies of the funding source governing personnel, facilities and equipment?

SECTION 13: PREPARING THE BUDGET

DOES THE PROPOSAL:

❏ Show that the applicant is aware of all regulations of either the local organization or the funding source governing the project's budget development and administration?

❏ Include sufficient resources to carry out the project's procedures and achieve its objectives?

❏ Provide some way to refer the reader back to that portion of the proposal's narrative which justifies major budget categories?

❏ Present the budget in the format desired by the funding source?

❏ Provide sufficient detail so that the reviewer can understand how various items were computed?

❏ Separate direct costs from indirect costs and describe what is covered in the latter, if appropriate?

❏ Include sufficient flexibility to cover unanticipated events?

❏ Organize the budget so that the general utilization of dollars can be compared to phases of the project?

❏ Specify the type and amount of any matching funds or cost-sharing?

❏ Include any attachments or special appendixes to justify unusual requests?

❏ Specify other sources of project revenue or plans for securing this?

❏ Indicate how the project will be continued in the future?

SECTION 14: PREPARING FOR REVIEW, SUBMISSION, NOTIFICATION AND RENEWAL

HAVE YOU:

❏ Read the final proposal carefully to check for typographical errors and to be certain that all requirements of the funding source have been met?

❏ Checked your proposal against the research on why applications are rejected and made certain that you have avoided the same mistakes?

❏ Made preliminary contacts with everyone who must review and approve the proposal prior to its submission and left the necessary time to complete these steps?

❏ Made certain that the proposal is cleared through the A-95 process, if necessary, and that it is routed to all appropriate external agencies?

❏ Obtained the necessary original signatures on the correct number of title pages?

❏ Made the necessary number of copies of the proposal and used the correct duplication process?

❏ Secured an appropriate letter of transmittal?

❏ Included letters of support from relevant audiences?

❏ Determined whether the submission deadline is a mailing deadline or a receipt deadline?

❏ Identified the best method for getting the proposals to the funding source?

❏ Determined how and when the funding source will notify you of the proposal's receipt?

❏ Found out how the funding source will review your proposal and the criteria that will be used?

❏ Obtained copies of any forms used by the funding source for review?

Continued

This handout taken from *Getting Funded: A Complete Guide to Proposal Writing* by Mary Hall, 1988.
Available from Continuing Education Publications, P.O. Box 1491, Portland, OR 97207.

❑ Made arrangements to obtain copies of reviewer comments?

❑ Determined how you will be notified if your project is approved and if negotiation is required?

❑ Discussed with more experienced persons how to approach negotiation?

❑ Arranged to have your organization's administrator or business officer present during negotiations?

❑ Given some thought to ways in which the budget might be cut and the necessary modifications that should be made in project objectives and procedures?

❑ Identified any increases in the budget that are needed because of factors that have occurred since the proposal's submission?

❑ Determined the procedures that will be followed by the funding source during negotiations and allocated sufficient time for this process?

❑ Requested that you be given, in writing and in advance, the major items that the funding source expects to negotiate, if appropriate?

❑ Determined when you will have to start efforts to get your proposal refunded?

❑ Identified the information that will be required in the continuation or renewal request and initiated steps to see that this is collected?

❑ Planned a timeline for developing the renewal request?

❑ Identified some other funding sources that might be interested in future phases of the project once the current source of support has ended?

❑ Begun preliminary discussion and contacts with other possible sources of support and developed a long-range plan for continued financing of the project activities and its possible spin-off ideas?

❑ Discussed with your organization the extent of support for project personnel and activities that can be expected once external funds are ended?

This handout taken from *Getting Funded: A Complete Guide to Proposal Writing* by Mary Hall, 1988. Available from Continuing Education Publications, P.O. Box 1491, Portland, OR 97207.